TZVETAN TODOROV

THE CONQUEST OF AMERICA

THE QUESTION OF THE OTHER

Translated from the French by Richard Howard

UNIVERSITY OF OKLAHOMA PRESS   NORMAN

Other books by Tzvetan Todorov
Translated by Richard Howard
  The Fantastic: A Structural Approach to a Literary Genre
  The Poetics of Prose
  An Introduction to Poetics

Translated by Catherine Porter
  Encyclopedic Dictionary of the Sciences of Language (with Oswald
    Ducrot)
  Symbolism and Interpretation
  Theories of the Symbol

Library of Congress Cataloging-in-Publication Data

Todorov, Tzvetan, 1939–
    [Conquête de l'Amérique. English]
    The conquest of America : the question of the other / Tzvetan
  Todorov ; translated from the French by Richard Howard.
        p.   cm.
    Originally published: New York : Harper & Row, c1984.
    Includes bibliographical references and index.
    ISBN 978–0–8061–3137–5 (paper)
        1. America—Discovery and exploration—Spanish. 2. Indians—First
  contact with Europeans.   3. Indians, Treatment of.   I. Title.
    E123.T6313   1999
    970.01′6—dc21   98-31639
                                                                      CIP

The paper in this book meets the guidelines for permanence and durability of the Committee on Production Guidelines for Book Longevity of the Council on Library Resources, Inc.∞

Oklahoma Paperbacks edition published 1999 by the University of Oklahoma Press, Norman, Publishing Division of the University, by arrangement with HarperCollins Publishers, Inc. Manufactured in the U.S.A. First printing of the University of Oklahoma Press edition, 1999.

6   7   8   9   10

The captain Alonso López de Avila, brother-in-law of the *adelantado* Montejo, captured, during the war in Bacalán, a young Indian woman of lovely and gracious appearance. She had promised her husband, fearful lest they should kill him in the war, not to have relations with any other man but him, and so no persuasion was sufficient to prevent her from taking her own life to avoid being defiled by another man; and because of this they had her thrown to the dogs.

Diego de Landa, *Relación
de las cosas de Yucatán*, 32

I dedicate this book to the memory of a Mayan woman devoured by dogs.

Contents

Illustrations

Foreword

Since its first publication in 1982, *The Conquest of America* has aroused a great deal of controversy. It has also, perhaps more than any other such work, established the European encounter with "the other" in America as a subject of urgent historical and moral importance. Part of the controversy was, indeed, created by Tzvetan Todorov's declared intention to write not a conventional work of history, but something more like a moral treatise, what he called—adopting a familiar eighteenth-century term—an "exemplary history." This is not, nor was it intended to be, a piece of empirical research (although the book is, in fact, meticulously researched), nor is it meant to be a simple narrative of the process of cultural confrontation in the Americas—or more precisely in Mexico and the Caribbean—in the hundred years after Columbus's first landfall. Instead, it is a form of dialogue in which the author has attempted to mediate between two extremes: on the one hand, the conventional historicist objective of reproducing "the voices of these figures 'as they really are,'" and on the other, the subjugation of "the other" to the self, so as "to make him [the other] into a marionette" whose strings are operated by the author. (p. 250) This dialogical approach was to alert the modern reader to the ethical implications of the European response to the presence of other cultural worlds, at one crucial and highly symbolic moment of its evolution: the moment when, as Todorov has written elsewhere (echoing David Hume and Adam Smith), "our modern history begins."[1]

Tzvetan Todorov was born in Stalinist Bulgaria and came to France in the early 1960s. It was this experience of internal "otherness," of being what his fellow Bulgarian Julia Kristeva has described as "strangers to ourselves,"[2] about which Todorov has written so movingly in *Nous et les autres* (translated as *On Human Diversity* 1989), that gradually led him to a concern with the relationship between "the diversity of human populations and the unity of the human race."[3] Prior to 1982, however, Todorov had been known as a highly influential and prolific literary theorist who had, among many other achievements, helped establish semiotics as a serious discipline and introduced the writings of Mikhaïl Bakhtin to Western Europe. *The Conquest of America* was his first venture into a new domain, one which he subsequently has made his own and in which he always has managed to fuse the personal and the professional into a highly individualistic vision of the moral dilemmas of the twentieth century.

For all that he has now wholly abandoned his previous literary studies, *The Conquest of America* is still predominantly a work concerned with signs. Semiotics is, by its very nature, synchronic. The signs that men use may change over time, but the processes by which they do so are not, in themselves, semiological ones. The American encounter was a "unique event in the history of humanity" in that two continental groups, who had had no prior existence of each other, came into sudden and violent contact.[4] But for all its uniqueness, the discovery and subsequent conquest of the peoples of the Americas is, as Todorov tells it, one narrative among many. Its exemplarity lies not in its uniqueness, but rather in what it can teach us about Europeans' ultimately lethal capacity to understand "others" and then to employ that knowledge in the pursuit of power over them. He has constructed this narrative from a collection of texts familiar to any student of the period: Columbus's famous letter to Ferdinand and Isabella; Hernán Cortés's *Letters of Relation*; Juan Ginés de Sepúlveda's notorious dialogue on Indian rationality, *Democrates Alter*; the voluminous writings of Bartolomé de Las Casas; and the ethnohistories of Diego Durán and Bernardino de Sahagún. Todorov's reading of these are, however, quite unlike the somewhat pedestrian and limited analyses to which they have generally been subjected.

For Todorov, what took place in America after 1492 was not merely the invasion and progressive subjugation of one group of peoples by another. It was also an encounter between two ways of interpreting the world, between two systems of signs. The predominantly preliterate Aztecs moved in a world of discourse that was, in Todorov's words, "past-orientated" and "tradition-dominated." Because the Aztec world had no formal script, it could not generate "signs" to communicate rapidly. And because of this the Aztecs were unable to adapt to situations wholly unforeseen, such as the arrival of Cortés and his men—situations in which, crucially, "the art of improvisation matters more than that of ritual." (p. 87) In contrast, the Europeans communicated with each other through language rather than directly to the world through external signs, and thus they were able to understand the Aztecs much better than the Aztecs were able to understand the Europeans. That understanding may have been superficial, and often misleading, but it was sufficient for Cortés to turn his opponents' cultural expectations against them. The answer to Todorov's question, "Did the Spaniards defeat the Indians by means of signs?" is clearly yes.

This thesis, which occupies a central part of the book, has received a great deal of attention, much of it critical. But the thrust of much of the critique—in particular that of Gananath Obeyesekere, which is perhaps the most telling—is based very largely on the supposition that Todorov is merely re-enforcing a myth of European superiority the Spaniards themselves had initiated.[5] Todorov is insistent, however, that the distinction he is making between semiliterate and fully literate communities is not, as it is with his Spanish sources, one of excellence ("Let us start with the assumption that on the linguistic or symbolic level there is no 'natural' inferiority on the Indians' side" [p. 63]). It is rather that certain cultural worlds may be less well adapted to resisting a predator like the European if they do not share that predator's specific cultural skills. Although Todorov does not say so, the Europeans were unable to conquer either the peoples of India or Asia not because the latter were technologically better-equipped than the Aztecs and the Circum-Caribbean tribes (they were not, and as Todorov is well aware, European firepower was of more symbolic than practical worth). It was precisely because in the Indian Ocean and the China Sea the various groups that came into conflict with one another "manipulated signs" in nearly identical ways.

Todorov has argued that in Europe *logos* has conquered *mythos*—reason has triumphed over fable—as language has taken the place of ritual and divination. His critics have maintained that this is an illusion, that mythos still "reigns there under the banner of logos."[6] No one, least of all Todorov, would defend the claim that western rationality is wholly transparent. Rather, his argument is that what took place in America after 1492, and continues to happen today, is the virtual obliteration of one cultural world by another, whose confidence in its own rationality and its possession of an instrument—language—enables it to understand the "other" to a much higher degree than "the other" is able to understand it. What Europe possessed was an undeniable "superiority in human communication." But it was a superiority achieved at a price. Not only have the European empires left in their wake a bitterly divided world, but Europe's communicative powers have cut us, their ultimate beneficiaries, off from the world. For Cortés, "the conquest of knowledge" led "to the conquest of power." What we—whoever we may now be—who live inescapably in a world shaped by those conquests have to learn is how to conquer knowledge in order "to resist power."

Todorov's objective was thus to understand the process of conquest in order to prevent it, in order to recognize it when we encounter it today. *The Conquest of America* was the first of Todorov's many writings to establish him—along with a somewhat younger generation of philosophers such as Luc Ferry, Alain Renault, and Pierre Manet—as one of the creators of a new strain in French political and moral thought, one that owes its inspiration not to Hegel, Nietzsche, and Heidegger (as most poststructuralist thought does), but to an older French liberal tradition going back to Tocqueville and Benjamin Constant (on which Todorov has just written a book-length essay).[7] It is a strain Todorov described in *Nous et les autres* as a "well-tempered humanism," a strain which attempts to revive the benign features of the Enlightenment against the ferocious critique to which its values have been subjected from the Romantics to the Postmoderns. *The Conquest of America* is therefore not only an important contribution to our understanding of the clash of cultures in the Americas in the early sixteenth-century. It is also an important contribution to contemporary moral thought.

Anthony Pagden

Notes

1. Tzvetan Todorov, *The Morals of History*, trans. Alyson Waters (Minneapolis: University of Minnesota Press, 1995), p. 17.
2. Julia Kristeva, *Etrangers à nous mêmes* (Paris: Fayard, 1988).
3. Tzvetan Todorov, *On Human Diversity: Nationalism, Racism and Exoticism in French Thought*, trans. Catherine Porter (Cambridge, Mass.: Harvard University Press), p. xi.
4. Todorov, *The Morals of History*, p. 17.
5. Gananath Obeyesekere, *The Apotheosis of Captain Cook: European Mythmaking in the Pacific* (Princeton: Princeton University Press, 1992), pp. 15–19. Obeyesekere's criticisms are directed primarily at Marshall Sahlins's extended analysis, and defense, of the claim that Cook was killed by the peoples of the Sandwich Islands because they took him for the god *Lono*.
6. Ibid., p. 11.
7. For an account of these developments, see Mark Lilla, ed. *New French Thought: Political Philosophy* (Princeton: Princeton University Press, 1994).

1.   DISCOVERY

The Discovery of America

My subject—the discovery *self* makes of the *other*—is so enormous that any general formulation soon ramifies into countless categories and directions. We can discover the other in ourselves, realize we are not a homogeneous substance, radically alien to whatever is not us: as Rimbaud said, *Je est un autre.* But *others* are also *"I"*'s: subjects just as I am, whom only my point of view—according to which all of them are *out there* and I alone am *in here*—separates and authentically distinguishes from myself. I can conceive of these others as an abstraction, as an instance of any individual's psychic configuration, as the Other—other in relation to myself, to *me;* or else as a specific social group to which *we* do not belong. This group in turn can be interior to society: women for men, the rich for the poor, the mad for the "normal"; or it can be exterior to society, i.e., another society which will be near or far away, depending on the case: beings whom everything links to me on the cultural, moral, historical plane; or else unknown quantities, outsiders whose language and customs I do not understand, so foreign that in extreme instances I am reluctant to admit they belong to the same species as my own. It is this problematics of the exterior and remote other that I have chosen—somewhat arbitrarily and because one cannot speak of everything all at once—in order to open an investigation that can never be closed.

But how to speak of such things? In Socrates' time, an orator was accustomed to ask his audience which genre or mode of expression was preferred: myth—i.e., narrative—or logical argumentation? In the age of the book, this decision cannot be left to the audience: the choice must be made in order for the book to exist, and one merely imagines (or hopes for) an audience that will have given one answer rather than the other; one also tries to listen to the answer suggested or imposed by the subject itself. I have chosen to narrate a history. Closer to myth than to argument, it is nonetheless to be distinguished from myth on two levels: first because it is a true story (which myth could, but need not, be), and second because my main interest is less a historian's than a moralist's; the present is more important to me than the past. The only way I can answer the question, How to deal with the other? is by telling an exemplary story (this will be the genre chosen), i.e., a story that will be as true as possible but in telling which I shall try never to lose sight of what biblical exegesis used to call its tropological or ethical meaning. And in this book, rather as in a novel, summaries or generalized perspectives will alternate with scenes or analyses of detail filled with quotations, and with pauses in which the author comments on what has just occurred, and of course with frequent ellipses or omissions. But is this not the point of departure of all history?

Of the many narratives available to us, I have chosen one: that of the discovery and conquest of America. For decorum's sake I have observed the unities: of time, taking the hundred years after Columbus' first voyage (i.e., the sixteenth century by and large); of place, taking the region of the Caribbean and Mexico (what is sometimes called Mesoamerica); and of action: the Spaniards' perception of the Indians will be my sole subject, with one exception—concerning Montezuma and those close to him.

There are two justifications—which I discerned after the fact—for choosing this theme as a first step into the world of the discovery of the other. First of all, the discovery of America, or of the Americans, is certainly the most astonishing encounter of our history. We do not have the same sense of radical difference in the "discovery" of other continents and of other peoples: Europeans have never been altogether ignorant of the existence of Africa, India, or China; some memory of these places was always there already—from the beginning. The moon is farther away than America from Europe, true enough, but today we know that our encounter with it is no encounter at all, and that this discovery does not occasion surprises of the same kind: for a living being to be photographed on the moon, an astronaut must stand in front of the camera, and in his helmet we see only one reflection, that of another earthling. At the beginning of the sixteenth century, the Indians of America are certainly present, but nothing is known about them, even if, as we might expect, certain images and ideas concerning other remote populations were projected upon these newly discovered beings (see fig. 1). The encounter will never again achieve such an intensity, if indeed that is the word to use: the sixteenth century perpetrated the greatest genocide in human history.

But the discovery of America is essential for us today not only because it is an extreme, and exemplary, encounter. Alongside this paradigmatic value, it has another as well—the value of direct causality. The history of the globe is of course made up of conquests and defeats, of colonizations and discoveries of others; but, as I shall try to show, it is in fact the conquest of America that heralds and establishes our present identity; even if every date that permits us to separate any two periods is arbitrary, none is more suitable, in order to mark the beginning of the modern era, than the year 1492, the year Columbus crosses the Atlantic Ocean. We are all the direct descendants of Columbus, it is with him that our genealogy begins, insofar as the word *beginning* has a meaning. Since 1492 we are, as Las Casas has said, "in that time so new and like to no other" (*Historia de las Indias*, I, 88*). Since that date, the world has shrunk (even if the universe has become infinite), "the world is small," as Columbus himself will peremptorily declare ("Lettera Rarissima," 7/7/1503; for an image of Columbus that communicates something of this spirit, see fig. 2); men have discovered the totality of which they are a part, whereas hitherto they formed a part without a whole. This book will be an attempt to understand what happened in that year, and during the century that followed, through the reading of several texts, whose authors will be my characters. These will engage in monologues, like Columbus; in the dialogue of actions, like Cortés and Montezuma, or in that of learned discourse, like Las Casas and Sepúlveda; or less obviously, like Durán and Sahagún, in the dialogue with their Indian interlocutors.

But enough preliminaries: let us proceed to the facts.

Columbus's courage is admirable (and has been admired many times over); Vasco da Gama and Magellan may have undertaken more difficult voyages, but they knew where they were going. For all his assurance, Columbus could not be certain that the Abyss—and there-

---

*Abbreviated references appear in the text; for complete titles, see the Bibliographic Note at the back of the book. The figures in parentheses, unless indicated otherwise, refer to chapters, sections, parts, etc. and not to pages.

Fig. 1 Ships and castles in the West Indies.

Fig. 2   Don Cristobal Colón.

fore his fall into it—did not lie on the other side of the ocean; or again, that this westward voyage was not the descent of a long downward slope (since we are at the earth's summit), which it would afterwards be impossible to reascend; in short, that his return was at all likely. The first question in our genealogical investigation will therefore be, What impelled him to set out? How could the thing have happened?

One might assume from reading Columbus's writings (diaries, letters, reports) that his essential motive was the desire to get rich (here as subsequently I am saying about Columbus what could be said about others; it happens that he was, frequently, the first, and therefore set the example). Gold—or rather the search for it, for not much is found at the start—is omnipresent in the course of Columbus's first voyage. On the very day following the discovery, October 13, 1492, he already notes in his diary: "I was attentive and worked hard to know if there was any gold," and he returns to this subject unceasingly: "I do not wish to delay but to discover and go to many islands to find gold" (15/10/1492). "The Admiral ordered that nothing should be taken, in order that they might surmise that the Admiral wanted nothing but gold" (1/11/1492). His very prayer has become: "Our Lord in his goodness guide me that I may find this gold" (23/12/1492); and, in a subsequent report ("Memorial for Antonio de Torres," 30/1/1494), he alludes laconically to "our activity, which is to gather gold." The signs he believes he has found of the presence of gold also determine his route: "I decided to go to the southwest to search for gold and precious stones" ("Journal," 13/10/1492). "He wished to go to the island which they call Venegue, where he had news, as ne understood, that there was much gold" (13/11/1492). "The Admiral believed that he was very near to the source, and that Our Lord would show him where the gold was born" (17/12/1492: for gold is "born" in this period). Thus Columbus wanders from island to island, for it is quite possible that the Indians had thereby found a means of getting rid of him. "At break of day, he made sail in order to lay a course in search of the islands that the Indians told him had much gold, and some of which had more gold than earth" (22/12/1492).

Is it, then, no more than greed that sent Columbus on his journey? It suffices to read his writings through to be convinced that this is anything but the case. Quite simply, Columbus knows the lure value of wealth, and of gold in particular. By the promise of gold he reassures others in difficult moments. "This day, they completely lost sight of land, and many sighed and wept for fear they would not see it again for a long time. The Admiral comforted them with great promises of lands and riches, to sustain their hope and dispel their fears of a long voyage" (F. Columbus, 18). "Here the men could stand it no longer and complained of the long voyage; but the Admiral cheered them as best he could, holding out good hope of the advantages they would have" ("Journal," 10/10/1492).

Not only the sailors hoped to grow rich; the very backers of the expedition, the rulers of Spain, would not have ventured upon the enterprise without the hope of a profit; since the journal Columbus keeps is intended for them, signs of the presence of gold must appear on every page (lacking gold itself). Recalling, on the occasion of the third voyage, the organization of the first, Columbus says quite explicitly that gold was, in some sense, the lure he offered so that the monarchs would agree to finance him: "It was needful also to speak of the temporal gain therein, foreshadowed in the writings of so many wise men, worthy of credence, who wrote histories and related how in these parts there are great riches" ("Letter to the Sovereigns," 31/8/1498). On another occasion he says he has gathered and preserved gold "so that their Highnesses might be pleased and might thus judge this situation on the basis of a number of large stones filled with gold" ("Letter to Doña Juana de Torres," November 1500). Furthermore, Columbus is not mistaken when he imagines the importance of these motives: is his disgrace not due, at least in part, to the fact that there was not more gold in these islands? "Then was born the defaming and disparagement of the undertaking which had been begun before, because I had not immediately sent caravels laden with gold" ("Letter to the Sovereigns," 31/8/1498).

We know that a long dispute will divide Columbus and the sovereigns (and later a trial will be instituted between the heirs of both sides), one that bears precisely on the amount of profits the Admiral is authorized to take from the "Indies." Despite all this, greed is not Columbus's true motive: if wealth matters to him, it is because wealth signifies the acknowledgment of his role as discoverer; but he himself would prefer the rough garment of a monk. Gold is too human a value to interest Columbus to any real degree, and we must believe him when he writes, in the journal of the third voyage: "Our Lord knows well that I do not bear these sufferings to enrich myself, for, certainly I know that everything in this age is vain except what is done for the honor and service of God" (Las Casas, *Historia,* I, 146). Or at the end of his account of the fourth voyage: "I did not come on this voyage for gain, honor or wealth, this is certain, for then the hope of all such things was dead. I came to Your Highnesses with honest purpose and sincere zeal; and I do not lie" ("Lettera Rarissima," 7/7/1503).

What is this honest purpose? In the journal of the first voyage, Columbus articulates it frequently: he wants to meet the Grand Khan, or the Emperor of China, of whom Marco Polo has left an unforgettable portrait. "I am determined to go to the mainland and to the city of Quisay and to present Your Highnesses' letters to the Grand Khan, and to beg a reply and to come home with it" (21/10/1492). This objective is somewhat lost sight of subsequently, the present discoveries being so distracting in themselves, but it is never actually forgotten. But why this obsession, which seems almost childish? Because, again according to Marco Polo, "the Emperor of Cathay some time since sent for wise men to teach him the religion of Christ" ("Lettera Rarissima," 7/7/1503), and Columbus seeks the route that would permit this desire to be realized. Infinitely more than gold, the spread of Christianity is Columbus's heart's desire, and he has set forth his feelings in the case very explicitly, notably in a letter to the pope. His future voyage will be "to the glory of the Holy Trinity and to that of the holy Christian religion," and for this he "hopes for the victory of God the Eternal, as He has ever granted it to me in the past"; what he does is "great and magnifying for the glory and growth of the Holy Christian religion." This, then, is his goal: "I hope in Our Lord to be able to propagate His holy name and His Gospel throughout the universe" ("Letter to Pope Alexander VI," February 1502).

The universal victory of Christianity—this is the motive that animates Columbus, a profoundly pious man (he never sets sail on Sunday), who for this very reason regards himself as chosen, as charged with a divine mission, and who sees divine intervention everywhere, in the movement of the waves as in the wreck of his ship (on a Christmas night!): "By many signal miracles God has shown Himself on the voyage" ("Journal," 15/3/1493).

Furthermore, the need for money and the desire to impose the true God are not mutually exclusive. There is even a relation of subordination between the two: one is a means, the other an end. In reality, Columbus has a more specific project than the exaltation of the Gospel in the universe, and the existence as well as the permanence of this project is indicative of his mentality: a kind of Quixote a few centuries behind his times, Columbus aspires to set off on a crusade to liberate Jerusalem! It happens that the notion is preposterous in his era, and since he is penniless as well, no one is willing to listen to him. How can a man without resources who wishes to found a crusade realize his dream in the fifteenth century? All he need do is discover America in order to obtain his funds. Or rather, merely sail to China by the "direct" western route, since Marco Polo and other medieval writers have confirmed the fact that gold is "born" there in abundance.

The reality of this project is amply confirmed. On December 26, 1492, during the first voyage, Columbus reveals in his journal that he hopes to find gold, "and that in so great quantity that the Sovereigns within three years would undertake and prepare to go and conquer the Holy Places," for so, says he, "I declared to Your Highnesses that all the gain of this my enterprise should be spent in the conquest of Jerusalem; and Your Highnesses smiled and said that it pleased you, and that even without this you had that strong desire." He refers again to this episode later on: "At the moment when I undertook to discover the Indies, it was with the intention of beseeching the King and the Queen, our Sovereigns, that they might determine to spend the revenues possibly accruing to them from the Indies for the conquest of Jerusalem; and it is indeed this thing which I have asked of them" ("Deed of Entail," 22/2/1498). This then was the project Columbus had set before the royal court, in order to seek the help necessary for his first expedition; as for Their Highnesses, they did not take it very seriously, and reserved the right to employ the potential profit of the undertaking for other purposes.

But Columbus does not forget his project and brings it up again in a letter to the pope: "This enterprise was undertaken in the intention of employing what would be gained from it in restoring the Holy See to the Holy Church. After having gone thither and having seen the land, I wrote to the King and to the Queen, My Sovereigns, that from that day for seven years I would require fifty thousand foot soldiers and five thousand horsemen for the conquest of the Holy See, and in the following five years fifty thousand more foot soldiers and five thousand more horse, which would come to ten thousand horse and one hundred thousand foot soldiers for the said conquest" (February 1502). Columbus does not surmise that the conquest will involve him continuously, but in an altogether different direction, very close to the lands he has discovered, and with many fewer soldiers after all. Hence his appeal does not provoke many reactions: "The other most notorious matter, which cries aloud for redress, remains inexplicable to this moment" ("Lettera Rarissima," 7/7/1503). This is why, seeking to confirm his intention even after his own death, he draws up a deed of entail and gives instructions to his son (or to the latter's heirs): to collect as much money as possible so that, if the sovereigns abandon the project, he can "proceed with it alone and with as much might as he can muster" (20/2/1498).

Las Casas has left a famous portrait of Columbus, one that nicely situates his crusading obsession in the context of his profound religiosity: "When gold or other precious objects were brought to him, he entered his chapel and said, 'Let us thank Our Lord who made us worthy of discovering so much wealth.' He was a most jealous keeper of the honor of God; eager to convert the peoples and to see the seed and faith of Jesus Christ spread everywhere, and especially devoted to the hope that God would make him worthy of helping to win back the Holy Sepulchre; and in this devotion and the confidence which he had that God would help him in the discovery of this World which He promised, he begged Queen Isabella to make a vow that she would spend all the wealth gained by the Crown as a result of the discovery in winning back the land and the House of Jerusalem, which the Queen did" (*Historia*, I, 2).

Not only did contacts with God interest Columbus much more than purely human affairs, but even his form of religiosity is quite archaic (for the period): it is no accident that the project of the crusades had been abandoned since the Middle Ages. Paradoxically, it will be a feature of Columbus's medieval mentality that leads him to discover America and inaugurate the modern era. (I must admit, and even assert, that my use of these two adjectives, *medieval* and *modern*, is anything but precise; yet I cannot do without them. Let them be understood first of all in their most ordinary sense, until the pages that follow can give them a more explicit content.) But, as we shall also see, Columbus himself is not a modern man, and this fact is pertinent to the course of the discovery, as though the man who was to give birth to a new world could not yet belong to it.

However, we may also discern in Columbus some features of a mentality closer to us. On one hand, then, he submits everything to an exterior and absolute ideal (the Christian religion), and every terrestrial event is merely a means toward the realization of that ideal. On the other, however, he seems to find in the activity in which he is most successful, the discovery of nature a pleasure that makes this activity self-sufficient; it ceases to have the slightest utility, and instead of a means becomes an end. Just as for modern man a thing, an action, or a being is beautiful only if it finds its justification in itself, for Columbus "to discover" is an intransitive action. "I wish to see and discover the most that I can," he writes on October 19, 1492, and on December 31 of that year: "And he says that he wished not to depart until he had seen all that country which there was to the eastward, and gone along the whole coast"; it is sufficient that he be informed of the existence of a new island for him to be overcome by a craving to visit it. In the journal of the third voyage, we find these powerful sentences: "He says that he would abandon everything to discover more lands and to probe their secrets" (Las Casas, *Historia*, I, 136). "What he most dearly desired, he says, was to discover more" (ibid., I, 146). At another moment he wonders: "I do not write how great will be the benefit to be derived hence. It is certain, Lord Princes, that when there are such lands there should be profitable things without number; but I tarried not in any harbor, because I sought to see the most countries that I could, to give the story of them to Your Highnesses" ("Journal," 27/11/1492). The profits which "should be" found there interest Columbus only secondarily: what counts are the "lands" and their discovery. This discovery seems in truth subject to a goal, which is the narrative of the voyage: one might say that Columbus has undertaken it all in order to be able to tell unheard-of stories, like Ulysses; but is not a travel narrative itself the point of departure, and not only the point of arrival, of a new voyage? Did not Columbus himself set sail because he had read Marco Polo's narrative?

Columbus as Interpreter

IN ORDER to prove that the land he sees before him is indeed the
continent, and not another island, Columbus engages in the following
reasoning (in his journal of the third voyage, transcribed by Las Casas):
"I have come to believe that this is a mighty continent which was
hitherto unknown. I am greatly supported in this view by reason of this
great river, and by this sea which is fresh, and I am also supported by
the statements of Esdras in his fourth book, the sixth chapter, which
says that six parts of the world consist of dry land and one part of water.
This work was approved by Saint Ambrose in his *Hexameron* and by
Saint Augustine. . . . Moreover I am supported by the statements of
several cannibal Indians whom I captured on other occasions, who
declared that there was mainland to the west of them" (*Historia*, I,
138).

Columbus cites three reasons in support of his conviction: the
abundance of fresh water; the authority of the sacred books; the opinion of other men he has met with. Now it is clear that these three
arguments are not to be set on the same level, but reveal the existence
of three spheres that articulate Columbus's world: one is natural, one
divine, and the third human. Hence it may not be an accident that we
can also find three motives for the conquest: the first human (wealth),
the second divine, and the third linked to a delight in nature. And in
his communication with the world, Columbus behaves differently depending on whether he is addressing (or being addressed by) nature,
God, or men. To return to the example of the mainland, if Columbus

is right it is solely because of the first argument (and we can see, in his journal, that this argument only gradually takes form, on contact with reality): observing that the water is fresh far out at sea, he deduces from this fact, quite perspicaciously, the river's might, and hence the distance it must have flowed; consequently, the land must be a continent. It is very likely, on the other hand, that he understood nothing of what the "cannibal Indians" had told him. Earlier in the same voyage he had reported his conversations as follows: "He [Columbus] says it is certain that it was an island, for that is what the Indians said," and Las Casas adds: "So it seems that he did not understand them" (*Historia*, I, 135). As for God . . .

We cannot, as a matter of fact, put these three realms on the same level, as Columbus did; for us there are only two real exchanges, with nature and with men; the relation to God does not involve communication, although it can influence or even predetermine every form of communication. This is precisely Columbus's case: there is a definite relation between the form of his faith in God and the strategy of his interpretations.

When we say that Columbus is a believer, the object is less important than the action: his faith is Christian, but we have the impression that, were it Muslim or Jewish, he would not have acted differently; what matters is the force of the belief itself. "Saint Peter leaped upon the sea and walked upon the water as long as the faith sustained him. He who has faith the size of a grain of corn will be obeyed by the mountains. Let he who has faith ask, for to him shall all be given. Knock, and it shall be opened unto you," he writes in the preface to his *Book of Prophecies* (1501). Further, Columbus believes not only in Christian dogma, but also (and he is not alone at the time) in Cyclopes and mermaids, in Amazons and men with tails, and his belief, as strong as Saint Peter's, therefore permits him to find them. "He understood also that far from there there were men with one eye, and others with dogs' heads" ("Journal," 4/11/1492). "The day before, when the Admiral went to the Rio del Oro, he said that he saw three mermaids who rose very high from the sea, but they were not as beautiful as they are painted, for they had something masculine in the countenance" (9/1/1493). "These women use no feminine exercises, but bows and arrows of cane, like the abovesaid; and they arm and cover themselves with plates of copper, of which they have plenty" ("Letter to Santangel," February–March 1493). "There remain to the westward two provinces where I have not been, one of which they call Avan, and there the people are born with tails" (ibid.).

Columbus's most striking belief is, true enough, of Christian origin: it concerns the earthly Paradise. He has read in Pierre d'Ailly's *Imago Mundi* that the earthly Paradise lies in a temperate region beyond the equator. He finds nothing of the kind in the course of his first visit to the Caribbean, which is hardly surprising; but on his return journey, in the Azores, he declares: "The earthly Paradise is at the end of the Orient, because it is a most temperate place, and so those lands which he had now discovered are, says he, at the end of the Orient" (21/2/1493). The theme becomes obsessive during the third voyage, when Columbus draws closer to the equator. At first he believes there is an irregularity in the earth's curvature: "I have been led to hold this concerning the world, and I find that it is not round as they describe it, but that it is the shape of the pear which is everywhere very round except where the stalk is, for it is very prominent, or that it is like a very round ball, and on one part of it is placed something like a woman's nipple, and that this part, where this protuberance is found, is the highest and nearest to the sky, and it is beneath the equinoxial line in this Ocean sea at the end of the Orient" ("Letter to the Sovereigns," 31/8/1498).

This elevation (a nipple on a pear!) becomes one more argument to assert that the earthly Paradise is there. "I believe that the earthly Paradise is here, and to it, save by the will of God, no man can come. . . . I do not hold that the earthly Paradise is in the form of a rugged mountain, as its description declares it to us, but that it is at the summit, there where I have said that the shape of the stalk of the pear is, and that, going toward it from a distance, there is a gradual ascent to it" (ibid.).

Here we can see how Columbus's beliefs influence his interpretations. He is not concerned to understand more fully the words of those who speak to him, for he knows in advance that he will encounter Cyclopes, men with tails, and Amazons. He sees clearly that the "mermaids" are not, as he has been told, beautiful women; but rather than conclude that mermaids do not exist, he corrects one prejudice by another: the mermaids are not so beautiful as is claimed. At another moment, in the course of the third voyage, Columbus wonders about the origin of the pearls the Indians sometimes bring him. The thing occurs before his eyes; but what he reports in his journal is the explanation given by Pliny, taken from a book: "Close to the sea there were countless oysters adhering to the branches of the trees that go into the sea, with their mouths open to receive the dew which falls from the leaves, until the drop falls, out of which pearls will be formed, as Pliny says, and he cites the dictionary called *Catholicon*" (Las Casas, *Historia*, I, 137). It is the same with the earthly Paradise: the sign that fresh water constitutes (hence a great river, hence a mountain) is interpreted, after a momentary hesitation, "in agreement with the opinion of those holy and wise theologians" (ibid.). "I am much more convinced in my own mind that the earthly Paradise is to be found there where I have said, and I rely upon the arguments and authorities given above" (ibid.). Columbus performs a "finalist" strategy of interpretation, in the same manner in which the Church Fathers interpreted the Bible: the ultimate meaning is given from the start (this is Christian doctrine); what is sought is the path linking the initial meaning (the apparent signification of the words of the biblical text) with this ultimate meaning. There is nothing of the modern empiricist about Columbus: the decisive argument is an argument of authority, not of experience. He knows in advance what he will find; the concrete experience is there to illustrate a truth already possessed, not to be interrogated according to preestablished rules in order to seek the truth.

Even if he was always a finalist, Columbus, as we have seen, was more perspicacious when he was observing nature than when he was trying to understand the natives. His hermeneutic behavior is not precisely the same in the one case as in the other, as we can now determine in some detail.

"From my tenderest years I have lived the life of sailors, as I am doing even today. This occupation leads those who follow it to wish to know the secrets of this world," Columbus writes at the beginning of the *Book of Prophecies* (1501). We shall insist here on the word *world* (in opposition to "men"): he who identifies himself with the sailor's occupation has dealings with nature rather than with his kind; and in his mind, nature has assuredly more affinities with God than men have: he writes in a single impulse, in the margin of Ptolemy's *Geography:* "Admirable are the tumultuous forces of the sea. Admirable is God in the depths." Columbus's writings, and most particularly the journal of the first voyage, reveal a constant attention to all natural phenomena. Fish and birds, plants and animals are the main characters of the adventures he recounts; he has left us detailed descriptions of them. "They fished also with nets, and caught among many others, one fish that looked like a proper pig not like a porpoise and of which it is said that it was all shell, very hard, and it had no soft place except the neck and eyes, and an opening underneath to discharge its superfluities. He ordered it salted, so that the Sovereigns might see it" (16/11/1492). "More than forty petrels came to the ship at once and with them two boobies; a boy of the caravel hit one with a stone; a frigate-bird came to the ship and a white one like a gull" (4/10/1492). "I saw many trees very unlike ours, and many of them have their branches of different kinds and all on one trunk, and one twig is of one kind and the other of another, and so unlike that it is the greatest wonder of the world. How great is the diversity of one kind from the other! For instance, one branch has leaves like a cane, others like mastic; and thus on one tree five or six kinds, and all so different" (16/10/1492). During the third voyage, he puts in at the Cape Verde islands, which serve the Portuguese at that time as a deportation center for all the lepers of the kingdom. The lepers are supposed to be cured by eating turtles and washing in their blood. Columbus pays no attention to the lepers and to their singular habits, but he immediately launches into a long description of the habits of turtles. The amateur naturalist becomes an experimental ethologist in the famous scene of the duel between a peccary and a monkey, described by Columbus at a moment when his own situation is almost tragic and when we do not expect to find him concentrating on the observation of nature: "There is a great abundance of animals, small and large, and very different from ours. At the time I had two pigs which an Irish hound dared not attack. An archer had wounded an animal which seemed to be a monkey, but much larger and with a man's face. He had pierced it with an arrow from breast to tail, and since the creature was ferocious, he had to cut off one arm and one leg. The pig, upon seeing the monkey, bristled and fled. When I saw that, I ordered the *begare*, as it is called in these parts, to be thrown to where the pig lay. When it was upon the pig, although more dead than alive and still wearing the arrow in its body, it coiled its tail round the hog's snout, took powerful hold, and with its remaining fore-claw grasped the boar round the neck, as if an enemy. This novel and beautiful combat has led me to write you this" ("Lettera Rarissima," 7/7/1503).

Attentive to animals and to plants, Columbus is even more concerned with all that touches navigation, even if this concern relates more to the sailor's practical sense than to any rigorous scientific observation. In conclusion to the preface of his first journal, he offers this injunction to himself: "And above all, it is of great importance that I forget sleep and be a very vigilant navigator, so that all may be properly done; which will require great effort," and we might say that he obeys it to the letter: not one day without notations concerning the stars, the winds, the sea's depth, the coastal relief; here theological principles do not intervene. Whereas Pinzón, commander of the second ship, vanishes in the search for gold, Columbus spends his time taking geographical notes: "All this night he remained hove to, as mariners say—which is bearing to windward without moving forward—and this in order to examine a pass, which is an opening in the sun as a kind of gorge between two peaks, which he had glimpsed at sunset and through which appeared two very high mountains" ("Journal," 13/11/1492).

The result of this vigilant observation is that Columbus performs, with regard to navigation, veritable exploits (despite the wreck of his ship): he always knows how to choose the best winds and the best sails; he initiates sidereal navigation and discovers magnetic variation; one of his companions on the second voyage, Michele de Cuneo, who makes no attempt at flattery, writes: "During navigations, it sufficed for him to glance at a cloud or by night at a star, in order to know what would ensue, and if there were to be heavy weather." In other words, he can interpret the signs of nature in terms of his interests; further, the only really effective communication he establishes with the natives rests on his knowledge of the stars. With a solemnity worthy of the adventures in boys' books, he takes advantage of his knowledge of the date of an imminent lunar eclipse. Stranded on the Jamaican coast for eight months, he can no longer persuade the Indians to bring him provisions without his having to pay for them; he then threatens to steal the moon from them, and on the evening of February 29, 1504, he begins to carry out his threat, before the terrified eyes of the caciques. . . . His success is instantaneous.

But two characters exist (for us) in Columbus, and whenever the navigator's profession is no longer at stake, the finalist strategy prevails in his system of interpretation: the latter no longer consists in seeking the truth but in finding confirmations of a truth known in advance (or, as we say, in wishful thinking). For instance, throughout the first crossing (Columbus takes a little over a month to sail from the Canaries to Guanahani, the first Caribbean island he sights), he is in search of signs of land; he finds them, of course, only one week after his departure. "They began sighting numerous clumps of green grass which seemed, according to the Admiral, to have been recently separated from the earth" (17/9/1492). "Out of the North appeared a great darkness, which signifies that it covers the earth" (18/9/1492). "There were several rainstorms without wind, which is a certain sign of land's proximity" (19/9/1492). "Two boobies came to the ship, then another, which was a certain sign of land's proximity" (20/9/1492). "They saw a whale, a sign that they were near land, because these creatures always keep near the coasts" (21/9/1492). Every day Columbus sees "signs," and yet we now know that these signs were lying to him (or that there were no signs), since land was touched only on October 12, over twenty days later!

At sea, all the signs indicate land's proximity, since that is Columbus's desire. On land, all the signs reveal the presence of gold: here, too, his conviction is determined far in advance. "He said again that he believes there are enormous riches, precious stones and spiceries" (14/11/1492). "The Admiral believed that there would be good rivers and much gold" (11/1/1493). Sometimes the assertion of this conviction is ingenuously combined with a confession of ignorance. "I believe that there are many plants and trees much esteemed in Spain for dyes and as medicines of spicery; but I do not know them, at which I am much aggrieved" (19/10/1492). "There are also trees of a thousand kinds, all with different fruits and all so fragrant that it is a wonder, and I am greatly distressed not to know them, for I am well assured they are all of great value" (21/10/1492). In the course of the third voyage, he pursues the same program of thought: he believes these lands are rich, for he greatly desires that they be so; his conviction is always anterior to the experience. "And he greatly desired to penetrate the secrets of these lands, for he did not believe it possible they did not contain things of great worth" (Las Casas, Historia, I, 136).

What are the "signs" which permit him to confirm his convictions? How does Columbus the interpreter proceed? A river reminds him of the Tagus. "Then he recalled that at the mouth of the river Tagus, near the sea, gold is found, and it appeared certain to him that this river must have gold" ("Journal," 25/11/1492); not only does a vague analogy of this kind prove nothing, but even the point of departure is false:

the Tagus does not carry gold in its course. Or again: "The Admiral said that where there is wax, there must be as well a thousand other good things" (29/11/1492); this inference is not even worth the famous "no smoke without fire"; the same is true of yet another one, in which the island's beauty leads him to believe in its riches.

One of his correspondents, Mosén Jaume Ferrer, had written him in 1495: "The great part of valuable things come from very hot regions, of which the inhabitants are black, or parrots." Blacks and parrots are therefore considered as the signs (the proofs) of heat, and heat as the sign of wealth. It is hardly surprising then that Columbus never fails to remark the abundance of parrots, the blackness of skins, and the intensity of the heat. "The Indians who came upon the ship had understood that the Admiral wanted a parrot" (13/12/1492); now we know why! During the third voyage, he heads farther south: "Here, the people are extremely black. And when, from this place, I sailed to the West, the heat was excessive" ("Letter to the Sovereigns," 31/8/1498). But the heat is welcome: "From the heat which, the Admiral said, they endured in this place, he argued that, in these Indies, and where they were going, there should be much gold" ("Journal," 21/11/1492). Las Casas remarks with some justice apropos of another such example: "It is a wonder to see how, when a man greatly desires something and strongly attaches himself to it in his imagination, he has the impression at every moment that whatever he hears and sees argues in favor of that thing" (*Historia*, I, 44).

The search for the location of *terra firma* (the mainland) represents another striking example of this behavior. On the first voyage Columbus recorded the pertinent information in his journal: "This island Hispaniola [Haiti] or the other island Yamaya [Jamaica] was only ten days by canoe from the mainland, which would be sixty to seventy leagues, and here the people do not go naked, but are clothed" (6/1/1493). He has his conviction, namely that the island of Cuba is a part of the continent (Asia), and he decides to eliminate all information tending to prove the contrary. The Indians Columbus encounters have told him that this land (Cuba) is an island; since the information does not suit his purposes, he challenges the quality of his informants. "And since these are bestial men who believe that the whole world is an island and who do not know what the mainland is, and have neither letters nor long-standing memories, and since they take pleasure only in eating and being with their women, they said that this was an island"

(Bernaldez transcribing the journal of the second voyage). We may wonder just how the love of women invalidates their assertion that this country is an island. Yet the fact is that toward the end of this second expedition, we are shown a famous and grotesque scene in which Columbus definitively renounces verifying by experience whether or not Cuba is an island, and determines to apply the argument of authority with regard to his companions: all disembark on land, and each one swears an oath asserting that "he had no doubt that this was the mainland and not an island, and that before many leagues, in navigating along the said coast, would be found a country of civilized people with some knowledge of the world. . . . A fine of ten thousand maravedis [Spanish currency] is imposed on anyone who subsequently says the contrary of what he now said, and on each occasion at whatever time this occurred; a punishment also of having the tongue cut off, and for the ship's boys and such people, that in such cases they would be given a hundred lashes of the cat-o'-nine-tails, and their tongue be cut off" ("Oath sworn regarding Cuba," June 1494). A remarkable oath, whereby one swears that one *will* find civilized inhabitants!

The interpretation of nature's signs as practiced by Columbus is determined by the result that must be arrived at. His very exploit, the discovery of America, proceeds from the same behavior: he does not discover it, he finds it where he "knew" it would be (where he thought the eastern coast of Asia was to be found). "He had always thought in his inmost heart," Las Casas reports, "whatever the reasons for this opinion [it was by reading Toscanelli and the prophecies of Esdras], that by crossing the ocean beyond the island of Hierro, after traversing a distance of seven-hundred and fifty leagues more or less, he would end by discovering the land" (*Historia*, I, 139). When seven hundred leagues are covered, he forbids navigating by night, for fear of missing the land, which he *knows* to be very near. This conviction is quite anterior to the voyage itself; Ferdinand and Isabella remind him of this in a letter that follows the discovery: "That which you had announced to us has come true as if you had seen it before having spoken of it to us" (letter of 16/8/1494). Columbus himself, after the fact, attributes his discovery of this a priori knowledge, which he identifies with the divine will and prophecies (actually quite slanted by him in this direction): "I have already said that for the execution of the enterprise of the Indies, reason, mathematics, and the map of the world were of no utility to me. It was a matter rather of the fulfillment of what Isaiah had predicted" (preface to the *Book of Prophecies,* 1501). In the same way, if Columbus discovers (in the course of the third voyage) the American continent strictly speaking, it is because he is seeking in a quite concerted manner what we call South America, as is revealed by his annotations in Pierre d'Ailly's book: for reasons of symmetry, there must be four continents on the globe—two in the north, two in the south; or, considered from another direction, two in the east, two in the west. Europe and Africa ("Ethiopia") form the first north-south pair; Asia is the northern element of the second; there remains to be discovered, no, to be *found* in its rightful place, the fourth continent. In this way the finalist interpretation is not necessarily less effective than the empiricist: other navigators dared not undertake Columbus's voyage because they did not possess his certainty.

This type of interpretation, based on prescience and authority, has nothing "modern" about it. But as we have seen, this attitude is balanced by another, much more familiar to us: the intransitive admiration of nature, experienced with such intensity that it is freed from any interpretation and from any function. Such delight in nature no longer has any finality, and Las Casas reports this fragment of the journal of the third voyage, which shows Columbus preferring beauty to utility: "He said that even if there were no profits to be gained here, if it were only the beauty of these lands . . . they would be no less estimable" (*Historia,* I, 131). There is no end to the enumeration of all of Columbus's admirations. "All this country has very high and beautiful mountains, not dry and rocky, but all accessible and with magnificent valleys. Like the mountains, the valleys are also filled with high and leafy trees, which it is glorious to look upon" ("Journal," 26/11/1492). "Here, the fish are so different from ours, that it is a wonder. There are some which, like dories, are decked out in the brightest colors of the world: blue, yellow, red, and all the colors. Others are painted in a thousand fashions, and the colors are so bright that there is no man who would not marvel and wonder at the sight of them. There are also whales" (16/10/1492). "Here and in all the island, the trees are green and the plants and grasses as well, as in the month of April in Andalusia. The singing of the small birds is such that it would seem that a man would never willingly leave this place. The flocks of parrots darken the sun. Birds great and small are of so many kinds and so different from ours that it is a wonder" (21/10/1492). Even the wind in this place "blows very lovingly" (24/10/1492).

In order to describe his admiration of nature, Columbus cannot leave off the use of the superlative. The green of the trees is so intense that it is no longer green. "The trees were here so luxuriant that their leaves ceased being green and became almost black by their very verdant force" (16/12/1492). "There rises from the earth a fragrance so good and so sweet, from the flowers or the trees, that it was the fairest thing in the world" (19/10/1492). "He said further that this island is the fairest that human eyes have ever seen" (28/10/1492). "He said that never had he seen a lovelier thing than this valley through the midst of which the river flows" (15/12/1492). "It is certain that the beauty of these islands, with their mountains and their sierras, their valleys watered with abundant rivers, is such to behold that no other land under the sun can appear finer, nor more magnificent" ("Memorial for Antonio de Torres," 30/1/1494).

Columbus is quite aware of the unlikeliness of these superlatives, and consequently how unconvincing they may be; but he runs the risk, declaring the impossibility of proceeding otherwise. "Upon seeing this harborage, he declared it such that none of those he had ever seen could equal it. And he seeks to excuse himself, saying that he has so greatly praised the others, that he no longer knows how to praise this one, and that he fears being accused of exaggerating everything beyond measure. But he defends his praises" ("Journal," 21/12/1492). He swears that he is exaggerating nothing: "He says such things of the fertility, the beauty, and the altitude of these islands found in this harborage, that he implores the sovereigns not to wonder at so many praises, for he assures them that he believes he had not spoken the hundredth part of their marvels" (14/11/1492). And he deplores the poverty of his language: "He said to the men who went in his company that, in order to make unto the sovereigns an account of all that they were seeing, a thousand tongues would not suffice to express it, nor his hand to write it, for it appeared that it was enchanted" (27/11/1492).

The conclusion of this uninterrupted admiration is quite logical: it is the desire never to leave this pinnacle of beauty. "He says that there was such great pleasure in seeing all this verdure, these forests, and these birds that he could not bring himself to leave them and return to his ships," we read in the entry for October 28, 1492. And he concludes a few days later: "This was a thing so marvelous for him, to see the trees and the foliage, the crystal water, the birds and the sweetness of the places, that he said he believed he never again wished to leave the place" (27/11/1492). Trees are Columbus's real Sirens: in their presence he forgets his interpretations and his search for gain, in order to reiterate tirelessly what serves no purpose, leads to nothing, and therefore can only be *repeated:* beauty. "He would tarry more than he wished because of his longing to see and the pleasure he took in gazing at the beauty and the freshness of these lands, wherever he sought to enter" (27/11/1492). Perhaps he thereby rediscovers a motive that has inspired all the great travelers, whether it was unknown to them or not.

The attentive observation of nature leads, then, in three different directions: to the purely pragmatic and effective interpretation concerning matters of navigation; to the finalist interpretation, in which signs confirm the beliefs and hopes entertained in any other regard; and finally, to that rejection of interpretation constituted by intransitive admiration, the absolute submission to beauty, in which one loves a tree because it is lovely, because it *is,* not because one might make use of it as a mast for one's ship or because its presence promises wealth. With regard to human signs, Columbus's behavior will be much simpler.

Between the two, there is a gap. The signs of nature are indices, stable associations between two entities, and it is enough that one be present for the immediate inference of the other to be possible. Human signs, i.e., the words of the language, are not simple associations—they do not directly link a sound to a thing, but pass through the intermediary of meaning, which is an intersubjective reality. Now, and this is the first striking phenomenon, with regard to language Columbus seems to pay attention only to proper names, which in some respects are what is closely related to natural indices. Let us first observe this attention and, to begin with, the concern with which Columbus surrounds his own name, to such a degree that, as we know, he changes its orthography several times during his life. Once more I cite the testimony of Las Casas, a great admirer of the Admiral and a unique source of countless items of information concerning him, who clearly reveals the meaning of these changes (*Historia,* I, 2): "But this illustrious man, renouncing the name established by custom, chose to be called Colón, restoring the ancient form less for this reason [that it was the ancient name] than, it would seem, because he was moved by the divine will which had elected him to achieve what his surname and given name signified. Divine providence habitually intends that the persons designated to serve should receive the given names and surnames corresponding to the task entrusted to them, as we see in many a place in the Scriptures; and the Philosopher says in chapter IV of his *Metaphysics,* 'Names should accord with the qualities and uses of things.' This is why he was called Cristobal, which is to say *Christum Ferens,* which means the bearer of the Christ, and it was thus that he often signed his name; for in truth he was the first to open the gates of the Ocean sea, in order to bear our Savior Jesus Christ over the waves to those remote lands and those realms hitherto unknown. . . . His surname was Colón, which means *repopulator,* a name befitting the man whose enterprise brought about the discovery of these peoples, these infinite numbers of souls who, thanks to the preaching of the Gospel, . . . have proceeded and will every day proceed to repopulate the glorious city of Heaven. It also befits this man, in that he was the first to bring the people of Spain (albeit not as they should have been) to found *colonies,* or new populations, which, being established amid the original inhabitants . . . should constitute a new . . . Christian Church and a happy republic."

Columbus (or, in the proper orthography, Colón) and after him Las Casas, like many of their contemporaries, believe then that names, or at least the names of exceptional persons, should be in the image of their being; and Columbus had noted in himself two features worthy to figure in his own name: the evangelizer and the colonizer; he was not mistaken, after all. The same attention to his name, which borders on fetishism, is manifest in the concern with which he surrounds his signature; for he does not sign documents, like everyone else, with his name, but with a specially elaborated siglum—so elaborated, indeed, that we have still not managed to solve its mystery; moreover it is an emblem he is not content to use for himself alone, but also imposes on his heirs; hence we read in his deed of entail: "My son Don Diego and any other person who might inherit this entail, from the moment when he will have thus inherited it and will have taken possession of it, will sign always with my own signature, as I use it now, that is with an X with an S above it; an M with a Roman A above it, and above this latter an S; and then a Y, with an S above it, with dashes and commas, as I make them now and as they can be seen in the present instance" (22/2/1498).

Even the commas and periods are determined in advance! This extreme attention to his own name finds a natural extension in his activity as a name-giver in the course of his voyages. Like Adam in the midst of Eden, Columbus is profoundly concerned with the choice of names for the virgin world before his eyes; and as in his own case, these names must be motivated. The motivation is established in several ways. At the beginning, we observe a kind of diagram: the chronological order of the baptisms corresponds to the order of importance of the objects associated with these names. These will be, successively, God, the Virgin Mary, the King of Spain, the Queen, the Royal Prince. "To the first one I came upon [he is speaking of islands], I gave the name of *San Salvador*, in homage to His Heavenly Majesty who has wondrously given us all this. The Indians call this island Guanahani. I named the second island *Santa María de Concepción*, the third *Fernandina*, the fourth *Isabella*, the fifth *Juana*, and so to each of them I gave a new name" ("Letter to Santangel," February–March 1493).

Hence Columbus knows perfectly well that these islands already have names, natural ones in a sense (but in another acceptation of the term); others' words interest him very little, however, and he seeks to rename places in terms of the rank they occupy in his discovery, to give them the *right* names; moreover nomination is equivalent to taking possession. Later on, having more or less used up the religious and royal hierarchies, he resorts to a more traditional motivation—by direct resemblance—for which he immediately gives us a justification. "I gave this cape the name *Formoso* because indeed it is fair" (19/10/1492). "He called them *Islas de Arena* [islands of sand] owing to the shallowness of the sea for some six leagues about them in their southern part" (27/10/1492). "He saw a cape covered with palm trees, and named it *Cabo de Palmas*" (30/10/1492). "There is a cape which extends far into the sea, sometimes lofty and sometimes low, and that is why he named it *Cabo Alto y Baxo*" (19/12/1492). "Flakes of gold were found in the pans of the casks and in those of the pipe-hoops. The Admiral bestowed upon this river the name *Rio de Oro*" (8/1/1493). "When he saw the land it was a cape which he named *Cabo de Padre y Hijo*, because in its tip it is divided into two rocky spurs, one greater than the other" (12/1/1493, I, 195). "I called this place the *Jardines* because it corresponded to that name . . ." ("Letter to the Sovereigns," 31/8/1498).

Things must have the names that correspond to them. On certain days this obligation plunges Columbus into a veritable naming frenzy. Thus on January 11, 1493: "He sailed four leagues to the East, reaching a cape which he called *Bel Prado*. From there, to the southwest rises the mountain which he called *Monte de Plata*, which he said was eight leagues away. At eighteen leagues to the East, a quarter southeast of the *Bel Prado*, is found the cape which he called *del Angel*. . . . Four leagues to the East one quarter Southeast, there is a point which the Admiral called *del Hierro*. Four leagues farther, in the same direction, is another point which he named *Punta Seca*, then six leagues farther is the cape which he called *Redondo*. Beyond, to the East is found *Cabo Franses*. . . ." His pleasure seems to be such that on certain days he gives two successive names to the same place (thus on December 6, 1492, a harborage named Maria at dawn becomes Saint Nicholas at vespers); if, on the other hand, someone else seeks to imitate him in his name-giving action, he cancels that decision in order to impose his own names: in the course of his escapade, Pinzón had named a river after himself (which the Admiral never does), but Columbus is quick to rebaptize it "River of Grace." Not even the Indians escape the cascade of names: the first men brought back to Spain are rebaptized Don Juan de Castilla and Don Fernando de Aragón. . . .

The first gesture Columbus makes upon contact with the newly discovered lands (hence the first contact between Europe and what will be America) is an act of extended nomination: this is the declaration according to which these lands are henceforth part of the Kingdom of Spain. Columbus disembarks in a boat decorated with the royal banner, and accompanied by his two captains, as well as by the royal notary armed with his inkwell. Before the eyes of the doubtless perplexed Indians, and without paying them the least attention, Columbus orders a deed of possession to be drawn up. "He called upon them to bear faith and to witness that he, before all men, was taking possession of the said island—as in fact he then took possession of it—in the name of the King and of the Queen, his Sovereigns . . ." (11/10/1492). That this should be the very first action performed by Columbus in America tells us a great deal about the importance the ceremony of naming assumed in his eyes.

Now, as we have said, proper names form a very particular sector of the vocabulary: devoid of meaning, they serve only for denotation, but not directly for human communication; they are addressed to nature (to the referent), not to men; they are, in the fashion of indices, direct associations between aural sequences of sounds and segments of the world. The share of human communication that occupies Columbus's attention is therefore precisely that sector of language which serves, at least in an initial phase, only to designate nature.

On the other hand, Columbus shows little interest in the rest of the vocabulary, revealing still further his naive conception of language, since he always perceives names as identified with things: the entire dimension of intersubjectivity, of the reciprocal value of words (in opposition to their denotative capacity), of the human and therefore arbitrary character of signs, escapes him. Here is a significant episode, a kind of parody of the ethnographic task: having learned the Indian word *cacique*, he is less concerned to know what it signifies in the Indians' conventional and relative hierarchy than to see to just which Spanish word it corresponds, as if it followed of itself that the Indians establish the same distinctions as the Spaniards, as if the Spanish usage were not one convention among others, but rather the natural state of things: "Until then, the Admiral had not been able to understand if this word [cacique] signified king or governor. They also had another name for grandee, which they call *nitayno*, but he did not know if they say this for hidalgo or governor or judge" ("Journal," 30/12/1492). Not for a moment does Columbus doubt that the Indians distinguish, as the Spaniards do, between nobleman, governor, and judge; his curiosity, quite limited moreover, bears only on the exact Indian equivalent for these terms. The entire vocabulary is, for him, in the image of proper names, and these derive from the properties of the objects they designate: the colonizer must be called Colón. Words are, and are only, the image of things.

Hence we shall not be surprised to see how little attention Columbus pays to foreign languages. His spontaneous reaction, which he does not always make explicit but which underlies his behavior, is that, ultimately, linguistic diversity does not exist, since language is natural. Which is all the more astounding in that Columbus himself is polyglot, and at the same time deprived of his mother tongue: he speaks equally well (or badly) Genoese, Latin, Portuguese, Spanish. But ideological certainties can always overcome individual contingencies. His very conviction of Asia's proximity, which gives him the courage to set out, rests on a specific linguistic misunderstanding. The common belief of his time holds that the earth is round; but it is supposed, with reason, that the distance between Europe and Asia by the western route is very great, even impassable. Columbus takes for his authority the Arab astronomer Alfraganus, who quite correctly indicates the earth's circumference, but who expressed himself in Arab nautical miles, which are about a third greater than the Italian nautical miles familiar to

Columbus. Now Columbus cannot imagine that such measurements are conventional, that the same term has different significations according to different traditions (or languages, or contexts); he therefore translates into Italian nautical miles, and so finds the distance within the measure of his powers. And although Asia is not where he believes it to be, he has the consolation of discovering America. . . .

Columbus's failure to recognize the diversity of languages permits him, when he confronts a foreign tongue, only two possible, and complementary, forms of behavior: to acknowledge it as a language but to refuse to believe it is different; or to acknowledge its difference but to refuse to admit it is a language. . . . This latter reaction is provoked by the Indians he encounters at the very beginning, on October 12, 1492; seeing them, he promises himself: "If it please Our Lord, at the moment of my departure I shall take from this place six of them to Your Highnesses, so that they may learn to speak" (these terms seemed so shocking to Columbus's various French translators that all of them corrected the statement to: "so that they may learn our language"). Later on, he is willing to admit that they do have a language, but he cannot bear the notion that it is different, and he persists in hearing familiar words in their remarks, and in speaking to them as if they must understand him, or in censuring their poor pronunciation of the names or words he supposes he recognizes. With this distorted understanding, Columbus engages in some absurd and imaginary dialogues, of which the most sustained example concerns the Grand Khan, the goal of his voyage. The Indians utter the word *Cariba*, designating the (man-eating) inhabitants of the Caribbean islands. Columbus hears *Caniba*, which is to say, the people of the khan. But he also understands that according to the Indians these persons have dogs' heads (from the Spanish *cane*, "dog") with which, precisely, they eat people. Now this seems to him no more than an invention, and he censures them for it: "The Admiral believed they were lying and thought that their captors must be under the signory of the Grand Khan" (26/11/1492).

When Columbus finally acknowledges the foreignness of one language, he insists at least that it be also the foreignness of all the others; on the one side, then, there are the Latin languages, and on the other, all foreign tongues; the resemblances are great within each group, to judge by Columbus's own facility for the former and, by the language specialist he takes with him, for the latter: when he hears mention of a great cacique in the interior, whom he imagines to be the khan, i.e., the emperor of China, he sends to him as emissary "a certain Luis de Torres, a converted Jew [who] had served the *adelantado* of Murcia and knew, it is said, Hebrew and Aramaic and also some Arabic" (2/11/1492). We may wonder in what language the negotiations between Columbus's envoy and the Indian cacique, alias the emperor of China, would have occurred; but this latter did not keep the rendezvous.

The result of this failure of attention to the other's language is predictable: indeed, throughout the first voyage, before the Indians taken back to Spain have learned "to speak," the situation is one of total incomprehension; or, as Las Casas says in the margin of Columbus's journal: "They were all groping in darkness, because they did not understand what the Indians were saying" (30/10/1490). This is not shocking, after all, nor even surprising; what is, on the other hand, is that Columbus regularly claims to understand what is said to him, while giving, at the same time, every proof of incomprehension. For instance, on October 24, 1492, he writes: "From what the Indians told me, [the island of Cuba] is of vast extent, great commerce, richly provided with gold and spices, visited by great ships and merchants." But two lines farther, on the same day, he adds: "I do not understand their language." What he "understands," then, is simply a summary of the books of Marco Polo and Pierre d'Ailly. "He believed he understood that here put in ships of great tonnage belonging to the Grand Khan, and that the mainland was ten days' sail distant" (28/10/1492). "I repeat then what I have said on several occasions: that Caniba is no other thing than the people of the Grand Khan who must indeed be near to this place." And he adds this dry commentary: "Each day, the Admiral said, we understand these Indians better, and they the same, although several times they have mistaken one thing said for another" (11/12/1492). We possess another narrative illustrating the way in which his men made themselves understood by the Indians: "The Christians, believing that if they disembarked only by two or three from the barges, the Indians would not fear them, advanced toward them in a party of three, shouting to them not to be afraid in their language, which they know a little from the conversation of those whom they had captured. In the end the Indians all took to their heels, so that not a trace of them remained" (27/11/1492).

Moreover, Columbus is not always the dupe of his illusions, and he admits that there is no communication (which makes all the more problematic the "information" he believes he derives from his conversations): "I do not know the language of the men here, they do not understand me, nor do I nor any of my men understand them" (27/11/1492). He did not understand their language, he says again, "save by conjecture" (15/1/1493); we realize, moreover, how untrustworthy this method is.

Nonverbal communication is scarcely more successful than the exchange of speech. Columbus prepares to land with his men on the shore. "One of the Indians [whom he sees facing him] advanced into the river near the prow of the barge, and delivered a long speech which the Admiral failed to understand [at which we are not surprised]. But he observed that the other Indians from time to time raised their hands toward the sky and uttered a great shout. The Admiral surmised that they were assuring him that his coming was a welcome event [typical example of wishful thinking], but he saw the face of the Indian whom he had taken with him (and who understands the language) change color, turn yellow as wax, and tremble mightily while saying by signs that the Admiral should leave the river because they sought to kill him" (3/12/1492). Again we may wonder if Columbus has realized what the second Indian was telling him "by signs." And here is another example of symbolic communication about as successful as the rest: "I greatly desired to hold converse with them, and yet I had nothing with me which I might show them to make them come near, except for a tambourine which I had brought upon the foredeck and which I ordered beaten so that several young men could dance to it, thinking that they would come to see the festivity. But as soon as they saw the tambourine beaten and the men dancing, all dropped the oars, took up their bows, stretched them, each man covering himself with his shield, and they began raining arrows upon us" ("Letter to the Sovereigns," 31/8/1498).

These failures are not due only to incomprehension of the language, to ignorance of the Indians' ways (though Columbus might have sought to overcome such obstacles): the exchanges with Europeans are not much more successful. Thus, on the return leg of the first voyage, in the Azores, we find Columbus making one mistake after the other in his communications with a Portuguese captain who is hostile to him: too credulous at first, Columbus sees his men arrested, whereas he had hoped for the most favorable reception; crudely dissembling thereafter, he fails to lure this captain onto his ship in order to imprison him in his turn. His perception of the very men who surround him is not very clear-sighted: those to whom he grants his entire confidence (such as Roldán, or Hojeda) immediately turn against him, whereas he neglects those who are genuinely devoted to him, such as Diego Mendez.

Columbus does not succeed in his human communications because he is not interested in them. We read in his journal for December 6, 1492, that the Indians he has taken on board his ship try to escape and are distressed to find themselves far from their island. "Moreover he did not understand them any better than they understood him, and they were greatly afraid of the people on this new island. Therefore, in order to make converse with its people, he would have had to tarry there for several days. But he did not do so, in order to see further lands and from doubt that the weather would hold." Everything is in the sequence of these few sentences: Columbus's summary perception of the Indians, a mixture of authoritarianism and condescension; the incomprehension of their language and of their signs; the readiness with which he alienates the other's goodwill with a view to a better knowledge of the islands he is discovering; the preference for land over men. In Columbus's hermeneutics human beings have no particular place.

Columbus and the Indians

COLUMBUS speaks about the men he sees only because they too, after all, constitute a part of the landscape. His allusions to the inhabitants of the islands always occur amid his notations concerning nature, somewhere between birds and trees. "In the interior of the lands, there are many mines of metal and countless inhabitants" ("Letter to Santangel," February–March 1493). "Hitherto, things had gone better and better for him, in that he had discovered so many lands as well as woods, plants, fruits and flowers as well as the people" ("Journal," 25/11/1492). "The roots of this place are as thick as a man's legs, and all the people, he says, were strong and brave" (16/18/1492): we readily see how the inhabitants are introduced, by means of a comparison necessary to describe the roots. "Here, they observed that the married women wore clouts of cotton, but the wenches nothing, save for a few who were already eighteen years old. There were also dogs, mastiffs and terriers. They found as well a man who had in his nose a gold stud the size of half a *castellano*" (17/19/1492): this allusion to the dogs among the remarks on the women and the men indicates nicely the scale on which the latter will be assessed.

The first mention of the Indians is significant: "Presently they saw naked people" (11/10/1492). The event is true enough; it is nonetheless revealing that the first characteristic of these people to strike Columbus is the absence of clothes—which in their turn symbolize culture (whence Columbus's interest in people wearing clothes, who might relate more closely to what is known of the Grand Khan; he is somewhat disappointed to have found nothing but savages). And the observation recurs: "They all go naked, men and women, as the day they were born" (6/11/1492). "This king and all his people went naked as their mothers bore them, and their women the same, without any shame" (16/12/1492): the women, at least, might have made an effort. Thereupon his remarks are frequently limited to the physical aspect of the people, to their stature, to the color of their skin (the more favored if it is lighter—i.e., more like his own). "They are of the color of the Canary Islanders, neither black nor white" (11/10/1492). "They are whiter than those of the other islands. Among others, he had seen two wenches as white as they might be in Spain" (13/12/1492). "And the women have very pretty bodies" (21/12/1492). And he concludes with astonishment that, although naked, the Indians seem closer to men than to animals. "All these people of the islands and of the mainland beyond, even if they seem bestial and go naked, . . . seem to him to be quite rational and of acute intelligence" (Bernaldez).

Physically naked, the Indians are also, to Columbus's eyes, deprived of all cultural property: they are characterized, in a sense, by the absence of customs, rites, religion (which has a certain logic, since for a man like Columbus, human beings wear clothes following their expulsion from Paradise, itself at the source of their cultural identity). Here there is also his habit of seeing things as it suits him; but it is significant that it leads him to the image of spiritual nudity: "It seemed to me that all these people were very poor in everything," he writes upon his first encounter, and again: "It has seemed to me that they belonged to no religion" (11/10/1492). "These people are very gentle and fearful, naked as I have already said, without weapons and without laws" (4/11/1492). "They have no religion, nor are they idolators" (27/11/1492). Already deprived of language, the Indians reveal themselves to be without law or religion; and if they have a material culture, it attracts Columbus's attention no more than their spiritual culture: "They brought skeins of spun cotton, parrots, darts and other trifles which it would be wearisome to describe" (13/10/1492). The important thing, of course, is the presence of the parrots. His attitude with regard to this other culture is, in the best of cases, that of the collector of curiosities, and it is never accompanied by any attempt at comprehension: observing for the first time certain masonry constructions (during the fourth voyage, on the coast of Honduras), he contents himself with ordering a piece of it to be broken off to keep as a souvenir.

He finds nothing astonishing in the fact that all these Indians, culturally virgin, a blank page awaiting the Spanish and Christian inscription, resemble each other. "The people were all like those of whom I have already spoken, of the same condition, as naked and of the same stature" (17/10/1492). "There came many of these people, like those of the other islands, as naked and likewise painted" (22/10/1492). "These people have the same natures and the same customs as those whom we have encountered hitherto" (1/11/1492). "These are, the Admiral said, people similar to the Indians I have already spoken of, of the same credulity" (3/12/1492). The Indians resemble each other in that they are all naked, deprived of distinctive characteristics.

Given this ignorance of the Indians' culture and their consequent identification with nature, we cannot expect to find in Columbus's writings a detailed portrait of the population. His initial image of them obeys the same rules as the description of nature: Columbus has decided to admire everything, and therefore first of all their physical beauty. "They were all very well made, stout in body and very comely of countenance" (11/10/1492). "All of splendid appearance. They are very handsome people" (13/10/1492). "These were the handsomest men and the most beautiful women whom he had hitherto encountered" (16/12/1492).

An author like Peter Martyr, who faithfully reflects the impressions (or the fantasies) of Columbus and of his first companions, delights in painting idyllic scenes. Here is how the Indians come to salute Columbus: "All the women were lovely. One might have supposed one was seeing those splendid naiads or those nymphs of the springs so celebrated by Antiquity. Holding up palm fronds, which they carried while performing their dances, accompanied by songs, they knelt and presented them to the *adelantado* [governor]" (I, 5; see fig. 3).

This admiration determined in advance also extends to morality. These people are good, Columbus declares at the start, without any concern to ground his affirmation. "They are the best people in the world and the most peaceable" (16/12/1492). "The Admiral said that he cannot believe that a man has ever seen people so good-hearted" (21/12/1492). "I do not believe that in all the world there are better men, any more than there are better lands" (25/12/1492): the ready enchantment with men and lands suggests the spirit in which Columbus writes, and the little confidence we can grant to the descriptive qualities of his remarks. Further, when he knows the Indians better, he

Fig. 3 Columbus lands in Haiti.

will leap to the other extreme, which is not thereby a source of information worthier of belief: shipwrecked on Jamaica, he sees himself "surrounded by a million savages filled with cruelty and inimical to us" ("Lettera Rarissima," 7/7/1503). Of course, what is striking here is the fact that Columbus finds, to characterize the Indians, only by adjectives of the *good/wicked* type, which in reality teach us nothing: not only because these qualities depend on the point of view adopted, but also because they correspond to specific states and not to stable characteristics, because they derive from the pragmatic estimate of a situation and not from the desire to know.

Two features of the Indians seem, at first sight, less predictable than the rest: their "generosity" and their "cowardice"; but as we read on in Columbus's descriptions, we perceive that these assertions tell us more about Columbus than about the Indians. Lacking words, Indians and Spaniards exchange, at the first meeting, various small objects; and Columbus unceasingly praises the generosity of the Indians, who give everything for nothing; it sometimes borders, he decides, on stupidity: why do they value a piece of glass quite as much as a coin, and a worthless piece of small change as much as a gold piece? "I have given," he writes, "many other things of slight value from which they took great pleasure" ("Journal," 11/10/1492). "All that they have they give for any trifle we offer them, so that they take in exchange pieces of crockery and fragments of glass goblets" (13/10/1492). "For anything at all we give them, without ever saying it is too little, they immediately give whatever they possess" (13/12/1492). "Whether it is a thing of value or a thing of little cost, whatever the object then given them in exchange and whatever it is worth, they are pleased" ("Letter to Santangel," February–March 1493). Nor more than in the case of languages does Columbus understand that values are conventional, that gold is not more precious than glass "in itself," but only in the European system of exchange. Hence, when he concludes this description of the exchanges by saying: "Even bits of broken cask-hoops they took in exchange for whatever they had, like beasts!" ("Letter to Santangel," February–March 1493), we have the impression that in this case it is Columbus who is worthy of the comparison: a different system of exchange is for him equivalent to the absence of system, from which he infers the bestial character of the Indians.

The feeling of superiority engenders a protectionist behavior: Columbus tells us that he forbids his sailors to make a swap he regards as scandalous. Yet we see Columbus himself offering preposterous presents, which are associated in our mind today with "savages," but which Columbus is the first to have taught them to admire and demand. "I sent for him and gave him a red cap, some little green glass beads which I attached to his arm, and two hawk's bells which I hung from his ears" ("Journal," 15/10/1492). "I gave him a very fine amber necklace which I was wearing round my neck, a pair of red slippers and a bottle of orange-flower water. He was so pleased with this that it was a wonder" (18/12/1492). "The lord now wore a shirt and gloves which the Admiral had given him" (26/12/1492). We understand that Columbus is shocked by the other's nakedness, but are the gloves, the red hat, and the slippers, in these circumstances, presents really more useful than the broken glass goblets? The Indian chiefs, in any case, can henceforth pay him a visit dressed. Subsequently we see that the Indians find other uses for the Spanish gifts, without their utility being demonstrated for all that. "Since they had no clothes, the people wondered what the needles could be used for, but the Spaniards satisfied their ingenuous curiosity, for they showed by signs that the needles serve to remove the thorns and splinters which often penetrate their skin, or else to pick their teeth; hence they began to prize them highly" (Peter Martyr, I, 8).

On the basis of these observations and these exchanges Columbus will declare the Indians the most generous people in the world, thereby making an important contribution to the myth of the noble savage. "They are without covetousness of another man's goods" (26/12/1492). "They are to such a degree lacking in artifice and so generous with what they possess, that no man would believe it unless he had seen such a thing" ("Letter to Santangel," February–March 1493). "And let it not be said, the Admiral said, that they give liberally only because what they gave was of little worth, for those who gave pieces of gold and those who gave a water calabash acted in the same way and just as liberally. And it is an easy thing," he adds, "to know, when a thing is given, that it is given with a free heart" ("Journal," 21/12/1492).

The thing is in fact less easy than it appears. Columbus has a presentiment of this when, in his letter to Santangel, he recapitulates his experience: "I could not learn if they possess private property, but I seemed to discern that all owned a share of what one of them owned, and particularly with regard to victuals" (February–March 1493).

Would a different relation to private property provide an explanation of this "generous" behavior? His son Fernando testifies as much, in relating an episode of the second voyage. "Certain Indies which the Admiral had brought from Isabella went into those cabins [which belonged to the local Indians] and made use of whatever they pleased; the owners gave no sign of displeasure, as if everything they owned were common property. The people, believing that we had the same custom, went at first among the Christians and took whatever they pleased; but they swiftly discovered their mistake" (51). Columbus thus forgets his own perception, and soon after declares that the Indians, far from being generous, are all thieves (a reversal parallel to the one that transforms them from the best men in the world into violent savages); thereby he imposes cruel punishments upon them, the same then in effect in Spain: "As on that voyage I made to Cibao, when it happened that some Indian stole something or other, if you discover that some among them steal, you must punish them by cutting off nose and ears, for those are the parts of the body which cannot be concealed" ("Instructions to Mosén Pedro Margarite," 9/4/1494).

The discourse concerning cowardice follows exactly the same course. First comes amused condescension: "They have no weapons, and are so fearful that one of our men suffices to chase away a hundred of them, even in jest" ("Journal," 10/11/1492). "The Admiral declares to the Sovereigns that with ten men one can chase away ten thousand of theirs, so timid are they, and cowardly" (3/12/1492). "They have neither iron, nor steel, nor weapons, and they are not made for such things; not that they are not strong and of fine stature, but because they are wondrously timid" ("Letter to Santangel," February–March 1493). The pursuit of the Indians by dogs, another of Columbus's "discoveries," rests on a similar observation: "For, against the Indians, one dog is the equal of ten men" (Bernáldez). Columbus therefore confidently leaves a troop of his men, at the end of the first voyage, on the island of Hispaniola; but, returning a year later, he is obliged to admit that they have all been killed by these same timid Indians who are so ignorant of weapons; has it taken a thousand of them to overcome each of the Spaniards? He then shifts to the other extreme, deducing in a sense their courage from their cowardice. "There are no people so wicked as the cowardly who never risk their life face to face, and you shall know that if the Indians find one or two men separated from the rest, it will not be surprising if they should kill them" ("Instructions to Mosén Pedro Margarite," 9/4/1494); their king Caonabo is "a man as wicked as he is bold" ("Memorial for Antonio de Torres," 30/1/1494). We do not have the impression that Columbus has thereby understood the Indians better afterwards than before: he never in fact escapes from himself.

At one moment of his career, it is true, Columbus makes a further effort. This occurs during the second voyage, when he asks a religious, Friar Ramón Pane, to describe in detail the Indians' manners and beliefs; and he himself provides, in a preface to this description, a page of "ethnographic" observations. He begins by a declaration of principle: "I have found among them neither idolatry nor any other religion," a thesis maintained despite the examples that immediately follow, under his own pen. For he describes, in effect, several "idolatrous" practices, adding however: "None of our men could understand the words which they uttered." His attention then turns to the revelation of a fraud: a talking idol was really a hollow object connected by a pipe to another room of the house in which the magician's assistant was sitting. The little treatise by Ramón Pane (preserved in the biography of Ferdinand Columbus, chapter 62) is much more interesting, but rather in spite of its author, who tirelessly repeats: "Since the Indians have neither alphabet nor writing, they do not speak their myths clearly, and it is impossible for me to transcribe them correctly; I am afraid I shall put the end at the beginning, and the other way around" (6). "Since I was writing in haste and without enough paper, I could not put everything in its place" (8). "I could learn nothing more on this matter, and what I write is of little worth" (11).

Can we guess, reading Columbus's notes, how the Indians, for their part, perceive the Spaniards? Hardly. Here again, all information is vitiated by the fact that Columbus has decided everything in advance: and since the tone, in the course of the first voyage, is one of admiration, the Indians too must admire. "They spoke many things among themselves which I could not understand, but I saw clearly that everything about us was a wonder to them" ("Journal," 18/12/1492): even without understanding, Columbus knows that the Indian "king" is in ecstasies in his presence. It is possible, as Columbus says, that the Indians wonder if the Spaniards are not beings of divine origin, which would certainly explain their initial fear and its disappearance before the Spaniards' altogether human behavior. "They are credulous; they know that there is a God in the heavens, and remain convinced that

that is where we have come from" (12/11/1492). "All of them believed that the Christians came from the heavens, and that the realms of the Sovereigns of Castile were to be found there and not in this world" (16/12/1492). "Today, long as they have been with me and despite numerous conversations, they remain convinced that I come from the heavens" ("Letter to Santangel," February–March 1493). We shall return to this belief when we can observe it in greater detail; we may note, nonetheless, that the ocean might well appear to Caribbean Indians quite as abstract as the space separating the sky from the earth.

The human side of the Spaniards is their thirst for earthly possessions: gold, from the beginning, as we have seen; and, soon after, women. There is a striking example of this in the remarks of one Indian, reported by Columbus: "One of the Indians taken by the Admiral spoke with their king, telling him how the Christians came from the sky and that they were seeking gold" ("Journal," 16/12/1492). This remark was true in more than one sense. We can say, in fact, simplifying to the point of caricature, that the Spanish conquistadors belong, historically, to that transitional period between a Middle Ages dominated by religion and a modern period that places material goods at the top of its scale of values. In practice, too, the conquest will have these two essential aspects: the Christians are generous with their religion, which they bring to the New World; from it they take, in exchange, gold and wealth.

Columbus's attitude with regard to the Indians is based on his perception of them. We can distinguish here two component parts, which we shall find again in the following century and, in practice, down to our own day in every colonist in his relations to the colonized; we have already observed these two attitudes in germ in Columbus's report concerning the other's language. Either he conceives the Indians (though without using these words) as human beings altogether, having the same rights as himself; but then he sees them not only as equals but also as identical, and this behavior leads to assimilationism, the projection of his own values on the others. Or else he starts from the difference, but the latter is immediately translated into terms of superiority and inferiority (in his case, obviously, it is the Indians who are inferior). What is denied is the existence of a human substance truly other, something capable of being not merely an imperfect state of oneself. These two elementary figures of the experience of alterity are both grounded in egocentrism, in the identification of our own values with values in general, of our *I* with the universe—in the conviction that the world is one.

On one hand, then, Columbus wants the Indians to be like himself, and like the Spaniards. He is an assimilationist in an unconscious and naive fashion; his sympathy for the Indians is "naturally" translated into the desire to see them adopt his own customs. He decides to take several Indians back to Spain in order that "upon their return they might be the interpreters of the Christians and might adopt our customs and our faith" (12/11/1492). They are disposed, he also says, "to be made to build cities, to be taught to wear clothes, and to adopt our customs" (16/12/1492). "Your Highnesses may have great joy of them, for soon you will have made them into Christians and will have instructed them in the good manners of your kingdoms" (24/12/1492). There is never a justification of this desire to make the Indians adopt the Spanish customs; its rightness is self-evident.

In general, this project of assimilation is identified with the desire to convert the Indians, to propagate the Gospel. We know that this intention is fundamental to Columbus's initial project, even if the idea is somewhat abstract at the start (no priest accompanies the first expedition). But as soon as he sees the Indians, the intention begins to grow more concrete. Immediately after having taken possession of the new lands by a formally established notarial action, Columbus declares: "I have known that they were people disposed to submit themselves and to convert to our Holy Faith much more readily by love than by force . . ." (11/10/1492). Columbus's "knowledge" is obviously a decision made in advance; further it concerns only the means to be used, not the end to be achieved, which he has no need to assert: it is, once again, self-evident. And he constantly returns to the notion that conversion is the principal goal of this expedition, and to his hope that the rulers of Spain will accept the Indians as their subjects altogether. "And I say that Your Highnesses must not permit any foreigner to conduct business with this country or to set foot in it if he is not a Catholic Christian, for the end and the beginning of this enterprise was the propagation and the glory of the Christian religion, and not to admit into these regions any man who may not be a good Christian" (27/11/1492). Such an attitude implies, among other things, a respect for the individual will of the Indians, since they are from the start placed on the same level as other Christians. "Since he already held these people for the Sovereigns of Castile and since there was no reason to work any harm upon them, he decided to release him [an old Indian man]" (18/12/1492).

Columbus's vision in this respect is facilitated by his capacity to see things as it suits him. In this case, the Indians seem to him already bearers of Christian qualities, already animated by the desire to convert. We have seen that, for Columbus, they belong to no "sect," are virgin of any religion; but more than this, they are already predisposed to Christianity. As though by accident, the virtues he imagines them to possess are Christian virtues: "These people have no religion, nor are they idolators, but very gentle and ignorant of evil, and do not even know how to kill one another. . . . They are very ready to say the prayers that we teach them and to make the sign of the Cross. Hence Your Highnesses must be persuaded to make Christians of them" (12/11/1492). This image can be arrived at, of course, only at the price of the suppression of every feature of the Indians that contradicts it— a suppression in the discourse concerning them, but also, if need be, in reality. In the course of the second expedition, the priests accompanying Columbus begin converting the Indians; but it is far from the truth that all of them submit and consent to venerate the holy images. "After having left the chapel, these men flung the images to the ground, covered them with a heap of earth, and pissed upon it"; seeing which, Bartholomé, Columbus's brother, decides to punish them in quite Christian fashion. "As lieutenant of the Viceroy and governor of the islands, he brought these wretched men to justice and, their crimes being duly attested to, he caused them to be burned alive in public" (Ramón Pane, in F. Columbus, 62, 26).

Whatever the case, spiritual expansion, as we now know, is indissolubly linked to material conquest (money is necessary to conduct a crusade); and thus a first flaw appears in a program that implied the equality of the partners: material conquest (and all that it implies) will be both the result and the condition of spiritual expansion. Columbus writes: "I believe that, if we begin, in a very short time Your Highnesses will succeed in converting to our Holy Faith a multitude of peoples while gaining great domains and wealth as well for all the peoples of Spain, because without any doubt there are in these lands great quantities of gold" (12/11/1492). This linkage becomes almost automatic for Columbus: "Your Highnesses have here another world in which our Holy Faith may be so propagated and whence may be taken so much wealth" ("Letter to the Sovereigns," 31/8/1498). The profit Spain takes from the enterprise is incontestable: "By the Divine will, I have thus placed another world under the authority of the King and of the Queen, our Sovereigns, and thereby Spain, which was reckoned poor, has become the richest realm of all" ("Letter to Doña Juana de Torres," November 1500).

Columbus behaves as if a certain equilibrium were established between the two actions: the Spaniards give religion and take gold. But, aside from the fact that the exchange is rather asymmetrical and does not necessarily benefit the other party, the implications of these two actions are contrary to each other. To propagate the faith presupposes that the Indians are considered his equals (before God). But what if they are unwilling to give their wealth? Then they must be subdued, in military and political terms, so that it may be taken from them by force; in other words, they are to be placed, from the human perspective this time, in a position of inequality (inferiority). Now, it is without the slightest hesitation that Columbus speaks of the necessity of subduing the Indians, not perceiving any contradiction between what each of his actions involves, or at least any discontinuity he thereby established between the divine and the human. This is why he remarks that the Indians were timid and did not know how to use weapons. "With fifty men Your Highnesses would hold them all in subjection and do with them all that you could wish" ("Journal," 14/10/1492): is it still the Christian speaking here? Is it still a matter of equality? Embarking for the third time for America, he asks permission to take with him criminals who would volunteer for the enterprise and thereby be pardoned: is this still the project of an evangelist?

"My desire," Columbus writes during the first voyage, "was to pass by no single island without taking possession of it" (15/10/1492); on occasion, he even offers an island here and there to one of his companions. At the beginning, the Indians must not have understood much about the ceremonies Columbus and his notaries were performing. But when it became apparent what they were doing, the Indians did not seem to be especially enthusiastic. In the course of the fourth voyage, the following episode occurs: "I built here a village and gave many presents to the *quibian*—for so they call the lord of this land—[gloves? a red hat? Columbus does not tell us] but I knew well that this peace would not last. These are, indeed, very wild people [we may translate: unwilling to submit to the Spaniards], and my men are very importunate; finally I took possession of lands belonging to this *quibian* [second half of the exchange: one gives gloves, one takes lands]. As soon as he saw the houses we had built and a lively trade going on, he determined to burn everything and to kill us all" ("Lettera Rarissima," 7/7/1503). The sequel of this story is even more sinister. The Spaniards manage to capture the *quibian*'s family as hostages; several of the Indians succeed in escaping nonetheless. "The remaining prisoners were seized with despair, for they had not escaped with their comrades, and it was discovered the next morning that they had hanged themselves from the bridge-poles, with some ropes they had managed to find there, bending their knees to do so, for otherwise there was not enough room for them to hang themselves properly." Ferdinand, Columbus's son, who reports this episode, was present at it; he was only fourteen years old at the time, and we may imagine that the reaction which follows was at least as much his father's as his own: "For those of us who were on board our ship, their death was not a great loss, but it seriously aggravated the situation of our men on land; the *quibian* would have been delighted to make peace in exchange for his children, but now that we had no hostages remaining, there was every reason to fear that he would wage war even more cruelly against our village" (99).

Whereupon war replaces peace; but we may assume that Columbus had never entirely overlooked this means of expansion, since from the first voyage he nurses a special project: "I set out this morning," he notes on October 14, 1492, "in search of a place where a fortress might be built." "Because there is a rocky cape on rather high ground, one might well build a fortress here" (5/11/1492). We know that he will fulfill this dream after his ship is wrecked, and that he will leave his men here. But is not the fortress, even if it proves rather ineffectual, already one step toward war, hence toward submission and inequality?

Thus, by gradual stages, Columbus will shift from assimilationism, which implied an equality of principle, to an ideology of enslavement, and hence to the assertion of the Indians' inferiority. We could already guess this from several summary judgments appearing in the first contacts. "They would make good and industrious servants" (11/10/1492). "They are fit to be ruled" (16/12/1492). In order to remain consistent, Columbus establishes subtle distinctions between innocent, potentially Christian Indians and idolatrous Indians, practicing cannibalism; and between pacific Indians (submitting to his power) and bellicose Indians who thereby deserve to be punished; but the important thing is that those who are not already Christians can only be slaves: there is no middle path. Hence he foresees that the ships that transport herds of cattle from Europe to America will be loaded with slaves on the return journey, in order to keep them from remaining empty and until gold is found in sufficient quantities, the equivalence implicitly established between beasts and men not being gratuitous, of course. "The conveyors could be paid in cannibal slaves, fierce but well-made fellows of good understanding, which men, wrested from their inhumanity, will be, we believe, the best slaves that ever were" ("Memorial for Antonio de Torres," 30/1/1494).

The Spanish sovereigns do not accept this suggestion of Columbus's they prefer to have vassals, not slaves—subjects capable of paying taxes rather than belonging to a third party; but Columbus nonetheless does not abandon his project, and writes again in September 1498: "From here one might send, in the name of the Holy Trinity, as many slaves as could be sold, as well as a quantity of Brazil [timber]. If the information I have is correct, it appears that we could sell four thousand slaves, who might be worth twenty millions and more" ("Letter to the Sovereigns," September 1498). The displacements might raise some problems at the beginning, but these will quickly be solved. "It is true that many of them die now; but this will not always be so. The Negroes and the Canarians had begun in the same fashion" (ibid.). This is indeed the meaning of his government of the island of Hispaniola, and another letter to the sovereigns, dated October 1498, is summarized thus by Las Casas: "In all that he says, there seems to emerge the fact that the profit he sought to bestow upon the Spaniards who were to be left in the place consisted in the slaves he would give them to be sold in Castile" (*Historia*, I, 155). In Columbus's mind, the propagation of the faith and the submission to slavery are indissolubly linked.

Michele de Cuneo, a member of the second expedition, has left one of the rare accounts describing in detail how the slave trade functioned at its inception; his narrative permits us no illusions as to how the Indians were perceived. "When our caravels . . . were to leave for Spain, we gathered in our settlement one thousand six hundred male and female persons of these Indians, and of these we embarked in our caravels on February 17, 1495, five hundred fifty souls among the healthiest males and females. For those who remained, we let it be known in the vicinity that anyone who wanted to take some of them could do so, to the amount desired; which was done. And when each man was thus provided with slaves, there still remained about four hundred, to whom permission was granted to go where they wished. Among them were many women with children still at suck. Since they were afraid that we might return to capture them once again, and in order to escape us the better, they left their children anywhere on the ground and began to flee like desperate creatures; and some fled so far that they found themselves at seven or eight days' distance from our community at Isabella, beyond the mountains and across enormous rivers; consequently they will henceforth be captured only with great difficulty." Such is the beginning of the operation; here now is the conclusion: "But when we reached the waters off Spain, around two hundred of these Indians died, I believe because of the unaccustomed air, which is colder than theirs. We cast them into the sea. . . . We disembarked all the slaves, half of whom were sick."

Even when there is no question of slavery, Columbus's behavior implies that he does not grant the Indians the right to have their own will, that he judges them, in short, as living objects. It is as such that, in his naturalist's enthusiasm, he always wants to take specimens of all kinds back to Spain: trees, birds, animals, and Indians; the notion of asking their opinion is foreign to him. "He says that he would capture some half dozen Indians in order to take them with him; but he says that he could not catch them because they had all left before nightfall. But the following day, Tuesday August 8, twelve men came in a canoe to the caravel: all were taken and brought to the Admiral's ship, and he selected six and sent the six others back to land" (Las Casas, *Historia*, I, 134). The figure is set in advance: a half dozen; the individuals do not count, but they are counted. On another occasion he wants women (not for lustful purposes, but in order to have a sampling of everything). "I have sent men to a house on the west bank of the river. They have brought me back seven head of women, girls and adults, and three infants" ("Journal," 12/11/1492). To be an Indian, and a woman to boot, immediately puts you on the same level as cattle.

Women: if Columbus is interested in them exclusively as a naturalist, such is not the case, need we remark, for the other members of the expedition. Let us read this account which the same Michele de Cuneo, a nobleman of Savona, provides of an episode occurring in the course of the second voyage—one story out of a thousand, but one that has the advantage of being told by its protagonist. "While I was in the boat, I captured a very beautiful Carib woman, whom the aforesaid Lord Admiral gave to me, and with whom, having brought her into my cabin, and she being naked as is their custom, I conceived the desire to take my pleasure. I wanted to put my desire to execution, but she was unwilling for me to do so, and treated me with her nails in such wise that I would have preferred never to have begun. But seeing this (in order to tell you the whole even to the end), I took a rope-end and thrashed her well, following which she produced such screaming and wailing as would cause you not to believe your ears. Finally we reached an agreement such that, I can tell you, she seemed to have been raised in a veritable school of harlots."

This account is revealing in more than one respect. The European finds the Indian women beautiful; obviously it does not occur to him to ask their consent to "put his desire to execution." Rather, he addresses this request to the Admiral, who is a man and a European like himself, and who seems to give women to his compatriots as readily as he distributed little bells to the native chiefs. Michele de Cuneo is writing of course to another man, and he masterfully adjusts the pleasure of the reading to his correspondent, since what is involved, in his eyes at least, is a story of pure pleasure. At first he assumes the absurd role of the humiliated male; but this is only to make his reader's satisfaction all the greater upon finding order reestablished and the white man triumphant. A last wink of complicity: our nobleman omits the description of the "execution," but lets it be deduced by its effects, apparently beyond his hopes. These effects also permit, in a striking example, the identification of the Indian woman with a whore: striking, for the woman who violently rejected sexual solicitation finds herself identified with the woman who makes this solicitation her profession. But is this not the true nature of every woman, which can be revealed by a certain number of lashes? Refusal can only be hypocritical; scratch resistance and reveal the whore. Indian women are women, or Indians to the second power; hence, they become the object of a double rape.

How can Columbus be associated with these two apparently contradictory myths, one whereby the Other is a "noble savage" (when perceived at a distance) and one whereby he is a "dirty dog," a potential slave? It is because both rest on a common basis, which is the failure to recognize the Indians, and the refusal to admit them as a subject having the same rights as oneself, but different. Columbus has discovered America but not the Americans.

The entire history of the discovery of America, the first episode of the conquest, is marked by this ambiguity: human alterity is at once revealed and rejected. The year 1492 already symbolizes, in the history of Spain, this double movement: in this same year the country repudiates its interior Other by triumphing over the Moors in the final battle of Granada and by forcing the Jews to leave its territory; and it discovers the exterior Other, that whole America which will become Latin. We know that Columbus himself constantly links the two events. "In this present year 1492, after Your Highnesses have brought to an end the war against the Moors . . . in this very month . . . Your Highnesses . . . determined to send me, Cristobal Colón, to the said regions of India. . . . Thus, after having driven all the Jews out of your realms and dominions, Your Highnesses in this same month of January commanded me to set out with a sufficient armada to the said countries of India," he writes at the head of the journal of the first voyage. The unity of the two endeavors, in which Columbus is prepared to see divine intervention, resides in the propagation of the Christian faith. "I hope in Our Lord that Your Highnesses will determine to send [priests] in great diligence in order to unite to the Church such great populations and to convert them, just as Your Highnesses have destroyed those who were unwilling to confess the Father, the Son and the Holy Ghost" (6/11/1492). But we can also see the two actions as directed in opposite, and complementary, directions: one expels heterogeneity from the body of Spain, the other irremediably introduces it there.

In his way, Columbus himself participates in this double movement. He does not perceive alterity, as we have seen, and he imposes his own values upon it; yet the term by which he most often refers to himself and which his contemporaries also employ is *extranjero*, "outsider"; and if so many countries have sought the honor of being his fatherland, it is because he himself had none.

2.   CONQUEST

The Reasons
for the Victory

THE encounter between Old World and New made possible by
Columbus's discovery is of a very special type: war, or rather, in the
term of the period, conquest. A mystery concerning the very outcome
of the combat still hovers over the conquest: why this lightninglike
victory, when the inhabitants of America are so superior in number to
their adversaries and fighting on their own territory as well? To confine
ourselves to the conquest of Mexico—the most spectacular, since the
Mexican civilization is the most brilliant of the pre-Columbian world
—how are we to account for the fact that Cortés, leading a few
hundred men, managed to seize the kingdom of Montezuma, who
commanded several hundred thousand? I shall try to find an answer in
the abundant literature to which this phase of the conquest gave rise
at the time: Cortés's own reports; the Spanish chronicles, the most
remarkable of which is that of Bernal Díaz del Castillo; lastly, the
native accounts, transcribed by the Spanish missionaries or written by
the Mexicans themselves.

Apropos of the use of this literature, one preliminary question arises
which did not have to be considered in the case of Columbus. The
latter's writings may have contained technically speaking, false statements; this in no way diminished their value, for I could interrogate
them chiefly as actions, not as descriptions. Here my subject is no
longer the experience of one man (who has written) but an event in
itself nonverbal, the conquest of Mexico; the documents analyzed are
no longer of concern solely (or chiefly) as actions, but as sources of
information about a reality of which they do not constitute a part. The

case of the texts expressing the Indians' point of view is especially problematic: as it happens, given the absence of native writings, they are all subsequent to the conquest and therefore influenced by the conquerors; I shall return to this point in the final chapter of this book. In a general way, I have an excuse and a justification to formulate here. The excuse: if we abjure this source of information, we cannot replace it by any other. Our only recourse is not to read these texts as transparent statements, but to try at the same time to take into account the action and circumstances of their utterance. As for the justification, it can be expressed in the language of the classical rhetoricians: the questions raised here refer less to a knowledge of the truth than to a knowledge of verisimilitude. That is, an event may not have occurred, despite the allegations of one of the chroniclers. But the fact that the latter could have stated such an event, that he could have counted on its acceptance by the contemporary public, is at least as revealing as the simple occurrence of an event which proceeds, after all, from chance. In a way, the reception of the statements is more revealing for the history of ideologies than their production; and when an author is mistaken, or lying, his text is no less significant than when he is speaking the truth; the important thing is that the text be "receivable" by contemporaries, or that it has been regarded as such by its producer. From this point of view, the notion of "false" is irrelevant here.

The chief stages of the conquest of Mexico are well known. Cortés's expedition, in 1519, is the third to land on the Mexican coasts; it consists of several hundred men. Cortés is sent by the governor of Cuba; but after the ships leave, this governor changes his mind and attempts to recall Cortés. The latter disembarks in Vera Cruz and declares himself to be under the direct authority of the king of Spain. Having learned of the existence of the Aztec empire, he begins a slow progress toward the interior, attempting to win over to his cause, either by promises or by warfare, the populations whose lands he passes through. The most difficult battle is waged against the Tlaxcaltecs, who will nevertheless become, subsequently, his best allies. Cortés finally reaches Mexico City, where he is cordially received; shortly thereafter, he decides to take the Aztec sovereign prisoner and succeeds in doing so. He then learns of the arrival on the coast of a new Spanish expedition, sent against him by the Cuban governor; the newcomers outnumber his own forces. Cortés sets out with some of these to meet this army, the rest remaining in Mexico to guard Montezuma, under the command of Pedro de Alvarado. Cortés wins the battle against his compatriots, imprisons their leader Panfilo de Narvaez, and convinces the rest to accept his command. But he then learns that during his absence things have gone badly in Mexico City: Alvarado has massacred a group of Mexicans in the course of a religious festival, and warfare has broken out. Cortés returns to the capital and joins his troops in their besieged fortress; at this point Montezuma dies. The Aztec* attacks are so insistent that Cortés decides to leave the city by night; his departure is discovered, and in the ensuing battle more than half his army is annihilated: this is the Noche Triste. Cortés withdraws to Tlaxcala, reorganizes his forces, and returns to besiege the capital; he cuts off all means of access and orders the construction of swift brigantines (at the time, the city was surrounded by lakes). After several months' siege, Mexico falls; the conquest has lasted about two years.

Let us first review the explanations commonly proposed for Cortés's victory. A first reason is the ambiguous, hesitant behavior of Montezuma himself, who offers Cortés virtually no resistance (this will therefore concern the first phase of the conquest, until Montezuma's death); such behavior may have, beyond certain cultural motivations to which I shall return, more personal reasons: in many respects, it differs from that of the other Aztec leaders. Bernal Díaz, reporting the remarks of the Cholula dignitaries, describes it thus: "They said that their lord Montezuma had known we were coming to Cholula, and that every day he was of many minds, unable to decide what to do about it. Sometimes he sent them instructions that if we arrived they were to pay us great honor and guide us on to Mexico, and at other times he said that he did not want us to come to his city and now recently the gods Tezcatlipoca and Huitzilopochtli, for whom they had great devotion, had proposed to him that we should be killed at Cholula or brought bound to Mexico" (83). One has the impression that there is a genuine ambiguity involved here, and not mere clumsiness, when Montezuma's messengers inform the Spaniards both that the Aztec kingdom is to be given to them as a present and that they are not to enter Mexico but to return whence they had come; but we shall see that Cortés deliberately sustains this equivocation.

In certain chronicles, Montezuma is depicted as a melancholy and

---

*It would be more accurate to speak of *Mexicas* rather than of *Aztecs*, and to write their "emperor's" name *Motecuhzoma*. But I have chosen to abide by common usage.

resigned man; it is asserted that he is a prey to his bad conscience, expiating in person an inglorious episode of earlier Aztec history: the Aztecs like to represent themselves as the legitimate successors of the Toltecs, the previous dynasty, whereas they are in reality usurpers, newcomers. Has this national guilt complex caused Montezuma to imagine that the Spaniards are direct descendants of the ancient Toltecs, come to reclaim what is rightfully theirs? We shall see that here, too, the idea is in part suggested by the Spaniards; it is impossible to declare with any certainty that Montezuma himself believed in it.

Once the Spaniards have arrived in his capital, Montezuma's behavior is even more singular. Not only does he let himself be taken captive by Cortés and his men (this captivity is Cortés's most startling decision, along with that of "burning"—in reality, scuttling—his own ships: with the handful of men under his command, he arrests the emperor, whereas he himself is surrounded by the all-powerful Aztec army), but also, once a prisoner, Montezuma's sole concern is to avoid all bloodshed. Contrary, for example, to what the final Aztec emperor, Cuauhtemoc, will do, Montezuma tries by every means in his power to keep war from breaking out in his city: he prefers to abandon his leadership, his privileges, and his wealth. Even during Cortés's brief absence, when the Spaniard has gone to face the punitive expedition sent against him, Montezuma will not attempt to take advantage of the situation in order to get rid of the invaders. "Many of those who had been with Pedro de Alvarado through the critical time said that if the uprising had been desired by Montezuma or started on his advice, or if Montezuma had had any hand in it, they would all have been killed. Montezuma had pacified his people and made them give up the attack" (Bernal Díaz, 125). History or legend (though it matters little which), in this case transcribed by the Jesuit Tovar, goes so far as to describe Montezuma, on the eve of his death, as ready to convert to Christianity; but as a final mockery, the Spanish priest, busy amassing gold, does not find the time. "It is said that he asked for baptism and converted to the truth of the Holy Gospel, and although there was a priest at hand, it is presumed that the latter was much more concerned to collect wealth than to catechize the poor king" (Tovar, p. 83).

Unfortunately we lack the documents that might have permitted us to penetrate the mental world of this strange emperor: in the presence of his enemies he is reluctant to make use of his enormous power, as if he were not convinced he wished to conquer; as Gomara, Cortés's chaplain and biographer, says: "Our Spaniards were never able to learn the truth, because at the time they did not understand the language, and afterward no one was found alive with whom Montezuma had shared the secret" (107). The Spanish historians of the period vainly sought the answer to these questions, seeing Montezuma sometimes as a madman, sometimes as a philosopher. Peter Martyr, a chronicler who remained in Spain, tends toward this latter solution: "He seemed to obey injunctions much harsher than the rules of grammar imposed upon little children, and with great patience endured everything in order to prevent an uprising of his subjects and his nobles. Any yoke seemed to him lighter than a revolt of his people. It was as if he sought to imitate Diocletian, who preferred to take poison than once more assume the reins of the empire he had abdicated" (V, 3). Gomara sometimes shows contempt for him: "Montezuma must have been a weak man of little courage, to let himself be seized and then, while a prisoner, never to attempt flight, even when Cortés offered him his freedom, and his own men begged him to take it" (89). But on other occasions he admits his perplexity, and the impossibility of settling the question: "the cowardice of Montezuma, or the love he bore Cortés and the Spaniards . . . " (91), or again: "in my opinion he was either very wise in disregarding the things he had to put up with, or very foolish, in not resenting them" (107). We are still subject to the same uncertainties.

The figure of Montezuma certainly counts for something in this nonresistance to evil. Yet such an explanation is valid only for the first part of Cortés's campaign, for Montezuma dies in the middle of events, as mysteriously as he had lived (probably stabbed by his Spanish jailers), and his successors at the head of the Aztec state immediately declare a fierce and pitiless war on the Spaniards. However, during the war's second phase, another factor begins to play a decisive role: this is Cortés's exploitation of the internal dissensions among the various populations occupying Mexican territory. He succeeds very well in this endeavor: throughout the campaign, he manages to take advantage of the struggles between rival factions, and during the final phase he commands an army of Tlaxcaltecs and other Indian allies numerically comparable to that of the Aztecs, an army of which the Spaniards are now merely, in a sense, the logistical support or command force: their units often seem to be composed of ten Spanish horse and ten thousand Indian foot soldiers! This is already the perception of contemporaries:

according to Motolinia, a Franciscan historian of "New Spain," "the conquistadors say that the Tlaxcaltecs deserve that His Majesty grant them much favor, and that if it had not been for them, they would all have been dead, when the Aztecs repulsed the Christians from Mexico, and that the Tlaxcaltecs offered them a haven" (III, 16). And indeed, for many years the Tlaxcaltecs enjoy numerous privileges granted them by the Spanish crown: exempted from taxes, they very often become administrators of the newly conquered lands.

We cannot avoid wondering, when we read the history of Mexico: why did the Indians not offer more resistance? Didn't they realize Cortés's colonizing ambitions? The answer displaces the question: the Indians in the regions Cortés first passed through are not more impressed by his imperialist intentions because they have already been conquered and colonized—by the Aztecs. Mexico at the time is not a homogeneous state, but a conglomerate of populations, defeated by the Aztecs who occupy the top of the pyramid. So that far from incarnating an absolute evil, Cortés often appears to them as a lesser evil, as a liberator, so to speak, who permits them to throw off the yoke of a tyranny especially detestable because so close at hand.

Sensitized as we are to the misdeeds of European colonialism, it is difficult for us to understand why the Indians do not immediately rebel, when there is still time, against the Spaniards. But the conquistadors merely fall into step with the Aztecs. We may be scandalized to learn that the Spaniards seek only gold, slaves, and women. "They were in fact concerned only to furnish themselves with some fine Indian women and to take a certain amount of booty," writes Bernal Díaz (142), and he tells the following anecdote: after the fall of Mexico, "Cuauhtemoc and all his captains complained to Cortés that some of our leaders who happened to be in the brigantines, as well as several who had fought on the highways, had carried off the wives and daughters of a great number of chieftains. They asked him to show mercy and to order that these women be returned. Cortés replied that he would have great difficulty taking them away from his comrades who already set great store by them, that he had sent for them, furthermore, and had them brought before him; that he would see if they had become Christians, declaring further that if they wished to return to their fathers and their husbands, he would make every effort to see that they did so." The result of the investigation is not surprising: "Most of the women chose to follow neither father, nor mother, nor husband;

but indeed to remain with the soldiers of which they had become the companions. Others hid themselves; some, moreover, declared that they no longer wished to be idolators. Indeed there were some who were already pregnant; so that only three returned to their people, Cortés having given specific orders to let them go" (157).

But it is precisely the same thing that the Indians complained of in the other parts of Mexico when they related the Aztecs' misdeeds: "The inhabitants of these villages . . . offered vigorous protests against Montezuma and especially against his tax-collectors, saying that they stole everything they possessed from them and that, if their wives and their daughters appeared to them worthy of attention, they violated them in the presence of the husbands and the fathers, and sometimes carried them off for good; that by their orders they were forced to work as if they were slaves, and to transport in canoes, or even overland, timber, stones, corn, without on the other hand leaving off the labor of their arms for sowing maize and other services of great number" (Bernal Díaz, 86).

The gold and precious stones that lure the Spaniards were already taken as taxes by Montezuma's functionaries; it does not seem that we can reject this allegation as a pure invention of the Spaniards seeking to legitimize their conquest, even if this is also a contributing factor: too many testimonies agree in this direction. The *Florentine Codex* reports the chiefs of the neighboring tribes coming to protest to Cortés the oppression imposed by the Aztecs: "For Montezuma and the Mexicans have caused us great grief and the Mexicans have brought us evil. They have brought poverty under our very noses, for they have imposed upon us all kinds of taxes" (XII, 26). And Diego Durán, a Dominican sympathizer and a cultural half-caste, one might say, discovers the resemblance precisely at the moment he reproaches the Aztecs: "If their hosts were inattentive or indifferent, the Aztecs pillaged and sacked the villages, despoiled the people of their clothes, beat them, stripped them of all their possessions and dishonored them; they destroyed the harvests and inflicted a thousand injuries and damages upon them. The whole country trembled before them. Wherever they came, they were given all they needed; but even when they were treated well, they behaved in this same fashion. . . . This was the cruellest and most devilish people that can be conceived, on account of the way in which they treated their vassals, which was much worse than the way in which the Spaniards treated them and treat them still" (III, 19).

"They did all the harm they could, as our Spaniards do today if they are not restrained from doing so" (III, 21).

There are many resemblances between old conquerors and new, as the latter themselves felt, since they described the Aztecs as recent invaders, conquistadors comparable to themselves. More precisely, and in this too the resemblance persists, the relation to the predecessor is that of an implicit and sometimes unconscious continuity, accompanied by a denial concerning this very relation. The Spaniards burn the Mexicans' books in order to wipe out their religion; they destroy their monuments in order to abolish any memory of a former greatness. But a hundred years earlier, during the reign of Itzcoatl, the Aztecs themselves had destroyed all the old books in order to rewrite history in their own fashion. At the same time the Aztecs, as we have seen, like to depict themselves as heirs of the Toltecs; and the Spaniards often choose a certain fidelity to the past, in religion or in politics; they are assimilated at the same time that they assimilate. One symbolic fact among others: the capital of the new state will be the same as that of the conquered Mexico. "Considering that Tenoxtitlan had been so great and so famous, we decided to settle in it. . . . If in the past it was the capital and the queen of all these provinces, it will be so, the same, henceforward" (Cortés, 3). Cortés seeks, in a sense, to constitute his legitimacy, no longer in the eyes of the king of Spain though this had been one of his great concerns during the campaign but in the eyes of the local population, by assuming a continuity with the kingdom of Montezuma. The viceroy Mendoza will resort to the fiscal records of the Aztec empire.

The same holds true in the realm of faith: religious conquest often consists in removing from a holy place certain images and establishing others there instead, preserving—and this is essential—the cult sites in which the same aromatic herbs are burned. Cortés tells the story: "The most important of these idols and the ones in which they have most faith I had taken from their places and thrown down the steps; and I ordered those chapels where they had been to be cleaned, for they were full of the blood of sacrifices; and I had images of Our Lady and of other saints put there" (2). And Bernal Díaz bears witness: "An order was given that the incense of their country should be burned before the holy image and the Blessed Cross" (52). "It is only just that what has served the worship of the demons should be transformed into a temple for the service of God," writes Fray Lorenzo de Bienvenida. The

Christian priests and friars will occupy exactly the places left empty after the repression of those professing the native religious worship, whom the Spaniards, moreover, called by that overdetermined name *popes* (contamination of the Indian term designating them and the word "pope"); Cortés made the continuity quite explicit: "The respect and welcome that they give to the friars is the result of the commands of the Marqués del Valle, Don Hernando Cortés, for from the beginning he ordered them to be very reverent and respectful to the priests, just as they used to be the the ministers of their idols" (Motolinia, III, 3).

To Montezuma's hesitations during the first phase of the conquest and the internal divisions among the Mexicans during the second, a third factor is frequently added: the Spanish superiority with regard to weapons. The Aztecs do not know how to work metal, and their swords, like their armor, are less effective; arrows (nonpoisoned arrows) are not as powerful as harquebuses and cannon; in their movements the Spaniards are much swifter: for land operations they have horses, whereas the Aztecs are always on foot; and on water they know how to build brigantines whose superiority over the Indian canoes plays a decisive role in the final phase of the siege of Mexico. Finally, the Spaniards also—unwittingly—inaugurate bacteriological warfare, since they bring smallpox, which ravages the opposing army. Yet these superiorities, in themselves incontestable, do not suffice to explain everything, if we take into account, at the same time, the numerical relation between the two camps. And there are in fact very few harquebuses, and even fewer cannon, whose power is not that of a modern bomb; further, the gunpowder is often wet. The effect of firearms and horses cannot be measured directly by the number of victims.

I shall not attempt to deny the importance of these factors, but rather to find a common basis for them which permits us to articulate and understand them, and at the same time to add many others, of which less account appears to have been taken. In doing so, I tend to take literally one reason for the conquest/defeat that we find in the native chronicles and which has hitherto been neglected in the West, doubtless being regarded as a purely poetic formula. The testimony of the Indian accounts, which is a description rather than an explanation, asserts that everything happened because the Mayas and the Aztecs lost control of communication. The language of the gods has become unintelligible, or else these gods fell silent. "Understanding is lost, wisdom is lost" (*Chilam Balam*, 22). "There was no longer any great teacher, any great orator, any supreme priest, when the change of rulers occurred upon their arrival" (ibid., 5). The Maya book *Chilam Balam* reiterates this piercing question, which can no longer receive an answer: "Where is the prophet, where is the priest who will give the true meaning of the language of this book?" (24). As for the Aztecs, they describe the beginning of their own end as a silence that falls: the gods no longer speak to them. "They asked the gods to grant them their favors and the victory against the Spaniards and their other enemies. But it must have been too late, for they had no further answer from their oracles; then they regarded the gods as mute or as dead" (Durán, III, 77).

Did the Spaniards defeat the Indians by means of signs?

Montezuma and Signs

INDIANS and Spaniards practice communication differently. But the discourse of difference is a difficult one. As we have already seen with Columbus, the postulate of difference readily involves the feeling of superiority, the postulate of equality that of indifference, and it is always hard to resist this double movement, especially since the final result of this encounter seems to indicate the victor explicitly enough: are not the Spaniards superior, and not merely different? But the truth, or what we regard as the truth, is not so simple.

Let us start with the assumption that on the linguistic or symbolic level there is no "natural" inferiority on the Indians' side: we have seen, for instance, that in Columbus's period it was they who learned the Other's language; and during the first expeditions to Mexico, it is again two Indians, called Melchior and Julian by the Spaniards, who serve as interpreters.

But there is much more, of course. We know, thanks to the texts of the period, that the Indians devote a great part of their time and their powers to the interpretation of messages, and that this interpretation takes remarkably elaborate forms, which derive from various kinds of divination. Chief among these is cyclical divination (of which, among us, astrology is an example). The Aztecs possess a religious calendar composed of thirteen months of twenty days; each of these days possesses its own character, propitious or unlucky, which is transmitted to actions performed on that day and even more to the persons born on it. To know someone's birthday is to know his fate; this is why, as soon as a child is born, the parents seek out a professional interpreter, who is also the priest of the community (see fig. 4).

"When a boy or girl was born, the father or relatives of the babe immediately went to visit the astrologers, sorcerers, or soothsayers, who were plentiful, begging them to state the destiny of the newborn boy or girl. . . . The astrologer and sorcerer-fortuneteller brought out the Book of the Horoscope, together with the calendar. Once the character of the day had been seen, prophecies were uttered, lots were cast, and a propitious or evil fate for the babe was determined by the consultation of a paper painted with all the gods they adored, each idol drawn in the square reserved for him. . . . One could learn whether the child was to be rich or poor, brave or cowardly, a priest or a married man, a thief or a drunkard, abstemious or lustful—all these things could be found in those prophetic pictures" (Durán II, 2).

To this preestablished and systematic interpretation, which derives from the fixed character of each calendar day, is added a second, contextual kind of divination, which takes the form of omens. Every event the least bit out of the ordinary, departing from the established order, will be interpreted as the herald of another event, generally an unlucky one, still to come (which implies that nothing in this world occurs randomly). For instance, that a prisoner should become depressed is an evil omen, for the Aztecs did not expect any such thing. Or that a bird should cry out at a specific moment, or a mouse run through the temple, or that one might make a slip of the tongue, or have a certain dream. Sometimes, it is true, these omens are phenomena that are not only rare but distinctly supernatural. "The dishes of food which had been sold by the Aztec women were served at the banquet and then there occurred a prodigious, fearsome thing, which bewildered everyone. As soon as the people had sat down to eat, the delicacies in the dishes turned into human hands, arms, heads, hearts, and vitals. In their terror the Xochimilca called their soothsayers and asked them what this meant. The soothsayers answered that it was an evil omen, since it meant the destruction of the city and the death of many" (Durán, III, 2). In the everyday realm as well as in the exceptional, then, "they believed in a thousand omens and signs" (Motolinia, II, 8): an overdetermined world will necessarily be an overinterpreted world as well.

Furthermore, when the signs are slow in coming, one does not hesitate to seek them out, and to this end one consults a professional .

Fig. 4 Consultation of the soothsayer and of the book.

soothsayer. The latter replies by resorting to one of his habitual techniques of divination: by water, by grains of corn, by cotton threads. This prognostication, which makes it possible to know whether an absent person is living or dead, whether or not a sick person will recover, whether or not an unfaithful husband will return to his wife, continues in the form of actual prophecies, and we find the great Aztec leaders regularly consulting soothsayers before undertaking any important activity. Further still, without their being asked various individuals declare they have been in communication with the gods and proceed to foretell the future. The whole history of the Aztecs, as it is narrated in their own chronicles, consists of realizations of anterior prophecies, as if the event could not occur unless it has been previously announced: departure from a place of origin, choice of a new settlement, victory or defeat. Here only what has already been Word can become Act.

The Aztecs are convinced that all such divinations come true, and only very rarely attempt to resist the fate declared to them; in Maya, the same word signifies "prophecy" and "law." "That which has been fated cannot be avoided" (Durán, II, 67). "These things shall be accomplished. No one shall cause them to cease" (*Chilam Balam*, 22). And such things indeed come to pass, since men do their best to bring them about; in other cases the prophecy is all the more accurate in that it will be formulated only in a retrospective fashion, after the event has taken place. In all cases these omens and divinations enjoy the greatest prestige, and if necessary one will risk one's life to obtain them, knowing that the reward is in proportion to the peril: the possessor of the prophecy is a favorite of the gods; the master of interpretation is, indeed, the master.

The world is from the start posited as overdetermined; men handle this situation by scrupulously regulating their social life. Everything is foreseeable, hence everything is foreseen, and the key word of Mesoamerican society is order. We read in the *Chilam Balam:* "They knew the measure of their days. Complete was the month; complete the year; complete the day; complete the night; complete the breath of life as it passed also; complete, the blood, when they arrived at their beds, their meals, their thrones. In due measure did they recite the good prayers; in due measure they sought the lucky days, until they saw the lucky stars enter into their reign; then they kept watch while the reign of the good stars began. Then everything was good" (5). Durán, one of the best observers of Aztec society, tells the following anecdote:

"One day I asked an old man why he was sowing a certain type of small bean so late in the year, considering that they are usually frostbitten at that time. He answered that everything has a count, a reason, and a special day" (II, 2). This regulation impregnates even the minutest details of life, which we might have supposed were left to the individual's free decision; ritual itself is only the most salient point of a society that is ritualized through and through; yet the religious rites are in themselves so numerous and so complex that they mobilize a veritable army of functionaries. "The number of rites was so great that it was not possible for a single minister to attend to all" (Durán, I, 19).

Hence, it is society as a whole—by the intermediary of the priests, who are merely the repository of social knowledge—that decides the fate of the individual, who is thereby not an individual in the sense we usually give this word. In Indian society of the period, the individual himself does not represent a social totality but is merely the constitutive element of that other totality, the collectivity. Durán also says, in a passage in which we feel his admiration tinged with nostalgia, for he no longer finds in his own society the values to which he aspires: "The nation had a special official for each activity, small though it were. Everything was so well recorded that no detail was left out of the accounts. There were even officials in charge of sweeping. The good order was such that no one dared to interfere with another's job or express an opinion, since he would be rebuffed immediately" (III, 41).

Certainly personal opinion and individual initiative are not what the Aztecs most prize. We have an additional proof of this preeminence of the social over the individual in the role taken by the family: parents are cherished, children adored, and the attention devoted to each absorbs much social energy. Reciprocally, the father and mother are held responsible for any misdeeds their son might commit; among the Tarascans, solidarity in responsibility extends even to the servants: "the tutors and nurses who had raised the son are killed, as are his servants, because they had taught him those bad customs" (*Relación de Michoacán*, III, 8. See III, 12).

But family solidarity is not a supreme value, for although transindividual the family cell is not yet the society; family links shift to the background, in fact, compared with the obligations toward the group. No personal quality makes one invulnerable with regard to the social law, and parents willingly accept penalties and punishments when these are applied to their children's misdeeds. "Even though the parents were distressed because of the ill treatment of their sons, whom these people loved dearly, they did not dare complain but acknowledged that the punishment had been just and good" (Durán, I, 21). Another account tells of King Nezajualpilli of Texcoco, famous for his wisdom, putting his own daughter to death because she permitted herself to be spoken to by a young man; to those attempting to intervene in his daughter's favor, he replies "that he must not break the law in anyone's behalf, for thereby he would be setting a bad example to other lords, and dishonoring himself" (Zorita, 9).

Indeed, death is a catastrophe only in a narrowly individual perspective, whereas, from the social point of view, the benefit derived from submission to group rule counts for more than the loss of an individual. This is why we see the intended sacrificial victims accepting their lot, if not with joy, in any case without despair; and the same is true of soldiers on the battlefield: their blood will help keep the society alive. Or more precisely, this is the image the Aztec people wants to have of itself, though it is not certain that all the persons constituting that people accept the arrangement: in order to keep prisoners from despairing on the eve of their sacrifice (a bad omen, as we have seen), they are given drugs; and Montezuma will need to rehearse the law to his tearful soldiers saddened by the death of their comrades: "That is why we were born! That is why we go to battle! That is the blessed death which our ancestors extolled" (Durán, III, 62).

In this overstructured society, one individual cannot be the equal of another, and hierarchic distinctions acquire a primordial importance. It is remarkable to find that when, in the middle of the fifteenth century, Montezuma I decides to codify the laws of his own society, he formulates fourteen prescriptions, of which only the last two suggest our own laws (punishment of adultery and of theft), whereas ten regulate what in our eyes would refer only to etiquette (I shall return to the two remaining laws): insignia, garments, the ornaments one is or is not entitled to wear, the type of house appropriate for each level of the population. Durán, ever nostalgic for a hierarchic society and disgusted by the nascent egalitarianism he perceives among the Spaniards, writes: "In the royal palaces and in the temples there were rooms and chambers which accommodated or received different qualities of persons, so that the first would not mingle with the second, so that those of good blood would not be on the same level with the lower class. . . . In good and orderly republics and communities, great attention was paid to these things, unlike the disorder which prevails in our modern republics, where one can barely tell who is the knight, who the muleteer, who the squire, who the sailor. . . . Therefore, in order to avoid this confusion and turmoil and so that each one would keep his place, the natives possessed important laws, decrees and ordinances" (Durán, I, 11).

As a consequence of this powerful integration, no one's life is ever an open and indeterminate field, to be shaped by an individual free will, but rather the realization of an order always preordained (even if the possibility of inflecting one's own fate is not altogether excluded). The individual's future is ruled by the collective past; the individual does not construct his future, rather the future is revealed; whence the role of the calendar, of omens, of auguries. The characteristic interrogation of this world is not, as among the Spanish conquistadors (or the Russian revolutionaries), of a praxeological type: "what is to be done?"; but epistemological: "how are we to know?" And the interpretation of the event occurs less in terms of its concrete, individual, and unique content than of the preestablished order of universal harmony, which is to be reestablished.

Would it be forcing the meaning of "communication" to say, starting from this point, that there exist two major forms of communication, one between man and man, the other between man and the world, and then to observe that the Indians cultivate chiefly the latter, the Spaniards the former? We are accustomed to conceiving of communication as only interhuman, for since the "world" is not a subject, our dialogue with it is quite asymmetrical (if there is any such dialogue at all). But this is perhaps a narrow view of the matter, one responsible moreover for our feeling of superiority in this regard. The notion would be more productive if it were extended to include, alongside the interaction of individual with individual, the interaction that occurs between the person and his social group, the person and the natural world, the person and the religious universe. And it is this second type of communication that plays a predominant part in the life of Aztec man, who interprets the divine, the natural, and the social through indices and omens, and with the help of that professional, the prophet-priest.

We must not suppose that this predominance excludes the knowledge of phenomena, what we might call more narrowly the collecting of information; on the contrary. It is the action on *others* by the intermediary of signs which here remains in the embryonic state; in return, one never fails to be informed as to the state of *things*, even living things: man is important here as an object of discourse, rather than its recipient. A war, we read in the *Relación de Michoacán*, will always be preceded by the sending of spies. After a careful reconnaissance, these spies return to account for their mission: "The spies know where the rivers are, as well as all the entrances, exits and dangerous parts of the village. When camp is made, the spies draw a clear map on the ground, tracing all these features for the captain-general, who shows it to the people" (III, 4). During the Spanish invasion, Montezuma never fails to send spies into the enemy camp, and he is thoroughly informed of the state of affairs: thus he learns of the arrival of the first expeditions while the Spaniards are still utterly unaware of his existence; we see him sending his instructions to the local governors: "Montezuma therefore commanded . . . and said to them: 'You shall order that guard be kept everywhere on the shores . . . wheresoever the strangers would come to land' " (*Florentine Codex*, XII, 3). Just as later on, when Cortés is in Mexico, Montezuma is immediately informed of Narvaez's arrival, which his guest is ignorant of. "By words, pictures and these memorials, they were often informed of that which passed. For this cause there were men of great agility who served as couriers to go and come, whom they did nourish in this exercise of running from their youth, laboring to have them well-breathed, that they might run to the top of a high hill without weariness" (j. de Acosta, *Historia*, VI, 10). Unlike the Tarascans of Michoacán, the Aztecs draw their maps and their messages on paper, and hence can transmit them over long distances.

But constant success in collecting information does not proceed in tandem here, as we might have expected, with a mastery of interhuman communication. There is something emblematic in Montezuma's repeated refusal to communicate with the intruders. During the first phase of the conquest, when the Spaniards are still close to the coast, the main message sent by Montezuma is that he does not want any exchange of messages to take place! He receives his information clearly, but this does not please him—quite the contrary; here is how the Aztec accounts describe him: "Montezuma lowered his head, and without answering a word, placed his hand upon his mouth. In this way he remained for a long time. He appeared to be dead or mute, since he was unable to give any answer" (Durán, III, 69). "When he heard this, Montezuma merely lowered his head; he remained in this attitude, and did not speak at all, but remained a long time full of affliction, as if he were beside himself"* (*Florentine Codex*, XII, 13). Montezuma is not simply alarmed by the content of the messages; he shows himself literally incapable of communicating, and the text establishes a significant parallel between "mute" and "dead." This paralysis does not merely weaken the gathering of information; it already symbolizes defeat, since the Aztec sovereign is above all a master of speech—the social action par excellence—and since the renunciation of language is the admission of failure.

Montezuma's fear of information received is associated quite coherently with fear of information sought by the Other, especially when this latter concerns his own person. "Each day, numerous messengers came and went, reporting to the King Montezuma all that occurred, saying how the Spaniards asked many questions in his regard, inquiring after his person, his behavior, and his household. By this he was much distressed, hesitating as to the way to take, to flee or to hide himself, or else to wait; for he dreaded the greatest evils and the greatest outrages for himself and his entire kingdom" (Tovar, p. 75). "And when Montezuma had heard that earnestly he was inquired after and asked about, that the gods urgently wished to behold him before their eyes, he felt torment and anguish in his heart" (*Florentine Codex*, XII, 89, p. 26). According to Durán, Montezuma's first reaction is to want to hide in a deep cave. According to the conquistadors, Montezuma's first messages declare that he will offer them everything in his kingdom, but on one condition: that they renounce any desire to come and see him.

This refusal of Montezuma's is not a personal action. The very first law promulgated by his ancestor Montezuma I says: "The king must never appear in public unless the occasion is extremely important" (Durán, III, 26), and Montezuma II applies it scrupulously, even forbidding his subjects to look at him when he must show himself in public. "If any common man dared to lift his eyes and look upon him, Montezuma ordered that he be slain." Durán, who reports this fact, complains of its deleterious effect on his work as a historian: "I once questioned an Indian as to the facial characteristics of Montezuma and

*Here we may note a stylistic feature of the Nahuatl texts: an expression is often followed by one or several synonyms. The method of parallelism is sufficiently common; but in addition Sahagún, interested in the expressive capacities of the language, had asked his informants to supply him, on each occasion, with all the expressions possible for one and the same thing.

about his height and general appearance, and this is the answer I received: 'Father, I will not lie to you or tell you of things I do not know. I never saw his face!' " (Durán, III, 53). It is not surprising to find this law heading the list of rules concerning the hierarchic differentiation of society: what is elided in both cases is the individual's pertinence to the social regulation. The king's body remains individual; but the king's function, more completely than any other, is a pure social effect; hence this body must be withdrawn from scrutiny. By letting himself be seen, Montezuma would contradict his values quite as much as by ceasing to speak: he leaves his sphere of action, which is the social exchange, and becomes a vulnerable individual.

It is quite as revealing to see Montezuma receiving information but punishing those who bring it, and hence failing on the level of human relations. When a man arrives from the coast to describe what he has seen, the king thanks him but orders his guards to cast him into prison and to keep a close watch on him. The magicians try to have prophetic dreams and to interpret the supernatural omens. "When he saw that the dreams were not in his favor but that they confirmed the earlier ill omens, he ordered that the dreamers be cast in prison. They were to be given food in small measures until they starved to death. After this no one wished to tell his dreams to Montezuma" (III, 68). But it turns out that they are no longer to be found in their prison; Montezuma then decides to punish them in an exemplary fashion: "He ordered the jailers to rise and go to the towns of all those who had prophesied evil things. 'Tear down their houses,' he cried, 'kill their wives and children and dig in the places where the houses had been, until you reach water. All their possessions are to be destroyed. And if any one of them is ever seen in a temple, he is to be stoned and his body thrown to the wild beasts!' " (ibid). We realize that, under these conditions, volunteers to provide or interpret information about the Spaniards' behavior will become quite infrequent.

Even when the information reaches Montezuma, his interpretation of it, though necessary, is made in the context of a communication with the world, not of that with men; it is his gods from whom he seeks advice about how to behave in these purely human affairs (indeed, this was how he had always behaved, as we know from the native histories of the Aztec people). "It seems that the prince was very devoted to his idols Tezcatlipoca and Huitzilopochtli, the god of war and the god of hell respectively, and sacrificed youths to them every day in hopes that they would tell him what to do about us" (Bernal Díaz, 41). "We learned on trustworthy authority that when the prince heard the news he was deeply grieved and angry, and that he immediately sacrificed some Indians to his idol Huitzilopochtli, the god of war, in order that the god might tell them what would be the outcome of our journey to Mexico and whether he should admit us into the city" (ibid, 83).

Hence it is quite natural that, when the rulers of the country wish to understand the present, they address themselves not to those who know men but to those who practice an exchange with the gods—the master interpreters. Thus in Tlaxcala: "It seems therefore that they were ill-disposed to listen to the envoys, and that their decision was to summon all the soothsayers, and those others whom they call *tacalnaguas*, who are like wizards and foretell the future, and ask them to discover by their witchcraft, charms and lots what sort of people we were and whether if they fought us continuously by day and night we could be conquered" (ibid, 66). But the reaction is precisely the same in Mexico: "The king immediately summoned his whole court and took counsel, telling them the bad news, asking what means might be employed in order to drive out of their country these cursed gods who came to destroy them, and by arguing the question at great length, as so serious a matter required, it was resolved to summon all the wizards and the necromancers who had a pact with the demon, in order that they might make the first attack, raising by their art dreadful visions which, by terror, would force these people to return to their own country" (Tovar, p. 75).

Montezuma knew how to inform himself concerning his enemies when these were called Tlaxcaltecs, Tarascans, Huastecs. But that was an exchange of information already perfectly well established. The identity of the Spaniards is so different, their behavior to such a degree unforeseeable, that the whole system of communication is upset, and the Aztecs no longer succeed precisely where they had previously excelled: in gathering information. If the Indians had known, Bernal Díaz writes on many occasions, "how few, weak and exhausted we were at that time . . ." All the Spaniards' actions take the Indians by surprise, in fact, as if it were the latter who were waging a regular war and as if the Spaniards were harassing them by guerrilla tactics.

We find a general confirmation of this attitude of the Indians in the very construction of their own narratives of the conquest. The latter invariably begin by the enumeration of the omens announcing the coming of the Spaniards. Moreover, Montezuma is apparently bombarded with messages that all predict the newcomers' victory. "In this time, the idol Quetzalcoatl, god of the Cholultecs, announced the coming of strange men who would seize the kingdom. Even so the king of Texcoco [Nezahualpilli], who had a pact with the demon, came one time to visit Montezuma at an untoward hour and assured him that the gods had told him that great trials and great sufferings were in store for him and all his kingdom; many sorcerers and magicians were saying the same thing" (Tovar, p. 69). We have similar indications concerning not only the Aztecs of central Mexico, but even the Carib Tainos "discovered" by Columbus, the Tarascans of Michoacán, the Mayas of Yucatán and Guatemala, the Incas of Peru, etc. One Maya prophet, Ah Xupan Nauat, apparently warned as early as the eleventh century that the invasion of the Yucatán would begin in 1527. Taken together, these accounts, proceeding from peoples very remote from each other, are striking in their uniformity: the arrival of the Spaniards is *always* preceded by omens, their victory is *always* foretold as certain. Further, these omens are strangely alike, from one end of the American continent to the other. There is always a comet, a thunderbolt, a fire, two-headed men, persons speaking in a state of trance, etc.

Even if we did not want to exclude the reality of these omens a priori, there is something about so many coincidences that should put us on our guard. Everything suggests that the omens were invented after the fact; but why? We see now that this way of experiencing the event is quite in agreement with the norms of communication practiced by the Indians. Instead of perceiving this fact as a purely human if unprecedented encounter—the arrival of men greedy for gold and power—the Indians integrate it into a network of natural, social, and supernatural relations, in which the event thereby loses its singularity: it is somehow domesticated, absorbed into an order of already existing beliefs. The Aztecs perceive the conquest—i.e., the defeat—and at the same time mentally overcome it by inscribing it within a history conceived according to their requirements (nor are they the only people to have done such a thing): the present becomes intelligible and at the same time less inadmissible, the moment one can see it already announced in the past. And the remedy is so well adapted to the situation that, hearing the narrative, everyone believes he remembers that the omens had indeed appeared *before* the conquest. But meanwhile, these prophecies exert a paralyzing effect on the Indians hearing them and further diminish their resistance; we know for example that Montejo will be particularly well received in the parts of Yucatán where the prophecies of *Chilam Balam* are promulgated.

This behavior contrasts with that of Cortés but not with that of all the Spaniards; we have already encountered a Spanish example of an astonishingly similar conception of communication: that of Columbus. Like Montezuma, Columbus carefully gathered information concerning things, but failed in his communication with men. More remarkable still, upon returning from his exceptional discovery, Columbus was eager to write his own *Chilam Balam:* he could not rest until he had produced a *Book of Prophecies,* a collection of formulas extracted from (or attributed to) the Sacred Books, which were supposed to predict his own expedition, and its consequences. By his mental structures, which link him to the medieval conception of knowledge, Columbus is closer to those whom he discovered than to some of his own companions: how shocked he would have been to hear it! Yet he is not alone. Machiavelli, theoretician of a world to come, writes a short time later in his *Discorsi:* "Both ancient and modern instances prove that no great events ever occur in any city or country which have not been predicted by soothsayers, revelations or by portents and other celestial signs" (I, 56). And Las Casas devotes a whole chapter of his *History of the Indies* to the following theme: "Wherein is seen how Divine Providence never permits important events, either for the good of the world or for its chastisement, to occur without their having first been heralded and predicted by the saints, or by other persons, even by infidels or wicked people, and even on certain occasions by the demons themselves" (I,10). Better prophecies made by demons than no prophecy at all! At the end of the century, the Jesuit José de Acosta is more prudent, but still testifies to the same structure of mind: "It appears very reasonable to think that a matter of this importance [the discovery of America] must be mentioned in the Holy Scriptures" (I, 15).

It is this particular way of practicing communication (neglecting the interhuman dimension, privileging contact with the world) which is responsible for the Indians' distorted image of the Spaniards during the first encounters, and notably for the paralyzing belief that the Spaniards are gods. This phenomenon seems very rare in the history of conquests and colonizations (we find it again in Melanesia, and it is responsible for the sad fate of Captain Cook); it can be explained only by an incapacity to perceive the other's human identity—i.e., to recognize him both as equal and as different.

The first, spontaneous reaction with regard to the stranger is to imagine him as inferior, since he is different from us: this is not even a man, or if he is one, an inferior barbarian; if he does not speak our language, it is because he speaks none at all, *cannot* speak, as Columbus still believed. It is in this fashion that European Slavs call their German neighbors *nemec*, "mutes"; the Mayas of Yucatán call the Toltec invaders *nunob*, "mutes"; and the Cakchiquel Mayas refer to the Mam Mayas as "stammerers" or "mutes." The Aztecs themselves call the people south of Vera Cruz *nonoualca*, "mutes," and those who do not speak Nahuatl they call *tenime*, "barbarians," or *popoloca*, "savages"; they share the scorn of all peoples for their neighbors, judging that the remotest ones, culturally or geographically, are not even suitable to be sacrificed and eaten (the sacrificial victim must be at once foreign and esteemed—i.e., in reality close at hand). "Our god does not like the flesh of those barbarous peoples. They are yellowish, hard, tasteless bread in his mouth. They are savages and speak strange tongues" (Durán, III, 28).

For Montezuma, differences between Aztecs, Tlaxcaltecs, and Chichimecs exist, of course, but they are immediately absorbed into the internal hierarchy of the Aztec world; the others are those who are subjugated and among whom are recruited the sacrificial victims. But even in the most extreme cases there is no sentiment of absolute strangeness: of the Totonacs, for instance, the Aztecs say both that they speak a barbarous language and that they lead a civilized life (*Florentine Codex*, X, 29)—i.e., one that can appear such to Aztec eyes.

Now, the otherness of the Spaniards is much more radical. The first witnesses of their arrival hasten to report their impressions to Montezuma: "We must tell him what we have seen, and this is a terrifying thing: nothing of the kind has ever been seen" (*Florentine Codex*, XII, 6). Unable to integrate them into the category of the Totonacs—whose alterity is not at all radical—the Aztecs, faced with the Spaniards, renounce their entire system of human otherness and find themselves obliged to resort to the only other device available: the exchange with the gods. Here again we may compare them with Columbus, and yet an essential difference also appears: like them, Columbus does not readily manage to see the other as human and different at the same time; but for this reason he treats the others as animals. The Indians' mistake will not last long, moreover; but just long enough for the battle to be definitively lost and America subject to Europe. As the *Chilam Balam* says on another occasion: "Those who die are those who do not understand; those who live will understand it" (9).

Now let us leave the reception and consider the production of discourses and symbols as practiced in the Indian societies at the period of the conquest. There is no need to go back as far as the *Popol Vuh*, the sacred book which makes the word the origin of the world, to realize that verbal practices are highly esteemed: nothing would be more mistaken than to suppose the Aztecs indifferent to this activity. Like many other peoples, the Aztecs interpret their own name as referring to their linguistic excellence, in opposition to other tribes: "The Indians of this New Spain derive, according to what is generally reported in their histories, from two diverse peoples: they give to the first the name Nahuatlaca, which means 'people who explain themselves and speak clearly,' thereby differentiated from the second people, at the time very wild and barbarous, concerned only with hunting, and to whom they gave the name of Chichimecs, which signifies 'people who go hunting' and who live by that primitive and uncouth occupation" (Tovar, p. 9).

To learn to speak constitutes part of family education; it is the first thing parents think of: "They took great care that their son should converse fittingly with others, that his conversation should be proper" (*Florentine Codex*, VIII, 20); and an ancient precept, addressed by parents to children, says: "Do not set a bad example or speak indiscreetly, or interrupt the speech of another. If someone does not speak well or coherently, see that you do not do the same; if it is not your business to speak, be silent" (Olmos, in Zorita, 9). The fathers invariably tell their sons: "You are to speak very slowly, very deliberately; you are not to speak hurriedly, not to pant, not to squeak, lest it be said of you that you are a groaner, a growler, a squeaker. Also you are not to cry out, lest you be known as an imbecile, a shameless one, a rustic, very much a rustic. . . . And you are to improve, to soften your words, your voice" (*Florentine Codex*, VI, 22).

That such attention be paid to what the Latin rhetorics called *actio* or *pronuntiatio* suggests that the Aztecs are not indifferent to other aspects of speech; and we know that this education is not left to parents alone, but is dispensed in special schools. As a matter of fact, the Aztec state has two kinds of schools, those in which students are prepared for the life of a warrior, and others that produce priests, judges, and royal dignitaries; it is in the latter schools, called *calmecac*, that particular attention is paid to language: "Very carefully were they taught good discourse. If one spoke not well, if one greeted others not well, then they drew blood from him with maguey thorns. . . . Carefully were they taught the songs which they called the gods' songs. These were inscribed in the books. And well were all taught the reckoning of the days, the book of dreams, and the book of years" (*Florentine Codex*, III, Appendix, 8). The *calmecac* is in fact a school of interpretation and speech, of rhetoric and hermeneutics. Thus every precaution is taken for students to become fine speakers and good interpreters.

Indeed, as another chronicler says (Juan Bautista Pomar, in the *Relación de Texcoco)*, they learned at the same time "to speak well and to govern well." In the Aztec civilization—as in many others—the high royal dignitaries are generally selected for their qualities of eloquence. Sahagún reports that "among the Mexicans, the learned, virtuous, and powerful rhetoricians were greatly esteemed" (VI, "Prologue," 2), and specifies: "The kings always kept by their side certain skillful orators, in order to speak and reply as would be necessary. They used such men from the first moments of their taking the throne" (VI, 12,8). Among the ancient Mayas, the function is even more important: the future leaders are chosen with the help of a procedure resembling a trial by riddles: they must be able to interpret certain figurative expressions, known as the language of Zuyua. Power demands wisdom, which is attested by the capacity to interpret. "These are the things to be understood in order to become chiefs of the town, when they are brought before the ruler. These are the words. If they are not understood by the chiefs of the town, ill-omened is the star adorning the night" (*Chilam Balam*, 91). If the candidates do not pass this test, they are severely punished. "The chiefs of the town shall be seized because they lack understanding. . . . They shall be hanged by the neck; the tips of their tongues shall be cut off; their eyes shall be torn out" (ibid., 92). Like the victims of the sphinx, the future chiefs are confronted with this dilemma: to interpret or die (though differing from certain characters of the *Arabian Nights* whose law is, instead, "Narrate or Die!" But no doubt there exist narrative civilizations and interpretative civilizations); and it is said that, once chosen, the chief is marked by the tattooing of pictograms on his body: his throat, his foot, his hand.

The association of power and language mastery is clearly marked among the Aztecs. The ruler himself is called *tlatoani*, which means, literally, "he who possesses speech" (something in the manner of our "dictator"), and the periphrasis designating the wise man is "the possessor of red ink and of black ink"—i.e., he who knows how to paint and interpret the pictographic manuscripts. The native chronicles describe Montezuma as "an excellent orator. His manner of speaking was so fine that he could attract and win over others with his reasoning, and all were delighted by his pleasant discourse" (Durán, III, 54). In Yucatán, the prophet interpreters—*chilanes*—enjoy the highest esteem and the greatest privileges: "It was the office of the priests to discourse and teach their sciences, to indicate calamities and the means of remedying them, preaching during the festivals, celebrating the sacrifice and administering the sacraments. The *chilanes* were responsible for giving those in the locality the oracles of the demons, and the respect paid them was so great that they did not ordinarily leave their houses except borne upon litters carried on the shoulders of bearers" (Landa, 27, p. 47).

Even after the conquest, the Spaniards cannot help admiring Indian eloquence. Fifteen years after the fall of the Aztec empire, Vasco de Quiroga writes: "Each of them thanked us in his turn with as much eloquence as if he had studied the art of oratory all his life" (p. 316). Sebastian Ramirez de Fuenleal, president of the second *audiencia* (the tribunal which was also the source of all legal power) of which Vasco de Quiroga is a member, experiences such pleasure hearing the Indians speak that he forgets the annoyance provoked by the tenor of the remarks: "Ten days ago, the chiefs of Michoacán and the sons of Cozonci [the local king] came to lodge their complaints with Your Majesty. So well ordered was their oratory that it was a veritable pleasure to hear the translation of it made for us by the interpreters."

The Spaniards of the period are equally fascinated by language. But the mere existence of an attention paid to verbal production by both Spaniards and Indians does not signify that the same aspects of language were being valued. The language privileged by the Aztecs is ritual speech—i.e., speech regulated in its forms and its functions, memorized and hence always quoted. The most striking form of ritual speech is constituted by the *huehuetlatolli*, discourses learned by heart, of varying length, covering a vast variety of themes and corresponding to a whole series of social circumstances: prayers, court ceremonies, rites of passage in the individual's life (birth, puberty, marriage, death), departures, encounters, etc. These are always formulated in carefully selected terms and are supposed to come out of the immemorial past, whence their stylistic archaism. Their function is that of all ritual speech in a society without writing: they materialize social memory, i.e., the body of laws, norms, and values to be transmitted from one generation to the next in order to assure the very identity of that collectivity; this also explains the exceptional importance given to public education, unlike what occurs in societies of the book, where the wisdom to which one can gain individual access counter-balances the values transmitted by the collective institution.

The absence of writing is an important element of the situation, perhaps even *the* most important. Stylized drawings, the pictograms used among the Aztecs, are not a lesser degree of writing: they note the experience, not the language. The unfamiliarity to the Indians of European writing creates reactions the literary tradition will exploit: the Indian is often represented bearing a fruit and a written message that mentions the fact; the Indian eats the fruit en route and is astonished to find himself confronted by the letter's recipient. "Thus the news spread through the island that the leaves speak in response to a sign from the Spaniards; and this obliges the islanders to be very careful of what is confided to them" (Peter Martyr, III, 8). The codex drawings only preserve the great landmarks of history, which as such remain unintelligible; they will be brought to comprehension by the ritual discourse accompanying them. We realize this today since certain drawings remain opaque to us, in the absence of any ancient commentary.

That the absence of writing is revelatory of symbolic behavior in general, and at the same time of the capacity to perceive the other, appears to be illustrated by another fact. The three great Amerindian civilizations encountered by the Spaniards are not located on precisely the same level of the evolution of writing. The Incas are the most unfamiliar with writing (they possess a mnemotechnical use of braided cords, moreover one that is highly elaborated); the Aztecs have pictograms; among the Mayas we find certain rudiments of phonetic writing. Now, we observe a comparable gradation in the intensity of the belief that the Spaniards are gods. The Incas firmly believe in this divine nature. The Aztecs do so only during the initial period of exposure. The Mayas raise the question to answer it in the negative:

rather than "gods," they call the Spaniards "strangers," or even "eaters of *anones*"—a fruit they themselves scorn to eat—or the "bearded ones," or at best "the powerful ones"; but never "gods." If we remark that they experienced a brief hesitation on this subject (as in the *Annals of Cakchiquels*—in Guatemala, but not in Yucatán), we also note that it very soon passes over and that their vision of the Spaniards remains fundamentally a human one. This is all the more remarkable in that only a few priests or nobles are initiated into the Mayan writing; but it is not the effective use of writing, writing as a tool, which matters here, but rather writing as an index of the evolution of mental structures. Yet we must add another explanation here (unless it is the same one): of the three groups only the Mayas have already undergone a foreign invasion (that of the Toltecs); they know what a different and at the same time a higher civilization is; and their chronicles will often inscribe the Spaniards within the rubric reserved for the Toltec invaders.

What is important here is that since writing cannot assume the role of memory support, speech must do so. This is why the *huehuetlatolli* have such importance, and also why, even outside these fixed genres, we notice in reading Sahagún's informants, for instance, that their answers express a knowledge they have learned by heart, without individual variations. Even if we suppose that these informants, doubtless old men, exaggerate the importance of ritual discourse to the detriment of improvised speech, we cannot help being impressed by the number and the length of such discourses, and hence by the place ritual occupies at the heart of the community's verbal life.

The essential feature of these discourses, then, is that they come from the past: not only their interpretation, but their production is dominated by the past rather than by the present; the very word *huehuetlatolli* signifies "speech of the ancients." These remarks, says one old man, "the men and the women of old left you, handed down to you, have been carefully folded away, stored up in your entrails, in your throat" (*Florentine Codex*, VI, 35). This is confirmed by other chroniclers: "In order to preserve [the orations and poems] word for word as declaimed by the orators and poets, the young lords who were to be their successors were drilled in them and, with constant repetition they committed them to memory without changing so much as a word," writes Tovar ("Letter to Acosta").

More generally, reference to the past is essential for the Aztec mentality of the period. We find a moving illustration of this in a quite exceptional document entitled *The Aztec-Spanish Dialogues of 1524*, only three years after the conquest. The first twelve Franciscans have arrived in Mexico and they have begun their work of conversion. But one day, in Mexico, a man stands up and protests: he is of course not capable of answering the Christians' theological arguments; but the Mexicans, too, have had their specialists in divine affairs, and the latter might confront the Franciscans and explain to them why the Aztec gods are not inferior to the god of the Spaniards. The Franciscans accept the challenge, and Cortés himself gives orders to organize the debate. Other discussions of the same kind doubtless occur in these first postconquest years; today we possess one Aztec narrative, collected by Sahagún, which is presented as an account of the Mexican confrontation of 1524, but which in reality must be a literary and generalized representation of such discussions. The debate as a whole is located within the context of Christian ideology, but its value as testimony remains very great.

Now, what will be the Aztec theologians' initial argument? Our religion, they say, is an ancient one; our ancestors have long adhered to it; hence, there is no reason to abandon it. "It is a new word, this one you tell them, and because of it we are distressed, because of it we are extremely frightened. Indeed, these our fathers, these who came to live on the earth, did not speak in this way. . . . They used to say that indeed they, the gods by whose grace we live, they deserved us. . . . And perchance now are we the ones who will destroy the ancient law?" (7, 950–6). The Franciscan fathers were not convinced by these arguments. In its way, the very narrative we possess illustrates the greater efficacy of the Christian discourse: this dialogue is quite asymmetrical, for the Evangelizers' words occupy a place that is not only greater, but growing; we get the impression that the voice of the Mexican priests, asserting attachment to the past, is gradually stifled by the abundant discourse of the Franciscans.

This is not an isolated example; we find an almost identical narrative by Cortés, who reports this improvised debate: "On hearing this I spoke to them, telling them to observe how vain and foolish was their belief, for they placed their trust in idols which could not even defend themselves and were so easily overthrown. They replied that they had been brought up in that belief by their fathers" (Cortés, 5). Forty or fifty years later, Durán still receives the same answer: "I have questioned certain elders regarding the origin of their knowledge of human destiny, and [the old men] answered that the ancient ones bequeathed it to them, taught it to them, and that is all they know. . . . It is clear that they have not acquired this knowledge from their own investigations" (Durán, II, 2).

From our present viewpoint, the Christians' position is not, in itself, "better" than that of the Aztecs, or closer to the "truth." Religion, whatever its content, is certainly a discourse transmitted by tradition and important as a guarantee of a cultural identity. The Christian religion is not in itself more rational than the Indian "paganism." But it would be illusory to regard the Aztec priests as anthropologists of religion. Knowing that religion is merely a traditional discourse does not afford them an outsider's perspective; quite the contrary, it is for this very reason that they cannot call religion into question. Personal opinion, as we have seen, is worthless in this context, and the Aztecs do not aspire to a knowledge the individual might have achieved by his own investigations. The Spaniards attempt to rationalize their choice of the Christian religion; it is this effort (or rather its failure) that generates, at this very period, the separation of faith and reason, and the very possibility of sustaining a nonreligious discourse concerning religion.

The submission of the present to the past therefore remains a significant characteristic of the Indian society of the period, and we can observe its traces in many realms other than religion—or, rather, religion extends far beyond the limits to which we are accustomed. Later commentators are frequently unable to restrain their admiration for a state that paid such attention to the education of children: rich and poor alike are schooled, either in a religious school or a military one. But it is clear that this is not a feature we can admire out of context: public education is essential in any society in which the past weighs heavily on the present, or, what comes to the same thing, in which the collectivity prevails over the individual. One of the fourteen laws of Montezuma I consecrates this preeminence of the ancient over the new and of the old over the young: "There are to be teachers and old men to chastise [the young] and to lead them in their exercises and not permit them to be idle or to waste their time" (Durán, III, 26). The riddle trials undergone by the Mayan chiefs do not call upon a random interpretative capacity: it is a matter of giving not an ingenious answer but the right answer—i.e., the traditional answer; to know the answer implies that one belongs to the right lineage, since it is transmitted from father to son. The Nahuatl word designating the truth, *neltiliztli*, is linked etymologically to "root," "base," "foundation"—the truth is allied with stability; and a *huehuetlatolli* regards two questions as parallel: "Does man possess the truth? Are there fixed and lasting things?" (*Colección*, 10, 15).

Into this past-oriented, tradition-dominated world erupts the conquest: an absolutely unpredictable event, surprising and unique (whatever the omens collected subsequently may say of it). It brings another conception of time, which combats the Aztec and Mayan conception. Two features of the Indian calendar, in which the latter conception is expressed particularly clearly, are relevant here. First of all a specific day belongs to a larger number of cycles than with us: there is the religious year of 260 days and the astronomic year of 365 days; the years themselves form cycles, in the manner of our centuries, but more consequentially, cycles of twenty, or fifty-two years, etc. Then, this calendar rests on the intimate conviction that time repeats itself. Our chronology has two dimensions, one cyclical, the other linear. If I say, "Wednesday, February 25," I am indicating the day's place within three cycles (week, month, year); but by adding "1981" I submit the cycle to the linear procedure, since the account of the years follows a succession without repetition, from the negative infinity to the positive infinity. Among the Mayas and Aztecs, on the contrary, the cycle prevails over linearity: there is a succession within the month, the year, or the "cluster" of years; but these latter, rather than being situated in a linear chronology, are repeated exactly from one to the next. There are differences within each sequence, but one sequence is identical with the next, and none is situated in an absolute time (whence the difficulties we encounter in translating Indian chronologies into our own). It is no accident that the graphic and mental image of time among the Aztecs and the Mayas is the wheel (whereas ours would probably be the arrow). As one (belated) inscription in the *Chilam Balam* says: "Thirteen score years, and then it will always return again" (22).

The ancient books of the Mayas and Aztecs illustrate this conception of time, as much by what they include as by the use they make of it. They are kept in each region by the priest-prophets and constitute (among other things) chronicles, books of history; at the same time, they make it possible to foretell the future because, since time repeats itself, knowledge of the past leads to that of the future—or rather, is the same thing. We see, therefore, in the Maya *Chilam Balam* that the event must always be located in its place within the system (a certain day of a certain month in a certain sequence of years) but that there will be no reference to the linear passage of time, even for events following the conquest; we have no doubt as to the day of the week on which a certain thing occurred, but we may hesitate among some twenty years! The very nature of events obeys this cyclical principle, since each sequence includes the same events; those occupying identical places in the different sequences have a tendency to be identified with each other. Hence in these books the Toltec invasion bears features incontestably proper to the Spanish conquest; but the converse is also true, so that although we know an invasion is in question, we cannot tell which one, though centuries separate them.

Not only do the sequences of the past resemble each other, but also those to come. This is why events are sometimes referred to the past, as in a chronicle, and sometimes to the future, in the form of prophecies: once again, past and future are the same thing. Prophecy is rooted in the past, since time repeats itself; the propitious or disastrous character of the days, months, years, centuries to come is established by the intuitive investigation of a denominator common to the corresponding periods of the past. Reciprocally, today we derive our information about the past of these peoples from their prophecies, which are often the only things to have been preserved. Durán reports that among the Aztecs, who distribute the years into cycles according to the cardinal points, "the years most feared by the people were those of the North and of the West, since they remembered that the most unhappy events had taken place under those signs" (Durán, II, 1). The Mayan account of the Spanish invasion inextricably mixes past and future, proceeding by retrospective anticipation. "These words are to be treasured as a precious jewel is treasured. They concern the coming introduction of Christianity" (*Chilam Balam*, 24, p. 164). "Thus it is that God, our Father, gives a sign when they shall come, because there is no agreement. The descendants [of the former rulers] are dishonored and brought to misery; we are Christianized, while they treat us like animals" (ibid., 11). One later copyist adds this significant note: "On this day of August 1766, occurred a hurricane. I have made a record of it in order that it may be seen how many years it will be before another one will occur" (ibid., 143). Once we establish the term of the series, the distance separating two hurricanes, we will be able to predict all the hurricanes to come. Prophecy is memory.

The same books exist among the Aztecs (though they have been less well preserved); to them are consigned, along with delimitations of territories or rates of tribute, the events of the past, and they are consulted when it is desired to know the future: past and future belong to the same book, pertain to the same specialist. It is to this book that Montezuma turns in order to learn what the foreigners will do. We see him first commissioning a picture to represent exactly what his messengers have seen at the coast. The most skillful painter in Mexico is assigned this task; the picture completed, Montezuma asks him: "Brother, I beg you to answer this question: by any chance do you know anything about what you have painted? Did your ancestors leave you a drawing or description of these men who were to arrive in this land?" (Durán, III, 70). We see how reluctant Montezuma is to admit that an entirely new event can occur, and that what the ancestors have not already known might come to pass. The painter's answer is negative, but Montezuma does not stop there; he consults all the other painters of the kingdom; still nothing. At the end he is told of an old man named Quilaztli, who is "well informed in all matters which concern ancient history and painted books." Quilaztli, who has not heard of the Spaniards' arrival, nonetheless knows everything about the imminent strangers, and he tells the king: " 'So that you may see that what I say is the truth, behold it drawn here! This picture was bequeathed to me by my ancestors.' He then took out an ancient picture on which were depicted the ship and the men dressed in the same manner as those which the king already knew through his painting. There he also saw other men mounted on horses or on flying eagles, all of them dressed in different colors, wearing their hats and swords" (ibid.).

The narrative is evidently very literary; it is nonetheless indicative of the Aztec conception of time and event: less that of Montezuma, of course, than of the narrator and his listeners. We cannot believe that there existed, long before the Spaniards' arrival, a drawing representing their ships and their swords, their clothes and hats, their beards and the color of their skin (and what are we to think of the men mounted on flying eagles?). Again, we are dealing with a prophecy fabricated a posteriori, a retrospective prospection. But that there should be a need to forge this history is revealing: no event can be entirely unprecedented; repetition prevails over difference.

In place of this cyclical, repetitive time frozen in an unalterable sequence, where everything is always predicted in advance, where the singular event is merely the realization of omens always and already present, in place of this time dominated by the system, appears the one-directional time of apotheosis and fulfillment, as the Christians then experience it. Further, the ideology and activity inspired by it lend support to this moment: the Spaniards see the ease of their conquest as a proof of the excellence of the Christian religion (this is the decisive argument employed in the course of the theological debates: the superiority of the Christian god is demonstrated by the Spaniards' victory over the Aztecs), whereas it is in the name of this excellence that they have undertaken the conquest: the quality of the one justifies the other, and reciprocally. And the conquest also confirms the Christian conception of time, which is not an incessant return but an infinite progression toward the final victory of the Christian spirit (a conception subsequently inherited by communism).

From this collision between a ritual world and a unique event results Montezuma's incapacity to produce appropriate and effective messages. Masters in the art of ritual discourse, the Indians are inadequate in a situation requiring improvisation, and this is precisely the situation of the conquest. Their verbal education favors paradigm over syntagm, code over context, conformity-to-order over efficacity-of-the-moment, the past over the present. Now, the Spanish invasion creates a radically new, entirely unprecedented situation, in which the art of improvisation matters more than that of ritual. It is quite remarkable, in this context, to see Cortés not only constantly practicing the art of adaptation and improvisation, but also being aware of it and claiming it as the very principle of his conduct: "I shall always take care to add whatever seems to me most fitting, for the great size and diversity of the lands which are being discovered each day and the many new secrets which we have learned from these discoveries make it necessary that for new circumstances there be new considerations and decisions; should it appear in anything I now say or might in future say to Your Majesty that I contradict what I have said in the past, Your Highness may be assured that it is because a new fact elicits a new opinion" (Cortés, 4). Concern for coherence has yielded to concern for the truth of each particular action.

Indeed, most of the Indians' communications to the Spaniards are notable for their ineffectiveness. In order to convince his visitors to leave the country, Montezuma sends gold each time: but nothing is more likely to persuade them to remain. Other chiefs offer them

women, with the same intent; these become both an additional justification for conquest and, as we shall see, one of the most dangerous
weapons—both defensive and offensive—to be put into the Spaniards'
hands. In order to discourage the intruders, the Aztec warriors inform
them that they will all be sacrificed and eaten, by themselves or by wild
beasts; and when on one occasion prisoners are taken, matters are
arranged so as to sacrifice them under the eyes of Cortés's soldiers; the
end is indeed just as was predicted: "Then they ate their flesh with a
sauce of peppers and tomatoes. They sacrificed all our men in this way,
eating their legs and arms, offering their hearts and blood to their idols,
as I have said, and throwing their trunks and entrails to the lions and
tigers and serpents and snakes that they kept in the wild-beast houses"
(Bernal Díaz, 152). But their comrades' unenviable fate can produce
only one effect on the Spaniards—to commit them to fighting with all
the more determination, since they now have but one choice: to conquer or to die in the cauldrons.

Or again, another touching episode reported by Bernal Díaz: Montezuma's first envoys paint a portrait of Cortés for him that is apparently a very close resemblance, since the next delegation is commanded
by "a great Mexican cacique who in face, features and body was very
like our Captain. . . . On account of this resemblance we in the camp
called them 'our Cortés' and 'the other Cortés'!" (Bernal Díaz, 39). But
this attempt to influence Cortés by a magic of resemblance (we know
that the Aztecs thus "personify" their gods) obviously produces no
effect whatever.

Just as the messages sent to (or against) the Spaniards turn out to
be ineffective, the Aztecs no longer manage to dominate communication with the other Indians in this new situation. Even in peacetime,
and before the Spaniards' arrival, Montezuma's messages are characterized by their ceremonial character, a potential obstacle for effectiveness: "He rarely answered, for usually his reply was given through his
intimates and familiars, who were always at his side for that purpose
and served as secretaries, as it were," writes Motolinia (III, 7). In the
state of improvisation imposed by conquest, new difficulties appear.
Montezuma's presents, which produce on the Spaniards an effect contrary to the one he has anticipated, also do him harm among his own
people, since they connote his weakness and thereby persuade other
leaders to change sides: "Their chiefs said among themselves that we
must be *teules* [beings of divine origin] indeed, for Montezuma was

afraid of us and sent us presents of gold. So if we had already a reputation for valor, henceforth it was greatly increased" (Bernal Díaz, 48).

Alongside these intentional messages which do not communicate what their authors have hoped, there exist others which do not seem intentional but which are quite as unfortunate in their effects: these proceeded from a certain incapacity of the Aztecs to dissimulate the truth. The war cry the Indians invariably utter when they do battle, and whose purpose is to alarm the enemy, actually reveals their presence and permits the Spaniards to orient themselves more effectively. Montezuma himself surrenders precious information to his jailers, and if Cuauhtemoc is captured, it is because he tries to escape in a boat richly decorated with royal emblems. We know that this is no accident. An entire chapter of the *Florentine Codex* is devoted to the "ornaments used by the kings in warfare" (VIII, 12), and the least we can say is that these decorations are not particularly discreet: "They wore the costly red spoonbill headdress, set off with gold, having very many quetzal feathers flaring from it, and with it, borne upon his back, the skin drum, upon a carrying frame and decorated with gold. And they dressed him in a red shirt, made of red spoonbill feathers, decorated with flint knives fashioned with gold; and his skirt of *sapote* leaves was set all about with quetzal feathers. The shield was ringed with thin gold, and its pendants were made of precious feathers" (*Florentine Codex*, VIII, 12, p. 33). We are also told, in the book devoted to the conquest, of the exploits of the warrior Tzilacatzin; the latter disguised himself in a thousand ways in order to deceive the Spaniards; however, the text adds, "his head went uncovered, so that it was apparent that he was an Otomi" (*Florentine Codex*, XII, 32). So we shall not be surprised to see Cortés winning a decisive battle, soon after his flight from Mexico on the Noche Triste, precisely as a result of this lack of dissimulation among the Aztecs. "As Cortés battled his way among the Indians, performing marvels in singling out and killing their captains who were distinguishable by their gold shields, and disregarding the common warriors, he was able to reach their general and kill him with one thrust of his lance. . . . When Captain Hernando Cortés killed their general, they began to retreat and give way to us" (Francisco de Aguilar).

Everything happens as if, for the Aztecs, signs automatically and necessarily proceed from the world they designate, rather than being a weapon intended to manipulate the Other. This characteristic of communication among the Indians gives rise, among authors favoring their cause, to a legend according to which the Indians are a people who know nothing of lying. Motolinia declares that the first Catholic priests noted two chief features among the Indians: "that they were a very veracious people, and that they would not take the property of others, even though it had been lying about the ground for a long time" (Motolinia, III, 5). Las Casas emphasizes the Indians' total lack of "duplicity," with which he contrasts the Spaniards' attitude: "The Spaniards have never respected their word nor the truth, with regard to the Indians" (Las Casas, *Relación*, "Peru"), so that, he declares, "liar" and "Christian" have become synonyms: "Not once but many times a Spaniard would ask an Indian if he was a Christian, and the Indian would reply: 'Yes, sir, I am a bit Christian because I have learned to lie a bit; another day I will lie big, and I will be a big Christian'" (*Historia*, III, 145). The Indians themselves might not disagree with this description; we read in Tovar: "No sooner was Captain Cortés finished with his peaceful speech, than the soldiers sacked the royal palaces and the residences of the dignitaries where they hoped to find riches, and thus the Indians began to consider the attitude of the Spaniards as very suspect" (Tovar, p. 80).

The facts, of course, belie the enthusiastic descriptions of the Indians' friends: we cannot conceive of a language without the possibility of lying, as there is no speech which does not know metaphor. But a society may favor or, quite the contrary, strongly discourage any discourse that, rather than faithfully describing things, is chiefly concerned with its effect and therefore neglects the dimension of truth. According to Alvarado Tezozomoc, "Montezuma promulgated a law whereby anyone caught telling a lie, however trivial, was to be dragged through the streets by the schoolboys of Tepochcalco until he had breathed his last breath" (103). Zorita also locates the origin of this character in the Indians' customs and education: "None dared swear falsely, fearing that the god by whom they swore would punish them with some grave infirmity. . . . Fathers warned their sons severely against lying, and a father punished a son who committed this offense by pricking his lip with a maguey thorn. As a result boys grew up accustomed to telling the truth. Aged Indians, asked why their people lie so much nowadays, reply that it is because falsehood goes unpunished. . . . The Indians say that they learned this trait from the Spaniards" (Zorita. 9).

During the first contact of Cortés's army with the Indians, the Spaniards (hypocritically) declare that they are not seeking war, but peace and love; "they did not trouble to reply in words but with a shower of arrows" (Cortés, 21). The Indians do not realize that words can be a weapon quite as dangerous as arrows. Several days before the fall of Mexico, the scene recurs: to the propositions of peace formulated by Cortés, who is in fact already the victor, the Aztecs stubbornly reply: "Do not talk to us any more about peace: words are for women, arms for men!" (Bernal Díaz, 154).

This distribution of labor is not accidental. One might say that the warrior/woman opposition plays a structuring role for the Aztec social image repertoire as a whole. Even if several paths lie open before the young man in search of a trade (soldier, priest, merchant), he has no doubt that the warrior's life is the most glamorous of all. Respect for speech does not go so far as to set specialists in discourse above military leaders (the head of state combines the two supremacies, since he is both warrior and priest). The soldier is the male par excellence, for he can administer death. Women, who give birth, cannot aspire to this ideal; yet their occupations and attitudes do not constitute a second valued pole of the Aztec axiology; it is no surprise that they are weak, but such weakness is never praised. And the society makes sure that no one is ignorant of the role he or she must take: if the newborn baby is a boy, a tiny sword and shield are put in the cradle; if a girl, then a toy shuttle and loom.

The worst insult, then, that can be addressed to a man is to treat him as a woman; on one occasion, the enemy warriors are forced to don women's clothes, for they have not accepted the challenge and fought. We see as well that the women have internalized this image (whose masculine origin we can easily imagine) and that they themselves contribute to the maintenance of the opposition, attacking young men who have not yet distinguished themselves on the battlefield: "Truly, he with the long, tangled hair of a youth also speaks! Do you speak indeed? . . . You with the evil-smelling, stinking forelocks, are you not only a woman like me?" And Sahagún's informant adds: "For thus the women could torment young men into battle; thus they moved and provoked them, thus the women prodded them into battle" (*Florentine Codex*, II, 213). Tovar reports a revealing scene, from the period of the conquest, when Cuauhtemoc, the incarnation of warrior values, attacks Montezuma, whose passivity identifies him with the women. Montezuma speaks to his people from the terrace of the palace, where he is kept prisoner by the Spaniards. "He had no sooner finished than a brave captain, eighteen years of age, named Cuauhtemoc, whom they already wished to choose for their king, shouted out: 'What matters what that coward Montezuma says, that woman of the Spaniards, for such we can call him, since he has surrendered himself like a woman, out of fear, and given us over to them bound hand and foot, and thus drawn all these evils upon us'" (Tovar, pp. 81–2).

Words for women, weapons for men . . . what the Aztec warriors did not know is that the "women" would win this war, if only figuratively; in the literal sense, women lose every war. Yet the identification is not entirely accidental, perhaps. The cultural model in effect since the Renaissance, even if borne and assumed by men, glorifies what we might call the feminine side of culture: improvisation rather than ritual, words rather than weapons. Not just any words, it is true: neither those that designate the world nor those that transmit the traditions, but those whose raison d'être is action upon others.

War, moreover, is only another field in which to apply the same principles of communication we can observe in peacetime; we find certain similar responses to both occasions. Initially, at least, the Aztecs fight a war subject to ritualization and to ceremonial: time, place, and manner are determined in advance, which is more harmonious but less effective. "It was the general practice in all the towns and provinces to leave, at the extreme boundary of each, a large barren stretch, cleared but uncultivated, for their wars" (Motolinia, III, 18). The combat begins and ends at a specific time. The goal of the combat is less to kill the enemy than to take prisoners (which operates distinctly in the Spaniards' favor). The battle begins with a first volley of arrows. "If the arrows did not strike anyone or draw blood, they retreated as best they could, because they considered it a certain omen that the battle would go badly for them" (Motolinia, "Letter of Introduction").

We find another striking example of this ritual attitude just before the fall of Mexico: having exhausted all other means, Cuauhtemoc decides to use the supreme weapon. What is it? The magnificent feather armor bequeathed to him by his father, a suit of clothes to which was attributed the mysterious virtue of putting the enemy to flight by its mere appearance; a brave warrior will be dressed in it and hurled against the Spaniards. But the quetzal feathers do not bring the Aztecs victory (*Florentine Codex*, XII, 38).

Just as there are two forms of communication, there are two forms of war (or two aspects of war, one valued by each side). The Aztecs cannot conceive and do not understand the total war of assimilation the Spaniards are waging against them; for them, war must be ended by a treaty establishing the amount of tribute to be paid the victor by the vanquished. Before winning the battle, the Spaniards had already won the decisive victory, which consisted in imposing their own type of war; their superiority was henceforth no longer in question. Nowadays it is difficult to imagine a war waged by any principle but effectiveness, even if the role of ritual is not completely dead: treaties forbidding the use of bacteriological, chemical, or atomic weapons are forgotten the day war is declared. Yet this is precisely how Montezuma understood matters.

Hitherto, I have described the symbolic behavior of the Indians in a systematic and synthetic form. In closing this chapter, I should like to follow a single account which I have not yet cited, that of the conquest of Michoacán (a region west of Mexico City), both to illustrate a description in its entirety and in order not to let "theory" prevail over narrative. This account was apparently given by a Tarascan noble to the Franciscan Martín de Jésus de la Coruña, who reported it in his *Relación de Michoacán*, written around 1540.

The narrative begins with omens: "These people say that during the four years before the Spaniards came to the land, their temples were burned from top to bottom, that they closed them and they would be burned again, and that the rock walls fell, as their temples were made of flagstones. They did not know the cause of this except that they held it to be an augury. Likewise, they saw two large comets in the sky. . . . (III, 19).

"A priest related that, before the Spaniards came, he had dreamed that people would appear bringing strange animals which turned out to be the horses which he had not known. . . . The priest also indicated that the priests of the mother of Cueravaperi, who were in a village called Cinapecuaro, had come to the father of the late Cazonci [the king before the preceding one] and reported the following dream or revelation prophesying the destruction of the house of their gods, an event which actually happened in Ucareo. . . . 'There will be no more temples or fireplaces, nor will any more smoke rise, everything shall become a desert because other men are coming to the earth' (ibid.).

"The people of the Hot Lands say that a fisherman in his boat was fishing in the river with a hook and that a very large fish took the hook, but the fisherman could not bring it in. An alligator appeared, from I do not know where in that river, snatched the fisherman from the boat, swallowed him and sank into very deep water. The fisherman grappled with the alligator and, defeating him, brought him to his own fine home. Upon arriving at his home, the fisherman bowed to the alligator, who then said to him: 'you shall see that I am a god; go to the city of Michoacán and tell the king, who is over all of us and whose name is Zuangua, that the signal has been given that there are now new men and all who have been born in all quarters of the land are to die. Tell this to the king' (ibid.).

"They say that there were other omens: that the cherry trees, even the small ones, would produce berries, the small magueys would produce stalks, and that little girls would become pregnant while still children" (III, 21).

The new event must be projected into the past, in the form of an omen, in order to be integrated into the narrative of the confrontation, for it is the past that prevails in the present: "How can we contradict what has been established?" (III, 19). If the event had not been predicted, one might simply not have acknowledged its existence. "Never have we heard of the coming of other people from our ancestors. . . . By this we shall be guided, since there was no recollection of this in days gone by nor did the old people tell one another that these men were to come" (III, 21). Thus speaks the Cazonci, king of the Tarascans, trusting more to the ancient narratives than to the new perceptions, and finding a compromise solution in the fabrication of omens.

Yet there is no lack of direct, firsthand information. Montezuma sends ten messengers to the Cazonci of Michoacán to ask for help. These men supply a specific account: "The Master of Mexico, called Montezuma, sends us and some other lords with orders to report to our brother the Cazonci about the strange men who have come and taken us by surprise. We have met them in battle and killed some two hundred of those who came riding deer and two hundred of those who were not mounted. Those deer wore coats of mail and carried something that sounds like the clouds, makes a great thundering noise and kills all those it meets leaving not one. They completely broke up our formation and killed many of us. They are accompanied by people from Tlaxcala, because these people have turned against us" (III, 20). Suspicious, the Cazonci decides to check this information. He seizes several Otomi and interrogates them; they confirm the preceding account. This does not satisfy him; he sends his own delegates into the besieged city; they return repeating the earlier information and specifying the military propositions of the Aztecs, who have foreseen in detail the Tarascans' possible military intervention.

At this point the old Cazonci dies; he is replaced by his oldest son. The Aztecs (under Cuauhtemoc rather than Montezuma) grow impatient and send a new delegation to repeat their proposals. The new Cazonci's reaction is revealing: without impugning the truth or usefulness of what the messengers declare, he decides to sacrifice them. "Let them follow my father to the inferno and present him with the petition there. Tell them to prepare themselves because this is the custom.'— The Mexicans were so informed, and they replied that as the Master had ordered it, it should be done, and they asked that it be done quickly, adding that there was nowhere for them to go; they had voluntarily come to their death. The Mexicans were made ready in the customary manner, after being informed that they were taking their message to the dead Cazonci, and were sacrificed in the temple of Curicaveri and Xaratanga" (III, 22).

The only positive step the Tarascans will take is to put the messengers to death; the Cazonci provides no active response to the Aztecs' request. First of all, he does not like them, they are the traditional enemy and, in fact, he is not so sorry that such disasters should befall them: "What purpose would I have in sending men to Mexico, for we are always at war when we approach each other, and there is rancor between us?" (III, 20). "For what purpose are we to go to Mexico? Each one of us might go only to die, and we know not what they will say about us afterwards. Perhaps they will sell us to these men who are coming and will be the cause of our being killed. Let the Mexicans do their own conquering or let them all come join us with their generals. Let the strangers kill the Mexicans . . ." (III, 22).

The other reason for the refusal to oppose the Spaniards is that they are taken for gods. "Where would they come from but from the heavens?" (III, 21). "Why would the strangers come without cause? A god has sent them, that is why they come!" (III, 21). "The Cazonci said that these were gods from the heavens and to each Spaniard he gave a round golden shield and blankets" (III, 23). It is in order to explain surprising facts that a divine hypothesis is resorted to: the supernatural is the child of determinism; and this belief paralyzse any attempt at resistance: "In the belief that they were gods, the dignitaries told the women not to harm them, for what those gods were carrying off belonged to them" (III, 26).

Thus the first reaction is the refusal to intervene on the human level, and the involvement of the divine sphere: "Let us wait and see. Let them come and try to take us. Let us do our best to hold our own a little longer in order to get wood for the temples" (III, 21; this wood is for the ritual fires). In the same spirit, when the Spaniards' advent seems inevitable, the Cazonci gathers his family and servants together so that they can all drown themselves in the waters of the lake.

At the last moment, he decides against this course of action; but his eventual attempts to resist continue on the level of communication familiar to him—communication with the world and not with men. Neither he nor his family manage to see through the conquistadors' hypocrisy. "Perhaps the fate which awaits us at the hands of the Spaniards is not so bad as that," says one of the Tarascan leaders. "I saw the Lords from Mexico who are coming with them; if these were slaves why would they be wearing turquoise collars round their necks, and rich blankets and green plumages as they do?" (III, 25). The Spaniards' behavior remains incomprehensible to them: "Why do they want this gold? These gods must eat it, that could be the only reason they want so much" (III, 26; Cortés, apparently, had offered this explanation: the Spaniards need gold as the cure for a sickness. The Indians, who identify gold with excrement, find this difficult to accept). Money, as a universal equivalent, does not exist among the Tarascans; the entire Spanish power structure eludes them. The production of symbols is no more fortunate than the interpretation; the first Spaniards bring the Cazonci, God knows why, ten pigs and a dog; he accepts them with thanks, but in reality dreads them: "He took them to be omens, and ordered the pigs and the dog killed and the people dragged them off and threw them in a weed patch" (III, 23). With more tragic consequences, the Cazonci reacts in the same way when he is brought Spanish weapons: "Whenever the Tarascans came into possession of firearms captured from the Spaniards, the weapons were offered to the gods in the temples" (III, 22). We realize why the Spaniards did not even have to wage war: they prefer, once they have arrived, to convoke the local leaders and fire their cannon into the air a few times: the

Indians fall to the ground in terror; the symbolic use of weapons proves to be sufficiently effective.

The Spaniards' victory in the conquest of Michoacán is swift and complete: no battle, no victims on the side of the conquistadors. The Spanish leaders—Cristobal de Olid, Cortés himself, then Nuño de Guzmán—promise, threaten, and extort all the gold they find. The Cazonci gives, always hoping it will be for the last time. In order to be more secure, the Spaniards take him prisoner; when they fail to obtain satisfaction, they do not hesitate to torture him and his family: they are hanged, their feet are scorched with burning oil, their genitals prodded with a metal rod. When Nuño de Guzmán decides that the Cazonci can no longer be of any use, he "condemns" him to a triple death: first, "he is attached to a piece of matting hooked to a horse's tail, the horse being ridden by a Spaniard" (III, 29). After having been dragged through the streets of the town, he is garroted, and finally his body is flung on a pyre and burned; his ashes will be scattered in the river.

The Spaniards win the war. They are incontestably superior to the Indians in the realm of interhuman communication. But their victory is problematic, for there is not just one form of communication, one dimension of symbolic activity. Every action has its share of ritual and its share of improvisation; all communication is, necessarily, both paradigm and syntagm, code and context; man has just as much need to communicate with the world as with men. The encounter of Montezuma with Cortés, of the Indians with the Spaniards, is first of all a human encounter; and we cannot be surprised that the specialists in human communication should triumph in it. But this victory from which we all derive, Europeans and Americans both, delivers as well a terrible blow to our capacity to feel in harmony with the world, to belong to a preestablished order; its effect is to repress man's communication with the world, to produce the illusion that all communication is interhuman communication; the silence of the gods weighs upon the camp of the Europeans as much as on that of the Indians. By winning on one side, the Europeans lost on the other; by imposing their superiority upon the entire country, they destroyed their own capacity to integrate themselves into the world. During the centuries to follow, they would dream of the noble savage; but the savage was dead or assimilated, and this dream was doomed to remain a sterile one. The victory was already big with its defeat; but this Cortés could not know.

Cortés and Signs

COMMUNICATION among the Spaniards is not, of course, precisely the contrary of that practiced by the Indians. Not being abstract notions, peoples both resemble and differ from each other. We have already seen Columbus's likenesses to the Aztecs on the typological level. The same is somewhat the case for the first expeditions to Mexico, those of Hernandez de Córdoba and Juan de Grijalva. These Spaniards apparently seek to collect as much gold as possible in the shortest amount of time, without trying to find out anything at all about the Indians. This is what we are told by Juan Diaz, chronicler of the second of these expeditions: "Many Indians were running along the shore with two banners which they raised and lowered, signaling us to approach; but the captain did not wish to. . . . The Indians sent one of the canoes ahead, to find out what we wanted. The interpreter told them we were looking for gold. . . . The captain told them we did not want anything but gold." Even when the opportunity arises, the Spaniards avoid it: "He also told us of other provinces, and said to our captain that he wished to come with us, but the captain did not agree to this, which angered all of us."

We have also seen that the first interpreters are Indians; the latter do not have the entire confidence of the Spaniards, who often wonder if the interpreter is accurately transmitting what he is told: "We thought the interpreter was deceiving us, for he was a native of this island and town." About "Melchior," Cortés's first translator, Gomara says: "This fellow was uncouth, being a fisherman, and it seemed he knew neither how to speak nor to answer" (11). The name of the province of Yucatán, for us a symbol of Indian exoticism and remote authenticity, is in reality the symbol of the misunderstandings that then prevailed: to the shouts of the first Spaniards landing on the peninsula, the Mayas answer: *Ma c'ubah than,* "we do not understand your words." The Spaniards, faithful to the tradition of Columbus, hear "Yucatán," and decide that this is the name of the province. During the first contacts, the Spaniards are not at all concerned with the impression their behavior makes on those they encounter: if they are threatened, they flee without hesitation, thereby showing they are vulnerable.

The contrast is striking once Cortés makes his appearance. Is he not an exception among conquistadors rather than the type? No: as is proved by the fact that his example will be immediately followed, and widely, even if never equaled. It required a remarkably gifted man to crystallize into a unique type of behavior elements hitherto so disparate: once the example is set, it spreads with impressive speed. The difference between Cortés and those who preceded him may lie in the fact that he is the first to have a political and even a historical consciousness of his actions. On the eve of his departure from Cuba, he probably did not differ in any way from the other conquistadors so greedy for wealth. Yet matters change very early in the expedition, and we can already observe this spirit of adaptation becoming the very principle of Cortés's conduct: at Cozumel, someone suggests that he send armed men to look for gold in the interior. "Cortés however answered with a laugh that he was not after such small game, but was here to serve God and the king" (Bernal Díaz, 30). As soon as he learns of the existence of Montezuma's kingdom, Cortés decides he will not be content with extorting gold, but must subjugate the kingdom itself. This strategy often vexes the soldiers of his army, who count on immediate and palpable profits; but Cortés remains intractable. Hence it is to him that we owe the invention, on the one hand, of conquest tactics, and on the other, of a policy of peacetime colonization.

What Cortés wants from the first is not to capture but to comprehend; it is signs which chiefly interest him, not their referents. His expedition begins with a search for information, not for gold. The first important action he initiates—and we cannot overemphasize the significance of this gesture—is to find an interpreter. He hears some Indians speak using Spanish words; he deduces that there may be Spaniards among them, castaways from previous expeditions; he makes inquiries, and his suppositions are confirmed. Then he orders two of his boats to wait eight days, after sending a message to these potential interpreters. After several reversals, Geronimo de Aguilar joins Cortés's men, who have difficulty recognizing him as a Spaniard: "They could not distinguish him from an Indian, for he was naturally dark, and had his hair untidily cut like an Indian slave. He carried a paddle on his shoulder and had an old sandal on his foot, the other sandal being tied to his belt" (Bernal Díaz, 29). This Aguilar, having become Cortés's official interpreter, will render him inestimable services.

But Aguilar speaks only the Mayan language, which is not that of the Aztecs. The second essential figure in this conquest of information is a woman, whom the Indians call Malintzin and the Spaniards Doña Marina, without our knowing which of these two names is a distortion of the other; the form most frequently given is La Malinche. She is offered as a gift to the Spaniards during one of the first encounters. Her mother tongue is Nahuatl, the language of the Aztecs; but she has been sold as a slave to the Mayas, and speaks their language as well. Hence there is a rather long chain of interpreters at first: Cortés speaks to Aguilar, who translates what he says to La Malinche, who in her turn speaks to the Aztec interlocutor. Her gift for languages is obvious, and she soon learns Spanish, which further increases her usefulness. We can imagine that she retains a certain rancor toward her own people, or toward some of their representatives; in any case she resolutely chooses to side with the conquistadors. In fact, she is not content merely to translate; it is evident that she also adopts the Spaniards' values and contributes as best she can to the achievement of their goals. On the one hand, she performs a sort of cultural conversion, interpreting for Cortés not only the Indians' words but also their actions; on the other hand, she can take the initiative when necessary, and addresses appropriate words to Montezuma (notably in the episode of his arrest) without Cortés's having spoken them previously.

All agree in recognizing the importance of La Malinche's role. Cortés considers her an indispensable ally, and this is readily seen by the importance he grants to their physical intimacy. Although he had "offered" her to one of his lieutenants immediately after having "received" her, and after the surrender he will marry her to another conquistador, La Malinche will be his own mistress during the decisive phase, from the departure from the coast to the fall of the Aztec capital. Without discussing the way in which men determine the fate of women, we may assume that this relationship has a strategic and military explanation rather than an emotional one: thanks to it, La Malinche can assume her essential role. But even after the fall of the kingdom, we always find her being appreciated for her real worth: "Cortés could not understand the Indians without her" (Bernal Díaz, 5, p. 51). The Indians, too, regard her as much more than an interpreter; all accounts mention her frequently, and she is present in every image. The *Florentine Codex* illustration of the first encounter between Cortés and Montezuma is quite characteristic in this regard: the two military leaders occupy the margins of the image, dominated by the central figure of La Malinche (see fig. 5). Bernal Díaz reports, for his part: "Doña Marina was a person of great importance, and was obeyed without question by all the Indians of New Spain" (86). Revealing, too, is the nickname the Aztecs give to Cortés: they call him Malinche (for once, it is not the woman who takes the man's name).

The Mexicans, since their independence, have generally despised La Malinche as an incarnation of the betrayal of indigenous values, of servile submission to European culture and power. It is true that the conquest of Mexico would have been impossible without her (or someone else playing the same role), so that she is responsible for what occurred. I myself see her in quite a different light—as the first example, and thereby the symbol, of the cross-breeding of cultures; she thereby heralds the modern state of Mexico and beyond that, the present state of us all, since if we are not invariably bilingual, we are inevitably bi- or tri-cultural. La Malinche glorifies mixture to the detriment of purity—Aztec or Spanish—and the role of the intermediary. She does not simply submit to the other (a case unfortunately much more common: we think of all the young Indian women, "offered" or not, taken by the Spaniards); she adopts the other's ideology and serves it in order to understand her own culture better, as is evidenced by the effectiveness of her conduct (even if "understanding" here means "destroying").

Later on, several Spaniards learn Nahuatl, and Cortés invariably benefits from this situation. For instance, he gives the imprisoned Montezuma a pageboy who speaks his language; information then circulates in both directions, but under the circumstances this is greatly to Cortés's advantage. "Then Montezuma asked Cortés that the page called Orteguilla, who already knew the language, might attend him, and this was of great benefit both to him and to us. For from this page

Fig. 5 La Malinche between Cortés and the Indians.

of whom he asked many questions, Montezuma learned a great deal about Spain, and we learned what his captains said to him" (95).

Being thus certain of understanding the language, Cortés neglects no occasion to gather new information. "When we had eaten, Cortés asked through our interpreters about the lord Montezuma" (61) . . . "Cortes took the *caciques* aside and asked them very detailed questions about the state of Mexico" (78). His questions are directly linked to the conduct of the war. Following a first confrontation, he immediately interrogates the defeated leaders: "How did it happen that they, with their great numbers, had fled from so few?" (Gomara, 22). Once such information is obtained, he never fails to reward, and generously, those who bring it to him. He is ready to listen to advice, even if he does not always follow it—since the information needs to be interpreted.

It is as a consequence of this perfected system of information that Cortés quickly gains a detailed knowledge of the existence of internal dissensions among the Indians—a fact whose decisive role for the final victory we have already observed. From the expedition's start he is attentive to all information of this kind. Now, such dissensions happen to be numerous; Bernal Díaz says: "They were constantly at war, province against province, town against town" (208), and Motolinia emphasizes this situation: "When the Spaniards came all the rulers and all the provinces differed greatly and were continually involved in wars against each other" (III, 1). Having reached Tlaxcala, Cortés is especially conscious of this situation: "When I saw the discord and animosity between these two peoples, I was not a little pleased, for it seemed to further my purpose considerably, and in consequence I might have the opportunity of subduing them more quickly, for, as the Scripture has it, 'divided they fall' " (3): it is curious to see that Cortés chooses to read this principle of the Caesars in the book of the Christians! The Indians will go so far as to solicit Cortés's intervention in their own conflicts; as Peter Martyr writes: "they hoped to secure protection of such heroes against their neighbors, for they likewise are afflicted by that malady which never disappears and is in some fashion inborn in humanity; like all men, they thirst for dominion" (IV, 7). Moreover, the effective conquest of information leads to the ultimate collapse of the Aztec empire: while Cuauhtemoc rashly parades the royal emblems on the boat that should allow him to escape, Cortés's officers, for their part, immediately gather all the information that might lead to his capture. "Immediately on receiving news that Cuauhtemoc was escaping, Sandoval ordered all his launches to stop destroying the houses and defences and follow the flight of the canoes" (Bernal Díaz, 156). "Garcia de Olguin, who commanded one of the brigantines, was told by an Aztec prisoner that the canoe he was following was that of the king" (Ixtlilxochitl, XIII, 173). The conquest of information leads to that of the kingdom.

We note a significant episode during Cortés's progress toward the capital. He has just left Cholula and, in order to reach the city of Mexico, must cross the mountain chain. Montezuma's envoys show him a pass; Cortés follows it reluctantly, fearing an ambush. At this moment, when in principle he should devote all his attention to this problem of protection, he perceives the peaks of the neighboring volcanoes, which are in eruption. His thirst for knowledge makes him forget his immediate concerns:

"Eight leagues from this city of Cholula are two very high and very remarkable mountains; for at the end of August there is so much snow on top of them that nothing else can be seen, and from one of them, which is the higher, there appears often both by day and by night a great cloud of smoke, as big as a house, which goes straight as an arrow up into the clouds and seems to come out with such force that even though there are very strong winds on top of the mountain, they cannot turn it. Because I have always wished to render Your Highness very particular account of all the things of this land, I wished to know the secret of this which seemed to me something of a miracle; so I sent ten of my companions, such as were qualified for such an undertaking, with some natives to guide them; and urged them to climb the mountain and discover the secret of this smoke, whence it came, and how" (Cortés, 2).

The explorers do not get all the way to the summit, and are content to bring back pieces of ice. But on the way down they glimpse another possible route toward Mexico which seems to present fewer dangers; this is the route Cortés will follow, and indeed he will meet with no nasty surprises on his way. Even at the most difficult moments, those which require his greatest attention, Cortés's passion to "know the secret" has not diminished. And, symbolically, his curiosity is rewarded.

It may be instructive to compare this ascent of the volcano to another, performed by the Mayas and reported in the *Annals of the Cakchiquels*. It, too, occurs during a military expedition. The volcano is reached: "The fire that emerged from inside the mountain was truly terrifying." The warriors want to go down inside it to take away a specimen of the burning lava, but no one has the courage to do so. Then they turn to their leader, Gagavitz (whose name means "volcano"), and say to him: "O you, our brother, you have arrived and you are our hope. Who will go to bring us the fire, and to try our luck in this manner, O my brother?" Gagavitz decides to do so himself, accompanied by another intrepid warrior; he descends inside the volcano, and emerges carrying the burning lava. The warriors exclaim: "Truly, it is terrifying—his magic power, his greatness and majesty; he has destroyed and made captive [the fire]." Gagavitz answers: "The spirit of the mountain has become my slave and my captive, O my brothers! When we conquered the secret of the mountain, we freed the stone of fire, the stone called Zacchog [flint]" (I).

On either side are both curiosity and courage. But the perception of the facts is different. Cortés perceives a singular natural phenomenon, a marvel of nature; his curiosity is intransitive; the practical consequence (discovery of a better route) is evidently accidental. For Gagavitz, man must measure himself against a magical phenomenon, combat the spirit of the mountain; the practical consequence is the domestication of fire. In other words, this account, which may have a historical basis, is transformed into a myth of the origins of fire: the stones whose impact produces sparks are apparently brought back by Gagavitz from the active volcano. Cortés remains on the purely human level; Gagavitz's narrative immediately sets up a network of natural and supernatural correspondences.

Communication among the Aztecs is above all a communication with the world, and here religious representations play an essential role. Religion is of course not absent from the Spanish side—it was even decisive in Columbus's case. But two important differences immediately confront us. The first resides in a specific feature of the Christian religion in relation to the pagan religions of America: what matters here is that Christianity is, fundamentally, universalist and egalitarian. "God" is not a proper noun: this word can be translated into any language, for it designates not *a* god—like Huitzilopochtli or Tezcatlipoca, though these are already abstractions—but *the* god. This religion seeks to be universal and is thereby intolerant. Montezuma gives evidence of what may appear to us as a fatal broad-mindedness during the religious conflicts: when Cortés attacks his temples, he tries to find compromise solutions. "Then Montezuma suggested placing our images on one side and leaving his gods on the other, but the Marqués [Cortés] refused" (Andrés de Tapia); after the conquest itself, the Indians continue trying to integrate the Christian god into their own pantheon, as one divinity among others.

This does not mean that any monotheist notion is alien to Aztec culture. Their countless divinities are merely the different names for god, invisible and intangible. But if god has so many names and so many images, it is because each of his manifestations and relations with the natural world is personified, his different functions are distributed among so many different personages. The god of the Aztec religion is both one and many. This is what causes Aztec religiosity to adapt itself so well to the addition of new divinities; and we know that, precisely in Montezuma's lifetime, a temple is built to receive all the "other" gods: "At that time king Montezuma decided that there should be a shrine where all the gods of the country could be adored. Moved by religious zeal, he ordered that one be built. . . . It was to be called Coatescalli, which means 'Temple of the Diverse Gods,' and it is called this because in it were housed many gods from the different provinces and lands . . ." (Durán, III, 58). The project will be completed, and this astonishing temple will function in the years preceding the conquest. The same is not true of the Christians, and Cortés's refusal proceeds from the very spirit of the Christian religion: the Christian god is not one incarnation which can be added to the rest, it is *one* in an exclusive and intolerant fashion, and leaves no room for other gods; as Durán says, "Since it is one, one Church adoring one True God, it cannot coexist with any other religion or belief in other gods" (I, "Introduction"). This fact contributes not a little to the Spaniards' victory: intransigence has always defeated tolerance.

Christianity's egalitarianism is part of its universalism: since God belongs to all, all belong to God; there is not, in this regard, a difference among peoples nor among individuals. As Saint Paul says: "There is neither Greek nor Jew, circumcision nor uncircumcision, Barbarian, Scythian, bond nor free: but Christ is all, and in all" (Col. 3:11), and "There is neither Jew nor Greek, there is neither bond nor free, there is neither male nor female: for ye are all one in Christ Jesus" (Gal. 3:28). These texts clearly indicate in what sense this egalitarianism of the early Christians is to be understood: Christianity does not combat inequalities (the master will remain a master, the slave a slave, as if this were a difference quite as natural as that between man and woman); but it declares them irrelevant with regard to the unity of all in Christ. These problems will recur in the moral debates following the conquest.

The second difference derives from the forms religious sentiment takes among the Spaniards of this period (but this too may be a consequence of Christian doctrine, and we may wonder to what degree an egalitarianizing religion leads, by its rejection of hierarchies, to the transcendence of religion itself): the Spaniards' God is an auxiliary rather than a Lord, a being to be used rather than enjoyed (in the language of theologians). In theory, and as Columbus wished (and even Cortés, of whom this is one of the most "archaic" mental features), the goal of the conquest is to spread the Christian religion; in practice, religious discourse is one of the means assuring the conquest's success: end and means have changed places.

The Spaniards hear the divine counsel only when the latter coincides with the suggestions of their informants or with their own interests, as is evidenced by the narratives of several chroniclers. "And we saw other very clear signs too, by which we knew it was God's wish that we settle in that land," says Juan Díaz, who accompanies Grijalva's expedition; and Bernal Díaz: "They advised us to go through Tlaxcala, which was friendly to them and hostile to the Mexicans. So we decided to take their advice, for God always guided us well" (61). During the episode of the volcano already discussed, Cortés also attributed to God the discovery of the best route. "As God has always shown diligence in guiding the Royal affairs of Your Sacred Majesty ever since Your childhood, and as I and those of my company traveled in Your Royal service, so He showed us another road which, although somewhat rough, was not so dangerous as the one by which they wished to lead us" (2). If the Spaniards fling themselves into battle shouting "Santiago!" this is less in the hope of an intervention of their tutelary saint than to give themselves courage and to frighten their enemies. The chaplain of Cortés's forces yields in nothing to a military leader: "Our troops were excited to a fever pitch under the influence of the encouragements of Fray Bartolomé de Olmedo, who exhorted them to hold fast in their goal to serve God and to extend his holy faith, promising the help of his sacred ministry and shouting to them to conquer or die in combat" (Bernal Díaz, 164). On Cortés's very banner we find this relation explicitly affirmed: "The flag that Cortés hoisted was of white and blue flames with a cross in the middle, and about the margins a

Latin motto which, translated, said: 'Friends, let us follow the Cross and with faith in this symbol we shall conquer'" (Gomara, 23).

A significant episode is reported during the campaign against the Tlaxcaltecs: in order to surprise the enemy, Cortés makes a night sortie with his cavalry. A first horse stumbles; Cortés sends it back to camp. A second does the same shortly after. "There were some who said to him, 'Surely, this seems a bad sign to us; let us return,' but he replied: 'I consider it a good sign. Onward'" (de Aguilar, see de Tapia). Whereas the Spaniards' arrival is only the fulfillment of a series of evil omens for the Aztecs (which moreover diminishes their combativeness), in comparable circumstances Cortés (unlike certain of his own companions) refuses to see divine intervention—or else it can only be in his favor, even if the signs seem to say the contrary! It is striking to see that in his declining phase, especially during the Honduras expedition, Cortés in his turn begins to believe in omens; and success no longer accompanies him.

This subordinate and finally limited role of the exchange with God gives way to a human communication in which the other will be clearly recognized (even if not esteemed). The encounter with the Indians does not create this possibility of recognition, it merely reveals it; the recognition exists for reasons belonging to the history of Europe itself. In order to describe the Indians, the conquistadors seek comparisons they find immediately either in their own pagan (Greco-Roman) past, or among others geographically closer and already familiar, such as the Muslims. The Spaniards call each of the first temples they discover a "mosque," and the first city glimpsed during the expedition of Hernandez de Córdoba will be named, Bernal Díaz tells us, Great Cairo. Trying to focus his impressions of the Mexicans, Francisco de Aguilar immediately remembers: "As a child and youth, I began reading many histories and antiquities of the Persians, Greeks and Romans. I also read about the rites performed in Portuguese India." We may wonder how much the flexibility of mind necessary to achieve the conquest, as evidenced by the Europeans of that period, is due to the singular situation that makes them the heirs of two cultures—Greco-Roman on one hand, and Judeo-Christian on the other (though in reality the merging of cultures was long since experienced in the assimilation of the Judaic tradition and the Christian, the Old Testament having been absorbed into the New). We shall have further occasion to observe the conflicts between these two elements of Renaissance culture; consciously or not, its representative must make a whole series of adjustments, translations, and occasionally very arduous compromises which allow him to cultivate a spirit of accommodation and improvisation destined to play so decisive a role in the course of the conquest.

European civilization of the period is "allocentric" rather than egocentric: for centuries its sacred site, its symbolic center, Jerusalem, has been not only exterior to European territory but subject as well to a rival civilization (the Muslims). In the Renaissance, this spatial decentering is linked to a temporal version: the ideal age is neither the present nor the future but the past, and a past that is not even Christian: that of the Greeks and the Romans. The center is elsewhere, which opens up the possibility for the Other to become, someday, central.

One of the things that most strikes the conquistadors' imagination, upon their entrance into Mexico, is what we might call Montezuma's zoo. The subject peoples offered various specimens of flora and fauna as tribute to the Aztecs, who had established places where these collections of plants, birds, serpents, and wild beasts could be observed. The collections not only were justified, it seems, by religious references (a certain animal corresponding to a certain divinity) but were admired for the rarity and variety of the species, or for the beauty of the specimens. Again this reminds us of Columbus's activity as a naturalist and an amateur who wanted samples of all that he encountered.

This institution, which the Spaniards admire in their turn (zoos do not yet exist in Europe), can be both related to and contrasted with another, which is virtually contemporary with it: the first museums. Men have always collected curiosities, natural or cultural; but it is only in the fifteenth century that the popes begin accumulating and exhibiting ancient remains as traces of another culture; this is also the period of the first works on the "life and manners" of remote peoples. Something of this spirit has passed into Cortés himself, for if, initially, his only concern is to knock down the idols and destroy the temples, soon after the conquest we see him preoccupied with preserving them, as testimony to the Aztec culture. A witness assigned to the trial Cortés is brought to some years later declares: "He showed great annoyance because he wanted those temples of the idols to remain as a memorial" (*Sumario*, I, p. 232).

What most nearly resembled a museum among the Aztecs was the Coateocalli, or Temple of the Diverse Gods. Yet we immediately perceive the difference: the idols brought into this temple from the four corners of the country provoke neither an aesthetic response of admiration nor, still less, a relativist consciousness of the differences among peoples. Once in Mexico, these divinities become Mexican, and their use remains purely religious, like that of the Mexican gods, even if their origin was different. Neither the zoo nor this temple bears witness to a recognition of cultural differences, as the nascent museum does in Europe.

The presence of a site reserved for the Other in the Spaniards' mental universe is symbolized by their constantly affirmed desire to communicate, which contrasts strongly with Montezuma's reticence. Cortés's first message is, "Since we had crossed so many seas and journeyed from such distant lands solely to see and speak with him in person, our Lord and great King cannot approve our conduct if we were to return now" (Bernal Díaz, 39). "The captain then answered them, giving them to understand that on no account would he leave until he had learned the secrets of the land and might send Your Majesties a true account of it" (Cortés, 1). The foreign sovereigns, like the volcanoes, exert an irresistible appeal to Cortés's desire to know, as if his sole goal were to write an account.

We might say that the very fact of thus assuming an active part in the process of interaction assures the Spaniards an incontestable superiority. They are the only ones to *act* in this situation; the Aztecs seek only to maintain the status quo, they are content to *react*. That it should be the Spaniards who have crossed the ocean to find the Indians, and not the converse, already heralds the result of the encounter; the Aztecs no longer have no further expansionist designs in the Americas. Significantly, in Mesoamerica it is the Aztecs who do not want to communicate or to change anything in their life (the two things are often identified), an attitude matching their veneration of the past and its traditions; the subject or dependent peoples participate much more actively in the interaction and find their advantage in the conflict: the Tlaxcaltecs, allies of the Spaniards, will be in many respects the real masters of the country in the century following the conquest.

Again let us consider the production of discourse and symbols. Initially Cortés has a constant concern for the interpretation which the Indians—the Others—make of his actions. He will severely punish pillagers in his own army because the latter *take* what must not be taken and *give* an unfavorable impression of themselves. "When he saw the town empty of its inhabitants and learned that Pedro de Alvarado had been to the other place and had taken fowls and hangings and other things of small value from the idols, also some gold that was half copper, he was as angry with our captain as he had been with the pilot, and reprimanded him severely, telling him that he would never pacify the country by robbing the natives of their possessions. . . . He had the gold, hangings and everything else restored to them, and in return for the fowls, which had already been eaten, he ordered that they should be given some beads and little bells. In addition he presented each Indian with a Spanish shirt" (Bernal Díaz, 25). Or again: "In one of these towns, Cortés happened to see a soldier called de Mora, from Ciudad Rodrigo, take two fowls from an Indian's house. Enraged that any soldier should do such a thing in a friendly town and before his very eyes, he immediately ordered a halter to be thrown around his neck" (51). The reason for these actions is precisely Cortés's desire to control the information the Indians receive: "In order to avoid the appearance of avarice on their part, and to dispel the notion that their single motive for coming was to acquire gold, all should pretend ignorance of it" (Gomara, 25); and in the towns: "Cortés had the crier announce that, on pain of death, no one was to touch anything but food—this in order to enhance his fame and good will among the natives" (Gomara, 29). We note the role incipiently taken by the vocabulary of pretense: "appearance" and "fame."

As for the messages he sends them, these too obey a perfectly coherent strategy. To begin with, Cortés wants the information the Indians received to be the same information he issues; he will therefore very carefully distill the truth in his own remarks, and he will be particularly pitiless with regard to spies: those whom he captures will have their hands cut off. At first the Indians are not sure that the Spaniards' horses are mortal beings; in order to sustain this uncertainty, Cortés has the animal corpses buried during the night after the battle. He will resort to many other stratagems in order to dissimulate his true sources of information, to make it appear that his information comes not from an exchange with human beings but from the supernatural realm. Concerning an informer's message, he reports: "As they have never discovered from whom I learned of their plot, they believe it was done by some magic art, and that nothing can be concealed from me. Having observed that in order to be certain of my road I have often taken out a ship's chart and a compass, especially when cutting the Cagoatzepan road which came through so accurately, they told many of the Spaniards that it was there that I had learned their secret. Some of them have even come to me and eager to show their good intentions, have begged me to look into the glass and at the map, so that I might see there that they spoke the truth, since through those objects I knew everything else. I encouraged this belief, giving them to understand that the compass and the chart did indeed reveal all things to me" (5).

Montezuma's behavior was contradictory (to welcome or reject the Spaniards?) and revealed the Aztec emperor's state of indecision, which would be exploited by his adversaries. Cortés's behavior is often quite as contradictory in appearance, but this contradiction is calculated and has as its goal—and effect—to "jam" its message, to leave its interlocutors in perplexity. One moment of his march toward Mexico is exemplary in this regard: Cortés is at Cempoala, received by the "great cacique" who hopes that the Spanish leader will help him throw off the Aztec yoke. At this moment five of Montezuma's envoys arrive to collect tribute; they are particularly vexed by the welcome given to the Spaniards. The cacique turns to Cortés to ask his advice; Cortés tells him to arrest the tax collectors. This is done, but when the Cempoalans propose sacrificing the prisoners, Cortés forbids this and adds his own soldiers to the prison guard. At nightfall, he orders his soldiers to bring him secretly two of the five prisoners, the most intelligent ones if possible; once they are before him, he pretends ignorance, is amazed to find them imprisoned, and offers to release them; in order to make certain of their escape, he himself conducts them outside Cempoalan territory. Liberated, they return to Montezuma and tell him what they owe Cortés. The next morning the Cempoalans discover the escape and prepare to sacrifice the three remaining prisoners, but Cortés forbids this as well; he expresses indignation at the negligence of the Cempoalan guards, and offers to keep the other three prisoners on his own boats. The cacique and his colleagues agree. But they also know that Montezuma will be informed of their rebellion, so they swear loyalty to Cortés and promise to help him in his struggle against the Aztec emperor. "Then in the presence of Diego de Godoy, the Notary, they took the oath of obedience to His Majesty, and sent messengers to all the other towns in the province to relate what had happened. As they now paid no more tribute and the tax-gatherers had disappeared, they could not contain their delight at having thrown off the tyranny of the Mexicans" (Bernal Díaz, 47).

Cortés's maneuvers have two recipients: the Cempoalans and Montezuma. With the former the matter is relatively simple: Cortés urges them to commit themselves irreversibly to his party. Since the Aztec tax-gatherers are quite close and the tribute very heavy—whereas the king of Spain is a pure abstraction and for the moment requires no taxes —the Cempoalans find justification enough to reach a decision. Matters are more complex with regard to Montezuma, who knows, on the one hand, that his envoys have been mistreated thanks to the presence of the Spaniards; but on the other, that they have had their lives saved thanks to these same Spaniards. Cortés presents himself simultaneously as an enemy and as an ally, making it impossible, or in any case unjustifiable, for Montezuma to take any action against him; by this device he imposes his power alongside that of Montezuma, since the latter cannot punish him. When he knew only the first part of the story, Montezuma "prepared to attack with a great force of many companies"; having learned the second, "this anger died down, and he resolved to find out something about us" (Bernal Díaz, 48). The result of Cortés's ambiguous message is that Montezuma no longer knows what to think, and must go in search of information.

Cortés's first concern, when weak, is to make others believe he is strong and not to let them discover the truth; this concern is a constant one: "As we had announced that that was the road we were to travel by, it did not seem wise to me to leave it or to turn back, for I did not wish them to believe we lacked courage" (2). "But I saw that to show the natives, especially those who were our allies, that we lacked courage, would suffice to turn them against us the sooner, and I remembered that Fortune always favors the bold" (2). "It seemed to me that although our road led elsewhere it would be cowardly to pass by without giving them a lesson, and our allies might think we were afraid" (3). Etc.

In a general way, Cortés is a man sensitive to appearances. When he is appointed to head the expedition, his first expenditures will be on an imposing outfit. "He began to adorn himself and to take much more care of his appearance than before. He wore a plume of feathers, with a medallion and a gold chain, and a velvet cloak trimmed with loops of gold. In fact he looked like a bold and gallant captain" (Bernal Díaz, 20); but we may assume that, unlike the Aztec leaders, he did not wear all these insignia into battle. Nor does he ever fail to surround his dealings with Montezuma's messengers by a whole ceremonial which must have been quite comical in the jungles, but which did not fail to achieve its effect any the less for that.

Cortés has the reputation of being an eloquent speaker; we know that he even wrote poems when he felt so inspired, and his reports to Charles V testify to a remarkable mastery of the language. The chronicler often show him at work, as much among his own soldiers as when he addresses the caciques through his interpreters. "Sometimes the captain gave us very good talks, leading us to believe that each one of us would be a count or a duke, and one of the titled; with this he transformed us from lambs to lions, and we went out against that large army without fear or hesitation" (de Aguilar; we shall return to this comparison with lions and lambs). "He was very friendly and a good conversationalist" (Bernal Díaz, 20); "Cortés won over all the caciques with kindly words" (36); "Cortés comforted them with kind words which he and Doña Marina were skillful in employing" (86). Even his sworn enemy Las Casas emphasizes his complete ease in communicating with men: he depicts him as a man who "is expert in human affairs" and "most alert and most versed in mundane wisdom" (ibid., III, pp. 114 and 115).

He is quite as concerned with his army's reputation, and contributes very astutely to its elaboration. When he and Montezuma climb one of the Aztec temples—114 steps high—the emperor invites him to rest. "Cortés replied that none of us was ever exhausted by anything" (Bernal Díaz, 92). Gomara has him reveal the secret of such behavior in a speech Cortés makes to his soldiers: "The outcome of war depends upon fame" (Gomara, 114). When he enters the Aztec capital for the first time, he refuses to be accompanied by an army of Indian allies, for that might be interpreted as a sign of hostility; on the other hand when, after the city's fall, he receives the messengers of a distant chief, he makes a great show of all his power: "So that they should see our strength and report it to their lord, I ordered the horsemen to parade and skirmish before them in a square. The foot soldiers were then sent out in formation, the harquebusiers discharged their weapons and I had them attack a tower" (3). And his favorite military tactic—since he must convince the enemy of his power when he is weak—will be to simulate weakness precisely when he is strong, in order to lead the Aztecs into murderous traps and ambushes.

Throughout the campaign, Cortés shows a preference for spectacular actions, being very conscious of their symbolic value. For example,
it is essential to win the first battle against the Indians; to destroy the
idols during the first challenge to the priests, in order to demonstrate
his invulnerability; to triumph during a first encounter between his
brigantines and the Indian canoes; to burn a certain palace located
within the city in order to show how irresistible his advance is; to climb
to the top of a temple so that he may be seen by all. He punishes seldom
but in an exemplary fashion, so that everyone will hear of it; we have
an example of this in the violent repression he inflicts on the region
of Panuco, following an uprising he has crushed; we note the attention
he pays to the spread of information: "Cortés ordered that each of
these caciques should bring his heir with him. This order was carried
out, and all the caciques were then burned on an enormous pyre, their
heirs witnessing the execution. Cortés afterwards summoned them
before him and asked if they had taken note of the sentence executed
upon their relatives; then, adopting a severe mien, he added that he
hoped this example would suffice, and that they would not henceforth
incur suspicion of disobedience" (Peter Martyr, VII, 2).

The very use Cortés makes of his weapons is of a symbolic rather
than a practical nature. A catapult is constructed which turns out not
to work; no matter: "Even if it were to have had no other effect, which
indeed it had not, the terror it caused was so great that we thought the
enemy might surrender" (3). At the very start of the expedition, he
organizes veritable *son et lumière* spectacles with his horses and cannons (which then serve for no other purpose); his concern for staging
is remarkable. He conceals a mare at a certain point, then brings in his
Indian guests and a stallion; the latter's noisy manifestations terrify
these persons, who have never seen a horse. Selecting a moment of
relative calm, Cortés has the nearby cannons fired. He has not invented
such stratagems, but he is doubtless the first to deploy them systematically. On another occasion, he leads his guests to where the ground is
hard, so that the horses can gallop rapidly, and once again has the great
cannon fired, though loaded only with gunpowder. We know from the
Aztec accounts that these performances did not fail of their purpose:
"The messengers lost their senses and fainted away. They fell down side
by side and lay where they had fallen" (*Florentine Codex*, XII, 5). Such
hocus-pocus is so effective that one good Father can write quite tran-
quilly, several years later: "These people have so much trust in us that

there is no longer any need for miracles" (Francesco da Bologna).

Cortés's behavior irresistibly suggests the almost contemporary teachings of Machiavelli. No question of a direct influence, of course, but rather of the spirit of a period which is manifest in the latter's writings as in the former's actions; further, the "Catholic" King Ferdinand, whose example Cortés certainly knew, is cited by Machiavelli as a model of the "new prince." How can we avoid the comparison between Cortés's stratagems and Machiavelli's precepts, which promote reputation and pretense to the forefront of the new values: "It is not, therefore, necessary for a prince to have all the above-named qualities, but it is very necessary to seem to have them; I would even be so bold as to say that to possess them and always to observe them is dangerous, but to appear to possess them is useful" (Machiavelli, *Prince*, 18). More generally, in the world of Machiavelli and of Cortés, discourse is not determined by the object it describes, nor by conformity to a tradition, but is constructed solely as a function of the goal it seeks to achieve.

Our best proof we can have of Cortés's capacity to understand and speak the other's language is his participation in the development of the myth of Quetzalcoatl's return. This will not be the first time that the Spanish conquistadors exploit the Indian myths in their own favor. For example, Peter Martyr tells the moving story of the deportation of the Lucays, inhabitants of what are now the Bahamas, who believe that after death their spirits go to the promised land, in a paradise where all pleasures will be showered upon them. The Spaniards, who need laborers and are failing to recruit volunteers, swiftly seize upon the myth and complete it to their own advantage. "As soon as the Spaniards understood the simple beliefs of the islanders regarding their souls, which after expiating their sins must leave the cold mountains of the north for the south, they sought to persuade them to quit their native soil of their own accord and allow themselves to be conducted to the southern islands of Cuba and Hispaniola. They succeeded in convincing them that they would thus reach the country where they would find their dead parents, their children, relatives and friends, and where they would enjoy every delight in the embraces of their loved ones. As their priests had already filled them with those false beliefs, when the Spaniards persuaded them, they left their country to pursue this vain hope. As soon as they understood that they had been deceived, since they found neither their parents nor any one they sought, and were on the contrary obliged to submit to severe fatigue and heavy labors to which they were unaccustomed, they were reduced to desperation. Their either killed themselves or, resolving to die of hunger and exhaustion, resisted both reasoning and force to make them eat. . . . Thus perished the unfortunate Lucayos" (Peter Martyr, VII, 4).

The story of Quetzalcoatl's return to Mexico is more complex, and its consequences more important. Here, in a few words, are the facts. According to Indian accounts from before the conquest, Quetzalcoatl is a figure at once historical (a leader) and legendary (a divinity). At a given moment, he is forced to leave his kingdom and flee to the east (toward the Atlantic); he vanishes but, according to certain versions of the myth, he promises (or threatens) to return some day to reclaim his own. We may note here that the notion of a Messiah's return does not play an essential role in Mexican mythology; that Quetzalcoatl is merely one divinity among others and does not occupy a privileged place (especially among the Aztecs, who perceive him as the god of the Cholultecs); and that only certain narratives promise his return, whereas others are content to describe his disappearance.

The Indian accounts of the conquest, especially those collected by Sahagún and Durán, tell us that Montezuma identified Cortés as Quetzalcoatl returning to recover his kingdom; this identification is given as one of the chief reasons for Monte zuma's failure to resist the Spanish advance. We cannot question the authenticity of accounts which report what the priests' informants believed. The notion of an identity between Quetzalcoatl and Cortés certainly existed in the years immediately following the conquest, as is also attested by the sudden recrudescence of cult objects linked to Quetzalcoatl. But there is an obvious hiatus between these two states of the myth: the old version, in which Quetzalcoatl's role is secondary and his return uncertain; and the new one, in which Quetzalcoatl is dominant and his return absolutely certain. Some force must have intervened to hasten this transformation of the myth.

This force has a name: Cortés, who effects a synthesis of varying data. The radical difference between Spaniards and Indians, and the relative ignorance of other civilizations on the part of the Aztecs led, as we have seen, to the notion that the Spaniards were gods. But which gods? Here Cortés must have provided the missing link, converting the rather marginal myth into the myth of Quetzalcoatl's return—perfectly adapted to the language of the Other. The accounts we find in Sahagún and Durán present the identification of Cortés with Quetzalcoatl as occurring to Montezuma himself. But this assertion merely proves that, for the Indians after the conquest, the thing was likely; Cortés's calculation must have been based on this possibility when he sought to produce an "authentic" Indian myth. In this regard, we possess more direct proofs.

One is that the first major source establishing the existence of this myth consists of Cortés's own letter reports. These reports, addressed to the Emperor Charles V, have more than a mere documentary value: for Cortés, as we have seen, speech is more a means of manipulating the Other than it is a faithful reflection of the world, and in his relations with his sovereign he has so many goals to achieve that objectivity is not the first of his concerns. Nonetheless, the evocation of this myth, as we find it in his account of the first meeting with Montezuma, is revealing in the extreme. Montezuma had declared, speaking to his Spanish guest and to his own dignitaries: "So because of the place from which you claim to come, namely from where the sun rises, and the things you tell us of the great lord or king who sent you here, we believe and are certain that he is our natural lord, especially as you say that he has known us for some time." To which Cortés replies, "As I thought most fitting, especially in making him believe that Your Majesty was he whom they were expecting" (2).

In order to characterize his own discourse, Cortés employs, significantly, the basic rhetorical notion of the "suitable," the "fitting": discourse is governed by its goal, not by its object. But Cortés has no interest in convincing Charles V that the latter is a Quetzalcoatl unaware of the fact; hence his report tells the truth in this regard. But in the facts reported we see his intervention twice over: Montezuma's initial conviction (or suspicion) is already the effect of Cortés's words ("because of the things that you tell us"), and especially of that ingenious argument whereby Charles V has known the Indians long since (it would not have been difficult for Cortés to produce proofs in this regard). And in reply, Cortés asserts the explicit identity of the two figures, thereby reassuring Montezuma, while remaining quite vague and appearing to confine himself to confirming a conviction his interlocutor had acquired by his own means.

Without being certain that Cortés is solely responsible for the identification of Quetzalcoatl with the Spaniards, we observe that he does his best to contribute to it. His efforts will be crowned with success, even if the legend must undergo some further transformations (dropping Charles V and directly identifying Cortés with Quetzal- coatl). This is because the legend's functioning is profitable on every level: Cortés can thus claim a legitimacy among the Indians; further, he affords them a means of rationalizing their own history: otherwise his coming would have no meaning and we can suppose that their resistance to it would have been much more intense. Even if Mon- tezuma does not take Cortés for Quetzalcoatl (moreover, he does not particularly fear Quetzalcoatl), the Indians who supply the accounts— i.e., the authors of the collective representation—do; this has incom- mensurable consequences. Thus by his mastery of signs Cortés ensures his control over the ancient Mexican empire.

Even if the Indian or Spanish chroniclers are mistaken or disingenu- ous, their works remain eloquent for us; each of them reveals its au- thor's ideology, even when the narrative of events is false. We have seen how much the Indians' semiotic conduct was united to the domi- nance of the hierarchic principle over the democratic principle, and of the social over the individual. Comparing narratives of the conquest itself—Indian and Spanish—we further discover the opposition of two types of very different ideology. Let us take two of the richest examples: Bernal Díaz's chronicle on the one hand; that of the *Florentine Codex*, collected by Sahagún, on the other. They do not differ in their docu- mentary value—both contain truths combined with errors—nor in their aesthetic quality—both are moving, even overwhelming. But they are not constructed similarly. The narrative in the *Codex* is the story of a people told by that people. Bernal Díaz's chronicle is the story of certain men told by one man.

Not that individual identifications are lacking in the *Codex*. Many a brave warrior is mentioned, even named, as well as the ruler's family, not to mention the latter himself; particular battles are evoked, the place where they occur is specified. Yet these individuals never become "characters:" they have no individual psychology inspiring their actions and differentiating them from each other. Fatality rules over the course of events and at no moment do we feel that things might have hap- pened otherwise. These individuals do not, by addition or fusion, form Aztec society. That society, on the contrary, is the initial datum and the hero of the account; the individuals are merely its instances.

Bernal Díaz tells the story of certain men—not only Cortés, but all those named are furnished with individual features, physical and moral.

Each is a complex mixture of virtues and defects whose actions cannot be predicted: from the world of the necessary we have shifted to the world of the arbitrary, since each individual can become the source of an action not to be anticipated by general laws. In this sense his chronicle is opposed not only to the Indian accounts (of which he knew nothing) but also to Gomara's, without which—out of a desire to contradict it—Bernal Díaz might not have written at all but would have been content to tell his story orally, as he must have done many times over. Gomara subjects everything to the image of Cortés, who thereby is no longer an individual, but an ideal figure. Bernal Díaz emphasizes the plurality and difference of his protagonists: if I were an artist, he says, "I could draw all those I have mentioned true to nature and even show how each one entered into battle" (Bernal Díaz, 206).

And we have seen to what degree his narrative swarms with "useless" (or rather unnecessary) details not imposed by the fatality of events: why tell us that Aguilar was wearing one sandal at his belt? Because this singularity of the event in his eyes constitutes its identity. Indeed, we find in the *Florentine Codex* certain details of the same kind: the lovely Indian women who cover their cheeks with mud in order to escape the Spaniards' lustful gaze; the Spaniards who must hold a handkerchief to their noses in order to escape the stench of corpses; Cuauhtemoc's dusty garments when he presents himself to Cortés. But they all appear in the last chapters, after the fall of Mexico, as if the empire's collapse were accompanied by the victory of the European narrative mode over the Indian style: the world of the post-conquest is cross-bred, in the fact as in the fashions of reporting it.

In the *Florentine Codex*, we do not know at any given moment who is speaking, or rather, we know that it is never an individual's account we hear but what the collectivity thinks. It is no accident that we do not know the names of the authors of these accounts; this is not due to Sahagún's negligence but to the irrelevance of the information. The narrative can report several events that have occurred simultaneously or in places quite remote from each other: it is never concerned to give us the sources of such information, to explain how all this has been discovered. Such information has no source, for it belongs to everyone, and that is precisely what makes it convincing; if it had a personal origin it would be, on the contrary, suspect.

Conversely, Bernal Díaz authenticates his information by personalizing its sources. Once again unlike Gomara, if he wants to write it is not because he regards himself as a good historian who is qualified to express a truth common to all; his singular, exceptional trajectory qualifies him as a chronicler: it is because *he was there* in person, because he has witnessed the events himself, that he must now speak. In one of his rare lyric flights, he exclaims: "For one who is not present in a war and does not see it or understand it, how is he able to speak of it? Are the clouds to utter praise or the birds that flew over us when we were fighting our battles? Only the captains and soldiers could do so" (Bernal Díaz, 212). And each time he describes the vicissitudes of which he was not a witness, he specifies from whom and how he heard the story—for he is not the only conquistador at the time to identify himself as a witness: "We always discussed matters," he writes, "with each other" (Bernal Díaz, 206).

We can pursue this comparison of the modalities of representation on the level of imagery. The figures shown in the Indian drawings are not individualized internally; if they are intended to refer to a particular person, a pictogram identifying that person appears alongside the image. Any idea of linear perspective, and hence of an individual viewpoint, is absent; the objects are represented in themselves, without possible interaction between them, and not as if someone were seeing them. Map and sketch are freely juxtaposed: one image (see fig. 6) representing the temple of Mexico shows each of its walls seen straight on, the whole subordinate to the ground plan, the human figures being as large as the walls. The Aztec sculptures are worked on all sides, including the base, even if they weigh several tons; this is because the object's observer is as little individual as its executant; representation gives us essences and is not concerned with the impressions of any one man. European linear perspective may not have originated from the concern to validate a single and individual viewpoint, but it becomes its symbol, adding itself to the individuality of the objects represented. It may seem bold to link the introduction of perspective to the discovery and conquest of America, yet the relation is there, not because Toscanelli, inspirer of Columbus, was the friend of Brunelleschi and Alberti, pioneers of perspective (or because Piero della Francesca, another founder of perspective, died on October 12, 1492), but by reason of the transformation that both facts simultaneously reveal and produce in human consciousness.

Cortés's semiotic conduct belongs indeed to his time and his place. In itself, language is not an unequivocal instrument: it serves as well

Fig. 6 The massacre perpetrated by Alvarado in the temple of Mexico.

for integration within the community as for manipulation of the other. But Montezuma privileges the former function, Cortés the latter. A last example of this difference is to be found in the role attributed on either side to the national language. The Aztecs or Mayas, who as we have seen venerated the mastery of a symbolic discourse, do not appear to have understood the political importance of a common language, and linguistic diversity makes their communication with foreigners difficult. Zorita writes, "Two or three different languages are spoken in many towns, and there is almost no contact or familiarity among the groups speaking these different languages" (9). Where the language is above all a means of designating the group speaking it and expressing the coherence proper to that group, it is not necessary to impose it on the other. Language itself remains situated in the space delimited by man's exchange with the gods and the world, rather than being conceived as a concrete instrument of action upon the Other.

Hence the Spaniards will establish Nahuatl as the national native language in Mexico, before effecting Hispanization; the Franciscan and Dominican priests will undertake the study of the native languages as they later assume the teaching of Spanish. The preparation for this conduct has begun much earlier, and the year 1492, which had already seen the remarkable coincidence of the victory over the Arabs, of the exile imposed on the Jews, and of the discovery of America, this year is also the one that sees the publication of the first grammar of a modern European language—the Spanish grammar of Antonio de Nebrija. The knowledge, here theoretical, of language testifies to a new attitude, no longer of veneration but of analysis and of a new consciousness of its practical utility; Nebrija writes in his Introduction these decisive words: "Language has always been the companion of empire."

3. LOVE

Understanding,
Taking Possession, and Destroying

CORTÉS understands relatively well the Aztec world that appears before him—certainly better than Montezuma understands the Spanish realities. And yet this superior understanding does not keep the conquistadors from destroying Mexican civilization and society; quite the contrary, we suspect that destruction becomes possible precisely because of this understanding. There is a dreadful concatenation here, whereby grasping leads to taking and taking to destruction, a concatenation whose unavoidable character we want to question. Should not understanding go hand in hand with sympathy? And should not even the desire to take, to profit at another's expense, imply a desire preserve that other as a potential source of wealth and profit?

The paradox of the understanding-that-kills might be readily resolved if we observed at the same time, among those who understand, an entirely negative value judgment of the Other; if success in knowledge were accompanied by an axiological rejection. We might imagine that, having come to know the Aztecs, the Spaniards judged them so contemptible that they declared them and their culture unworthy to exist. Yet if we read the conquistadors' writings, we find that this is anything but the case, and that on certain levels at least, the Aztecs provoke the Spaniards' admiration. When Cortés must pass judgment on the Indians, he invariably compares them with the Spaniards themselves; this is more than a stylistic or narrative device: "The natives of these parts are of much greater intelligence than those of the other islands; indeed they appeared to us to possess such understanding as is sufficient for an ordinary citizen to conduct himself in a civilized country" (3). "These people live almost like those in Spain, and in as much harmony and order as there, and considering that they are barbarous and so far from the knowledge of God and cut off from all civilized nations, it is truly remarkable to see what they have achieved in all things" (2). It will be noted that, for Cortés, exchanges with *another* civilization can explain a high level of culture.

The Mexicans' cities, Cortés believes, are as civilized as those of the Spaniards, and he gives a curious proof of the notion: "There are many poor people who beg from the rich in the streets, as the poor do in Spain and in other civilized places" (2). As a matter of fact the comparisons are always in Mexico's favor, and we cannot help being struck by their specificity, even if we take into account Cortés's desire to parade the merits of the country he is presenting to his emperor. "The Spaniards . . . said that they had seen fortified lodgings larger and stronger and better built than the Burgos Castle" (2). "It seems like the silk market in Granada, except here there is a much greater quantity" (2); "The most important of these towers is higher than that of the cathedral of Seville" (2); "The marketplace of Tenoxtitlan is a square much larger than that of Salamanca" (3). Another chronicler says: "Even had the Spaniards done it, it would not have been better executed" (Diego Godoy). In short: "I shall not attempt to describe it at all, save to say that in Spain there is nothing to compare with it" (Cortés, 2). These comparisons testify of course to the desire to grasp the unknown by means of the known, but they also contain a systematic and revealing distribution of values.

The manners of the Aztecs, or at least of their leaders, are more refined than those of the Spaniards. Cortés marvels at the heated dishes in Montezuma's palace: "Because the climate is cold, beneath each plate and bowl they brought a brazier with hot coals so that the food should not go cold" (2), and Bernal Díaz does the same with regard to the toilets: "On all the roads they have shelters made of reeds or straw or grass so that they can retire when they wish to do so, and purge their bowels unseen by passers-by, and also in order that their excrement shall not be lost" (92).

But why be limited to Spain alone? Cortés is convinced that the wonders he sees are the greatest in the world. "It cannot be believed that any of the princes of this world, of whom we know, possess any things of such high quality" (2); "They were such that in all the world there could be none like them, nor any of such varied and natural colors or such workmanship" (2); "They are so well constructed in both their stone and woodwork that there can be none better in any place" (2); "So realistic in gold and silver that no smith in the world could have made better" (2); "Their city was indeed the most beautiful thing in the world" (3). And the only comparisons Bernal Díaz finds are taken from the romances of chivalry (the conquistadors' favorite reading, it is true): "These great towns and *cues* [temples] and buildings rising from the water, all made of stone, seemed like an enchanted vision from the tale of Amadis. Indeed some of our soldiers asked whether it was not all a dream" (87).

So much enchantment, yet followed by such complete destruction! Bernal Díaz, evoking his first vision of Mexico, writes with characteristic melancholy: "I say again that I stood looking at it, and thought that no land like it would ever be discovered in the whole world. . . . But today all that I then saw is overthrown and destroyed; nothing is left standing" (87). Far from being dissipated, then, the mystery only grows more intense: not only did the Spaniards understand the Aztecs quite well, they admired them—and yet they annihilated them; why?

Let us reread Cortés's admiring observations. One thing is striking about them: with very few exceptions, they all concern *objects:* the architecture of houses, merchandise, fabrics, jewelry. Like today's tourist who admires the quality of Asian or African craftsmanship though he is untouched by the notion of sharing the life of the craftsmen who produce such objects, Cortés goes into ecstasies about the Aztec productions but does not acknowledge their makers as human individualities to be set on the same level as himself. An episode following the conquest illustrates this attitude: when Cortés returns to Spain, some years after the conquest, we find him making a significant sampling of everything he considered remarkable in the conquered country. "He had already collected many birds differing from those found in Castile, which was a thing well worth seeing, and two tigers, and many kegs of coagulated liquid amber and balsam, and another of oil; and four Indians skilled in juggling with a stick with their feet, a thing remarkable in Castile and in all other countries, skillful dancers who were accustomed to use some sort of contrivance, so that to all appearance they seem to fly in the air while dancing; and he took three Indian hunchbacks who were monstrosities, for their bodies appeared broken, and they were very dwarfish" (Bernal Díaz, 194; see fig. 7). We know that these jugglers and monsters provoked admiration at the Spanish court as at that of Pope Clement VII, where they were subsequently sent.

Things have changed a little since Columbus, who, it will be recalled, also captured the Indians in order to complete a kind of naturalist's collection, in which they took their place alongside plants and animals, but who was interested only in number: six head of women, six of men. In the latter case, the Other was reduced, we might say, to the status of an object. Cortés does not have the same point of view, but the Indians have still not become subjects in the full sense of the word, i.e., subjects comparable to the *I* who contemplates and conceives them. They occupy rather an intermediate status in his mind: they are subjects, certainly, but subjects reduced to the role of producers of objects, artisans or jugglers whose performances are admired— but such admiration emphasizes rather than erases the distance between them and himself; and the fact that they belong to the series of "natural curiosities" is not altogether forgotten. When Cortés compares their performances to those of the Spaniards, even if it is to grant them primacy in all generosity, he has not abandoned his egocentric point of view, has not even sought to do so: is it not true that the Spaniards' emperor is the greatest of all, that the Christians' God is the most powerful? And it just so happens that Cortés, who thinks this, is a Spaniard and a Christian. On this level—that of the subject in relation to what constitutes him as such, and not to the objects he produces—there can be no question of attributing a superiority to the Indians. When Cortés must express his opinion on Indian slavery (as he does in a memorandum addressed to Charles V), he envisages the problem only from one point of view: that of the profitability of the enterprise; it is never a question of what the Indians, for their part, might want (not being subjects, they have no desires). "There is no doubt that the natives must obey the royal orders of Your Majesty, whatever their nature": such is the point of departure of his reasoning, which subsequently seeks out the forms of submission which would be most advantageous to the king. It is striking to see how Cortés, in his will, remembers all who are to receive his money: his family and his servants, convents, hospitals and schools; but there is never any question of the Indians, though they are the sole source of his wealth.

Cortés is interested in the Aztec civilization, and at the same time remains altogether alien to it. Nor is he the only one; this is the behavior of many enlightened men of his time. Albrecht Dürer, around

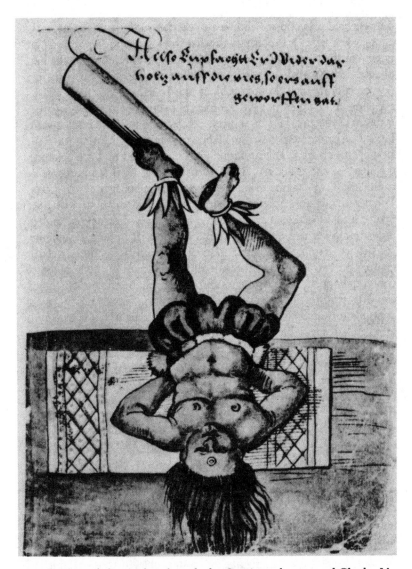

Fig. 7 One of the acrobats brought by Cortés to the court of Charles V.

1520, admires the works of Indian craftsmanship Cortés sends to the royal court, but it does not occur to him to try making anything of the kind; the Indian images themselves as drawn by Dürer remain entirely faithful to the European style. These exotic objects quickly vanish into dust-covered collections; "Indian art" exerts no influence on sixteenth-century European art (contrary to what will happen in the case of "art nègre" in the twentieth). To formulate matters differently: in the best of cases, the Spanish authors speak well *of* the Indians, but with very few exceptions they do not speak *to* the Indians. Now, it is only by speaking to the other (not giving orders but engaging in a dialogue) that *I* can acknowledge *him* as subject, comparable to what I am myself. Hence we can now specify the relation among the words that form the title of this chapter: unless grasping is accompanied by a full acknowledgment of the other as subject, it risks being used for purposes of exploitation, of "taking"; knowledge will be subordinated to power. What remains still obscure, then, is the second relation: why does taking lead to destroying? For there is certainly destruction, and in order to answer this question, we must review its principal elements.

Let us examine the destruction of the Indians in the sixteenth century on two levels, quantitative and qualitative. In the absence of contemporary statistics, the question of the number of Indians killed could constitute the object of mere speculation, involving the most contradictory answers. The early authors propose figures, it is true; but, in a general way, when a Bernal Díaz or a Las Casas says "a hundred thousand" or "a million," we may doubt that they ever had the possibility of counting, and if these figures are ultimately to mean anything, it is very vague: "a great many." Hence we have not taken seriously Las Casas's "millions" in his *Brevíssima relacíon de la destruccíon de las Indias,* when he tries to calculate the number of Indians killed. However matters have altogether changed, for today's historians, by ingenious methods, have managed to estimate with great plausibility the population of the American continent on the eve of the conquest, in order to compare that population with what the Spanish calculations report fifty or a hundred years later. No serious argument has yet been raised against these figures, and those who, even today, continue to reject them do so simply because, if the thing is true, it is profoundly shocking. Indeed, these figures justify Las Casas: not that his estimates are trustworthy, but his figures are comparable to those established today.

Without going into detail, and merely to give a general idea (even if we do not feel entirely justified in rounding off figures when it is a question of human lives), it will be recalled that in 1500 the world population is approximately 400 million, of whom 80 million inhabit the Americas. By the middle of the sixteenth century, out of these 80 million, there remain ten. Or limiting ourselves to Mexico: on the eve of the conquest, its population is about 25 million; in 1600, it is one million.

If the word genocide has ever been applied to a situation with some accuracy, this is here the case. It constitutes a record not only in relative terms (a destruction on the order of 90 percent or more), but also in absolute terms, since we are speaking of a population diminution estimated at 70 million human lives. None of the great massacres of the twentieth century can be compared to this hecatomb. It will be understood how vain are the efforts made by certain authors to dissipate what has been called the "black legend" of Spain's responsibility for this genocide. Blackness there is indeed, even if there is no legend. The Spaniards are not worse than the other colonial powers; it just so happens that they are the people who occupied America at the time, and that no other colonizing power has had the opportunity, before or since, to cause the death of so many at once. The British and the French, in the same period, behave no differently; only their expansion is not on the same scale, hence the damages they can cause are not on such a scale either.

But it may be objected that there is no point in attempting to establish responsibilities, or even to speak of genocide rather than of a natural catastrophe. The Spaniards did not undertake a direct extermination of these millions of Indians, nor could they have done so. If we examine the forms taken by the diminution of the population, we realize that there are three, and that the Spaniards' responsibility is inversely proportional to the number of victims deriving from each of them:

1. By direct murder, during the wars or outside of them: a high number, nonetheless *relatively* small; direct responsibility.

2. By consequence of bad treatment: a higher number; a (barely) less direct responsibility.

3. By diseases, by "microbe shock": the majority of the population; an indirect and diffused responsibility.

I shall return to the first point, examining the destruction of the Indians on the qualitative level; first let us look at the Spaniards' responsibility in the second and third forms of death.

By "bad treatment" I mean chiefly the labor conditions imposed by the Spaniards, especially in the mines, but not only there. The conquistador-colonists have no time to lose, they must become rich at once; consequently, they impose an unendurable rhythm of labor, with no concern to preserve the health, hence the life, of their workers; the average life expectancy of a miner of the period is twenty-five years. Outside the mines, the tribute and taxes are so extreme that they lead to the same result. The first colonists pay no attention to this situation, for the conquests succeed each other so rapidly that the death of an entire population does not particularly disturb them: another can always be brought in from newly conquered lands. Motolinia observes: "The tributes demanded of the Indians were so great that many towns, unable to pay, would sell to the money-lenders among them the lands and children of the poor and as the tributes were very frequent and they could not meet them by selling all that they had, some towns became entirely depopulated and others were losing their population" (III, 4). Enslavement also provokes, directly and indirectly, massive diminutions of the population. The first bishop of Mexico, Juan de Zumarraga, thus describes the activities of Nuño de Guzmán, conquistador and tyrant: "When he began to govern this province, it contained 25,000 Indians, subjugated and peaceful. Of these he has sold 10,000 as slaves, and the others, fearing the same fate, have abandoned their villages."

Alongside the increase of the death rate, the new living conditions also provoke a diminution of the birthrate: "They no longer approach their wives, in order not to beget slaves," the same Zumarraga writes to the king; and Las Casas explains: "Thus husbands and wives were together once every eight or ten months, and when they met they were so exhausted and depressed on both sides that they had no mind for marital intercourse, and in this way they ceased to procreate. As for the newly born, they died early because their mothers, overworked and famished, had no milk to nurse them with, and for this reason, while I was in Cuba, 7000 children died in three months. Some mothers even drowned their babies from sheer desperation, while others caused themselves to abort with certain herbs which produced still-born children" (Historia, 11, 13). Las Casas also remarks in the same volume that his conversion to the cause of the Indians was effected by reading these words in Ecclesiasticus, 34:21: "the bread of the needy is their life: he that defraudeth him thereof is a man of blood." Certainly the question is one of economic murder in all these cases, for which the colonizers bear the entire responsibility.

Matters are less clear-cut with regard to diseases. Epidemics decimated the European cities of the period, as they did those in America, though on another scale: not only did the Spaniards unwittingly communicate this or that microbe to the Indians, but had they wished to combat the epidemics (as was the case of certain priests), they could not have done so in any sufficiently effective manner. It is now established, however, that the Mexican population was declining even exclusive of the great epidemics, as a consequence of malnutrition, other common diseases, or the destruction of the traditional social fabric. Further, we cannot consider even these murderous epidemics as a purely natural phenomenon. The half-caste Juan Bautista Pomar, in his *Relación de Texcoco*, finished around 1582, reflects on the causes of depopulation, which he estimates, quite accurately moreover, on the order of a reduction of ten to one; there are diseases, of course, but the Indians were especially vulnerable to diseases, for they were exhausted by hard labor and had lost the will to live; the blame goes to "affliction and fatigue of their spirits because they had lost the liberty God had given them; for the Spaniards treat them worse than slaves."

Whether or not this explanation is acceptable on the medical level, it is certain that the conquistadors see the epidemics as one of their weapons: they do not know the secrets of bacteriological warfare, but if they could, they would not fail to make use of disease quite deliberately; we can also assume that in most cases they did nothing to prevent the spread of epidemics. That the Indians die like flies is the proof that God is on the conquerors' side. The Spaniards may have presumed a little with regard to divine benevolence on their behalf, but, on the evidence, the outcome was incontestable.

Motolinia, a member of the first group of Franciscans to land in Mexico in 1524, begins his *Historia* with an enumeration of the ten plagues sent by God to chastise this land; their description occupies the first chapter of the first book of his work. The reference is clear: like biblical Egypt, Mexico has incurred the wrath of God, and is justly punished. The integration of the following events into a single succession is not without interest.

"The first was a plague of smallpox," brought by one of Narvaez's soldiers. "As the Indians did not know the remedy for the disease and were very much in the habit of bathing frequently, whether well or ill, and continued to do so even when suffering from smallpox, they died in heaps, like bedbugs. Many others died of starvation, because, as they were all taken sick at once, they could not care for each other, nor was there anyone to give them bread or anything else." For Motolinia, too, disease is not alone responsible; ignorance, lack of care and of nourishment are equally so. Materially, the Spaniards could have suppressed these other sources of mortality, but nothing was farther from their intentions: why combat a disease when it is sent by God to punish the unbelievers? Eleven years later, Motolinia continues, a new epidemic began—of measles; but bathing was now forbidden and the sick were cared for; many died, but many fewer than the first time.

"The second plague was the great number of those who died in the conquest of New Spain, especially around the city of Mexico." Which is how those who were killed by arms join the victims of smallpox.

"The third plague was a very great famine which came immediately after the taking of the city of Mexico." During the war, there could be no sowing; and even if some grain was sown, the Spaniards destroyed the harvests. Even the Spaniards, Motolinia adds, had difficulty finding corn—which says everything.

"The fourth plague was that of the *calpixques*, or overseers, and the Negroes." Both served as intermediaries between the colonists and the bulk of the population; these were Spanish peasants or former African slaves. "Because I do not wish to disclose their defects, I shall keep silent about what I think and only say that they make themselves feared and insist upon service as if they were the absolute and natural masters. They never do anything but demand, and however much people give them they are never content, for wherever they are they infect and corrupt everything, as foul as putrid flesh. . . . In the first years, these overseers were so absolute in their mistreatment of the Indians, overloading them, sending them far from their land, and giving them many other tasks, that many Indians died because of them and at their hands."

"The fifth plague was the great taxes and tributes that the Indians paid." When the Indians had no gold left, they sold their children; when they had no children left, they had nothing more to offer but their lives: "When they were unable to do so, many died because of it, some under torture and some in cruel prisons, for the Spaniards treated them brutally and considered them less than beasts." Was this a further source of wealth for the Spaniards?

"The sixth plague was the gold mines. . . . It would be impossible to count the number of Indians who have, to the present day, died in these mines."

"The seventh plague was the building of the great city of Mexico. . . . In the construction some were crushed by beams, others fell from heights, others were caught beneath buildings which were being torn down in one place to be built up again in another; especially did this happen when they tore down the principal temples of the devil. Many Indians died there." How to avoid seeing divine intervention in the death inflicted by the stones of the Great Temple? Motolinia adds that not only were the Indians not paid in any form for this labor, but they paid for the building material themselves, or were forced to bring it with them, and they were not fed; and since they could not both demolish temples and work in the fields, they went to work hungry; whence, perhaps, a certain increase in "labor accidents."

"The eighth plague was the slaves whom the Spaniards made in order to put them to work in the mines." At first those who were already slaves of the Aztecs were taken; then those who had given evidence of insubordination; finally all those who could be caught. During the first years after the conquest, the slave traffic flourished, and slaves often changed master. "They produced so many marks on their faces, in addition to the royal brand, that they had their faces covered with letters, for they bore the marks of all who had bought and sold them." Vasco de Quiroga, in a letter to the Council of the Indies, has also left a description of these faces transformed into illegible books, like the victims' bodies in Kafka's *Penal Colony:* "They are marked with brands on the face and in their flesh are imprinted the initials of the names of those who are successively their owners; they pass from hand to hand, and some have three or four names, so that the faces of these men who were created in God's image have been, by our sins, transformed into paper."

"The ninth plague was the service in the mines, to which the heavily laden Indians travelled sixty leagues or more to carry provisions; the food which they carried for themselves sometimes gave out when they reached the mines and sometimes on the way back before they reached home; sometimes they were kept by the miners for several days to help them get out the mineral or to build houses for them or to serve them, and when their food gave out they died, either at the mines or on the road, for they had no money to buy food and there was no one to give it to them. Some reached home in such a state that they died soon after. The bodies of these Indians and of the slaves who died in the mines produced such a stench that it caused a pestilence, especially at the mines of Guaxaca. For half a league around these mines and along a great part of the road one could scarcely avoid walking over dead bodies or bones, and the flocks of birds and crows that came to feed upon the corpses were so numerous that they darkened the sun, so that many villages along the road and in the district were deserted."

"The tenth plague was the divisions and factions which existed among the Spaniards in Mexico." We may ask how this harmed the Indians, and the answer is simple enough: since the Spaniards argue among themselves, the Indians suppose they can take advantage of their disputes to get rid of them; whether or not the thing is true, the Spaniards regard it as a fine excuse to execute a great number of Indians, including Cuauhtemoc, a captive at the time.

Motolinia starts with the biblical image of the ten plagues, supernatural events caused by God in order to punish Egypt. But his narrative is gradually transformed into a realistic and accusatory description of life in Mexico during the first years after the conquest; it is men who are, obviously, responsible for these "plagues" and in reality Motolinia does not countenance their actions. Or rather, while condemning exploitation, cruelty, and bad treatment, he considers the very existence of these "plagues" as an expression of the divine will and a punishment of the infidels (without implying that he approves of the Spaniards, the immediate cause of so much wretchedness). Those directly responsible for each of these disasters (before they become "plagues") are known to all: the Spaniards.

Now let us return to the qualitative aspect of the destruction of the Indians (though such an adjective scarcely seems fitting here). I mean by it the particularly impressive and perhaps modern character this destruction assumes.

Las Casas had devoted his *Brevíssima Relación* to the systematic evocation of all the horrors caused by the Spaniards (see figs. 8 and 9). But the *Relación* generalizes without citing proper names or individual circumstances; hence, some have maintained that his account was a great exaggeration, if not a pure invention of the Dominican's perhaps pathological or even perverse mind; it is obvious that Las Casas did not observe all he reports. Hence, I have chosen to cite only a few narratives of eye witnesses; they may afford a certain impression of monotony, but so, no doubt, did the reality that they evoke.

The oldest among them is the report of a group of Dominicans addressed to M. de Xeries, the minister of Charles I (the future Charles V), in 1519; it concerns events in the Carib islands.

As to the way in which children were treated: "Some Christians encounter an Indian woman, who was carrying in her arms a child at suck; and since the dog they had with them was hungry, they tore the child from the mother's arms and flung it still living to the dog, who proceeded to devour it before the mother's eyes. . . . When there were among the prisoners some women who had recently given birth, if the new-born babes happened to cry, they seized them by the legs and hurled them against the rocks, or flung them into the jungle so that they would be certain to die there."

As to relations with the workers in the mines: "Each of them [the foremen] had made it a practice to sleep with the Indian women who were in his work-force, if they pleased him, whether they were married women or maidens. While the foreman remained in the hut or the cabin with the Indian woman, he sent the husband to dig gold out of the mines; and in the evening, when the wretch returned, not only was he beaten or whipped because he had not brought up enough gold, but further, most often, he was bound hand and foot and flung under the bed like a dog, before the foreman lay down, directly over him, with his wife."

As to the treatment of the labor force: "Each time that the Indians were transferred, there was so great a number of them who were dying of hunger on the way that the wake they left behind the ship would have sufficed, one might think, to guide another landing party to the port. . . . More than eight hundred Indians having been led to a harbor of this island, known as Puerto de Plata, there was a wait of two days before they were made to go down into the caravelle. Six hundred of them died, who were flung into the sea; they rolled upon the waves like logs."

Here is an account by Las Casas which does not figure in the *Relación* but in his *History of the Indies*, and reports an event of which he was more than a witness: a participant; this is the massacre at Caonao in Cuba, perpetrated by Narvaez's troops which he serves as chaplain (III, 29). The episode begins with an accidental circumstance:

Figs. 8 and 9   Cruelties of the Spaniards.

"And the Spaniards, on the morning of the day they arrived at the town, stopped to breakfast in a riverbed that was dry but for a few shallow pools. This riverbed was full of whetstones, and all longed to sharpen their swords upon them."

Having reached the village after this picnic, the Spaniards decide to test whether their swords are as sharp as they seem. "A Spaniard, in whom the devil is thought to have clothed himself, suddenly drew his sword. Then the whole hundred drew theirs and began to rip open the bellies, to cut and kill those lambs—men, women, children and old folk, all of whom were seated, off guard and frightened, watching the mares and the Spaniards. And within two credos, not a man of all of them there remains alive. The Spaniards enter the large house nearby, for this was happening at its door, and in the same way, with cuts and stabs, begin to kill as many as they found there, so that a stream of blood was running, as if a great number of cows had perished."

Las Casas finds no explanation for these incidents except the desire to test whether the swords were sufficiently sharp. "To see the wounds which covered the bodies of the dead and dying was a spectacle of horror and dread: indeed, since the devil, who inspired the Spaniards, furnished them these whetstones with which they sharpened their swords, on the morning of that very day, in the bed of the stream where they broke their fast, everywhere where they wielded their weapons upon these stark naked bodies and this delicate flesh, they cut a man quite in half with a single blow."

Here now is an account concerning the expedition of Vasco Nuñez de Balboa, transcribed by someone who has heard many conquistadors telling their own adventures: "The Spaniards cut off the arm of one, the leg or hip of another, and from some their heads at one stroke, like butchers cutting up beef and mutton for market. Six hundred, including the cacique, were thus slain like brute beasts. . . . Vasco ordered forty of them to be torn to pieces by dogs" (Peter Martyr, III, 1).

Time passes but habits remain: as we observe from the letter which the monk Jerónimo de San Miguel sends to his king on August 20, 1550: "Some Indians they burned alive; they cut off the hands, noses, tongues, and other members of some; they threw others to the dogs; they cut off the breasts of women."

And here is an account by the bishop of Yucatán, Diego de Landa, who does not particularly favor the Indians: "And this Diego de Landa says that he saw a tree near the town from whose branches a captain hanged many Indian women, and from their feet he also hanged the infant children. . . . There the Spaniards committed the most unheard-of cruelties; they cut off hands, arms, and legs, and women's breasts; and they threw the Indians into deep lakes, and stabbed the children because they could not walk as fast as their mothers. If those whom they had chained together by the neck fell ill or did not walk as fast as the others, they cut off their heads so as not to have to stop to release them" (15).

And to conclude this macabre enumeration, a detail reported by Alonso de Zorita, around 1570: "I had known an *oidor* [judge] to say publicly from his dais, speaking in a loud voice, that if water were lacking to irrigate the Spaniards' farms, they would have to be watered with the blood of Indians" (10).

What are the immediate motivations that produce such an attitude in the Spaniards? One is incontestably the desire for instant wealth, which implies the neglect of others' well-being or even life: torture is inflicted in order to discover the hiding places of treasure; human beings are exploited in order to obtain profits. The authors of the period already gave this reason as the principle explanation of what had happened—for example, Motolinia: "If anyone should ask what has been the cause of so many evils, I would answer: covetousness, the desire to store in one's chest a few bars of gold for the benefit of I know not whom" (I, 3); and Las Casas: "I do not say that they want to kill them [the Indians] directly, from the hate they bear them; they kill them because they want to be rich and have much gold, which is their whole aim, through the toil and sweat of the afflicted and unhappy" ("Entre los remedios," 7).

And why this desire to be rich? Because money leads to everything, as everyone knows: "With money men acquire all the temporal things that they need and desire, such as honor, nobility, estate, family, luxury, fine clothes, delicate foods, the pleasure of vices, vengeance on their enemies, great esteem for their person" (ibid.).

Certainly the desire for riches is nothing new, the passion for gold has nothing specifically modern about it. What is new is the subordination of all other values to this one. The conquistador has not ceased to aspire to aristocratic values, to titles of nobility, to honors, and to esteem; but it has become quite clear to him that everything can be obtained by money, that money is not only the universal equivalent of all material values, but also the possibility of acquiring all spiritual values. It is certainly advantageous, in Montezuma's Mexico as in preconquest Spain, to be rich; but one cannot purchase status, or in any case not directly. This homogenization of values by money is a new phenomenon and it heralds the modern mentality, egalitarian and economic.

In any case, the desire for wealth is far from explaining everything; and if it is eternal, the forms taken by the Indians' destruction, as well as its proportions, are entirely unprecedented and sometimes even exceptional; the economic explanation is here proved inadequate. We cannot justify the massacre at Caonao by any form of greed, nor the hanging of mothers from trees, and children from the mothers' feet; nor the tortures in which the victim's flesh is torn off with pincers, bit by bit; slaves do not work better if the master sleeps with their wives over their supine bodies. Everything occurs as if the Spaniards were finding an intrinsic pleasure in cruelty, in the fact of exerting their power over others, in the demonstration of their capacity to inflict death.

Here again we might evoke certain immutable features of "human nature," for which the psychoanalytic vocabulary reserves terms such as "aggression," "death instinct," or even *Bemächtigungstrieb*, instinct for mastery; or, with regard to cruelty, we might recall various characteristics of other cultures, and even of Aztec society in particular, which has the reputation of being "cruel" and of not making much of the number of victims (or rather of doing just that, but in order to glorify itself thereby!): according to Durán, 80,400 persons were sacrificed in Mexico by King Ahuitzotl during the inauguration of a single new temple. We might also assert that each people, from the beginning of time to our own day, sacrifices its victims with a kind of murderous madness, and we might speculate if this is not a characteristic of male-dominated societies (since these are the only ones known).

But it would be a mistake to erase all differences in this way and to abide by affective rather than descriptive terms (such as "cruelty"). Murders are like the ascent of volcanoes: in each case, one reaches the top and climbs back down; yet one does not report the same thing. Just as it has been necessary to set the society valuing ritual in opposition to the society favoring improvisation, or code to context, here we may speak of sacrifice-societies and massacre-societies, of which the Aztecs and the sixteenth-century Spaniards would be the respective representatives.

Sacrifice, from this point of view, is a religious murder: it is performed in the name of the official ideology and will be perpetrated in public places, in sight of all and to everyone's knowledge. The victim's identity is determined by strict rules. He must not be too alien, too remote (we have seen that the Aztecs believed that the flesh of distant tribes was not acceptable to their gods), but he must not, on the other hand, belong to the same society: one's fellow citizen is not sacrificed. The victims come from limitrophic countries, speaking the same language but having an autonomous government; further, once captured, they are kept in prison for some time, thereby partially—but never completely—assimilated. Neither identical nor totally different, the sacrificial victim also counts by his personal qualities: the sacrifice of brave warriors is more highly appreciated than that of just anyone; as for invalids of all kinds, they are immediately declared unsuitable for sacrifice. The sacrifice is performed in public and testifies to the power of the social fabric, to its mastery over the individual.

Massacre, on the other hand, reveals the weakness of this same social fabric, the desuetude of the moral principles that once assured the group's coherence; hence it should be performed in some remote place where the law is only vaguely acknowledged: for the Spaniards, America or even Italy. Massacre is thus intimately linked to colonial wars waged far from the metropolitan country. The more remote and alien the victims, the better: they are exterminated without remorse, more or less identified with animals. The individual identity of the massacre victim is by definition irrelevant (otherwise his death would be a murder): one has neither time nor curiosity to know whom one is killing at that moment. Unlike sacrifices, massacres are generally not acknowledged or proclaimed, their very existence is kept secret and denied. This is because their social function is not recognized, and we have the impression that such action finds its justification in itself: one wields the saber for the pleasure of wielding the saber, one cuts off the Indian's nose, tongue, and penis without this having any ritual meaning for the amputator.

If religious murder is a sacrifice, massacre is an atheistic murder, and the Spaniards appear to have invented (or rediscovered; but not borrowed from their immediate past, for the Inquisition's stakes were more closely related to sacrifice) precisely this type of violence, which we encounter in our own more recent past, whether on the level of individual violence or on that of violence perpetrated by states. It is as though the conquistadors obeyed the rule of Ivan Karamazov: "everything is permitted." Far from the central government, far from royal law, all prohibitions give way, the social link, already loosened, snaps, revealing not a primitive nature, the beast sleeping in each of us, but a modern being, one with a great future in fact, restrained by no morality and inflicting death because and when he pleases. The "barbarity" of the Spaniards has nothing atavistic or bestial about it; it is quite human and heralds the advent of modern times. In the Middle Ages, we find that a woman's breasts or a man's arms will be cut off as a punishment or revenge; but such things were done in one's own country, or were just as likely to be done in one's own country as elsewhere. What the Spaniards discover is the contrast between the metropolitan country and the colony, for radically different moral laws regulate conduct in each: massacre requires an appropriate context.

But what if we do not want to have to choose between a civilization of sacrifice and a civilization of massacre?

Equality or Inequality

THE desire for wealth and the impulse to master—certainly these two forms of aspiration to power motivate the Spaniards' conduct; but this conduct is also conditioned by their notion of the Indians as inferior beings, halfway between men and beasts. Without this essential premise, the destruction could not have taken place.

From its first formulation, this doctrine of inequality will be opposed by another, which affirms the equality of all men; hence we are listening to a debate, and we must pay attention to the two voices in contention. Now, this debate does not only oppose equality to inequality, but also identity to difference; and this new opposition, whose terms are no more ethically neutral than those of the preceding one, makes it more difficult to bring a judgment to bear on either position. We have already seen as much with Columbus: difference is corrupted into inequality, equality into identity. These are the two great figures of the relation to the other that delimit the other's inevitable space.

Las Casas and other defenders of equality have so often accused their adversaries of regarding the Indians as animals that we may wonder if there has not been an exaggeration. Hence, we must turn to the defenders of inequality themselves in order to determine if this is the case. The first interesting document in this regard is the famous *Requerimiento,* or injunction addressed to the Indians. It is the work of the royal jurist Palacios Rubios and dates from 1514; it is a text born of the necessity to regulate conquests hitherto somewhat chaotic. Henceforth, before a country is conquered, its inhabitants must have this text read to them. Some historians have occasionally regarded this procedure as the crown's desire to prevent unjustified wars, to grant certain rights to the Indians; but this interpretation is too generous. In the context of our debate, the *Requerimiento* is clearly on the side of inequality, implied rather than affirmed, it is true.

This text, a curious example of an attempt to give a legal basis to the fulfillment of desires, begins with a brief history of humanity, whose culminating point is the appearance of Jesus Christ, declared "master of the human lineage," a kind of supreme sovereign who has the entire universe under his jurisdiction. Once this point of departure is established, things follow quite simply: Jesus has transmitted his power to Saint Peter, the latter to the popes who have followed him; one of the last popes has bestowed the American continent upon the Spaniards (and in part upon the Portuguese). The juridical reasons for the Spanish domination being thus posited, it remains only to establish one thing: that the Indians be informed of the situation, for they may have been unaware of these successive gifts which the popes and emperors were making to one another. This unawareness will be remedied by the reading of the *Requerimiento*, in the presence of an officer of the king (though no interpreter is mentioned). If the Indians show themselves convinced following this reading, one has no right to take them as slaves (it is here that this text "protects" the Indians by according them a certain status). If however they do not accept this interpretation of their own history, they will be severely punished. "But if you do not do this, and wickedly and intentionally delay to do so, I certify to you that, with the help of God, we shall forcibly enter into your country and shall make war against you in all ways and manners that we can, and shall subject you to the yoke and obedience of the Church and of their Highnesses; we shall take you and your wives and your children, and shall make slaves of them as their Highnesses may command; and we shall take away your goods, and we shall do all the harm and damage that we can as to vassals who do not obey and refuse to receive their lord, and resist and contradict him."

There is an obvious contradiction, which adversaries of the *Requerimiento* will not fail to emphasize, between the essence of the religion that is supposed to establish all the Spaniards' rights and the consequences of this public reading: Christianity is an egalitarian religion; yet in its name, men are reduced to slavery. Not only are spiritual power and temporal power identified, which is the tendency of every state ideology whether or not it derives from the Gospel, but further, the

Indians can choose only between two positions of inferiority: either they submit of their own accord and become serfs; or else they will be subjugated by force and reduced to slavery. To speak of legality, under these conditions, is absurd. The Indians are posited as inferiors from the start, for it is the Spaniards who determine the rules of the game. The superiority of those who promulgate the *Requerimiento*, one might say, is already contained in the fact that it is they who are speaking, while the Indians listen.

We know that the conquistadors had no scruple in applying the royal instructions as it suited them and in punishing the Indians in case of resistance. As late as 1550 Pedro de Valdivia reports to the king that the Arawaks, inhabitants of Chile, were unwilling to submit; consequently he has waged war against them and, having won, he has not failed to punish them: "Two hundred had their hands and noses cut off for their contumacy, inasmuch as I had many times sent them messengers and given them commands as ordered by Your Majesty."

We do not know in just which language Valdivia's messengers expressed themselves and how they managed to make the contents of the *Requerimiento* intelligible to the Indians. But we do know how in other cases the Spaniards deliberately neglected resorting to interpreters, since such neglect ultimately simplified their task: the question of the Indians' reaction no longer came up. The historian Oviedo, one of the champions of the thesis of inequality and himself a conquistador, has left several accounts of the matter. The first thing is to capture the Indians: "After they had been put in chains, someone read the *Requerimiento* without knowing their language and without any interpreters, and without either the reader or the Indians understanding the language they had no opportunity to reply, being immediately carried away prisoners, the Spaniards not failing to use the stick on those who did not go fast enough" (I, 29, 7).

During another campaign, Pedrarias Davila asks Oviedo himself to read the famous text. The latter answers his captain: "Good sirs, it appears to me that these Indians will not listen to the theology of this *Requerimiento*, and that you have no one who can make them understand it; would Your Honor be pleased to keep it until we have one of these Indians in cage, in order that he may learn it at his leisure and my Lord Bishop may explain it to him" (ibid.).

As Las Casas says in analyzing this document, we do not know "whether to laugh or cry at the absurdity of it" (Las Casas, *Historia*, III, 58).

Palacios Rubios's text will not be preserved as the juridical basis of the conquest. But the more or less weakened traces of its spirit are to be noted even among the conquistadors' adversaries. The most interesting example is perhaps that of Francisco de Vitoria, theologian, jurist, and professor at the University of Salamanca, one of the pinnacles of Spanish humanism in the sixteenth century. Vitoria demolishes the contemporary justifications of the wars waged in America, but nonetheless conceives that "just wars" are possible. Among the reasons that can lead to the latter, two types are particularly interesting for us. On the one hand there are those based on reciprocity: they apply without differentiation to the Indians and the Spaniards. This is the case of violations of what Vitoria calls "the natural right to society and communication" (*De Indis*, 3, 1, 230). This right to communication can be understood on several levels. It is first of all natural that persons should be able to move freely outside their country of origin, it must be "permitted to each to go and to travel into all countries he so desires" (3, 2, 232). The same can be posited of freedom of trade, and Vitoria here recalls the principle of reciprocity: "The Indian princes cannot prevent their subjects from engaging in commerce with the Spaniards, and conversely the Spanish princes cannot forbid commerce with the Indians" (3, 3, 245). As for the circulation of ideas, Vitoria thinks only of the Spaniards' freedom to preach the Gospels to the Indians, and never of the Indians' freedom to propagate the *Popul Vuh* in Spain, since Christian "salvation" is an absolute value for him. Nonetheless, we might link this case to the two preceding ones.

On the other hand, matters proceed otherwise with another group of reasons advanced by Vitoria in order to justify wars. He considers, it turns out, that an intervention is permissible if it is made in the name of the innocent against the tyranny of native leaders or laws, a tyranny that consists "for instance of sacrificing innocent men or even of putting to death innocent men in order to eat them" (3, 15, 290). Such a justification of war is much less obvious than Vitoria would suggest, and in any case does not derive from reciprocity: even if this rule were applied alike to Indians and Spaniards, it is the latter who have decided on the meaning of the word *tyranny*, and this is the essential thing. The Spaniards, unlike the Indians, are not only subject to the decision but also its judge, since it is they who select the criteria according to which the judgment will be delivered; they decide, for instance, that human sacrifice is the consequence of tyranny, but massacre is not.

Such a distribution of roles implies that there is no real equality between Spaniards and Indians. In reality, Vitoria does not conceal the fact; his final justification of war against the Indians is quite clear in this regard (it is true that it is presented in a dubitative mode). "Although these barbarians are not altogether mad," he writes, "yet they are not far from being so. . . . They are not, or are no longer, capable of governing themselves any more than madmen or even wild beasts and animals, seeing that their food is not any more agreeable and scarcely better than that of wild beasts." Their stupidity, he adds, "is much greater than that of children and madmen in other countries" (3, 18, 299–302). Hence, it is licit to intervene in their countries in order to exercise the rights of guardianship. But even admitting that one is to impose "the good" on others, who, once again, decides what is barbarity or savagery and what is civilization? Only one of the two parties to the agreement, between whom subsists no equality or reciprocity. We are accustomed to seeing Vitoria as a defender of the Indians; but if we question, not the subject's intentions, but the impact of his discourse, it is clear that his role is quite different: under cover of an international law based on reciprocity, he in reality supplies a legal basis to the wars of colonization which had hitherto had none (none which, in any case, might withstand serious consideration).

Alongside these juridical expressions of the doctrine of inequality, we find a great many more in the letters, reports, and chronicles of the period; all tend to present the Indians as imperfectly human. I select two testimonies among a thousand, simply because their authors are a priest and a man of letters and learning—i.e., because they belong to social groups that are generally the most well intentioned toward the Indians. The Dominican Tomás Ortiz writes to the Council of the Indies:

"On the mainland they eat human flesh. They are more given to sodomy than any other nation. There is no justice among them. They go naked. They have no respect either for love or for virginity. They are stupid and silly. They have no respect for truth, save when it is to their advantage. They are unstable. They have no knowledge of what foresight means. They are ungrateful and changeable. . . . They are brutal. They delight in exaggerating their defects. There is no obedience among them, or deference on the part of the young for the old, nor of the son for the father. They are incapable of learning. Punishments have no effect upon them. . . . They eat fleas, spiders and worms raw, whenever they find them. They exercise none of the human arts or industries. When taught the mysteries of our religion, they say that these things may suit Castilians, but not them, and they do not wish to change their customs. They are beardless, and if sometimes hairs grow, they pull them out. . . . The older they get the worse they become. About the age of ten or twelve years, they seem to have some civilization, but later they become like real brute beasts. I may therefore affirm that God has never created a race more full of vice and composed without the least mixture of kindness or culture. . . . The Indians are more stupid than asses, and refuse to improve in anything" (Peter Martyr, VII, 4).

This text, it seems to me, requires no commentary.

The second author is once again Oviedo, a rich source of xenophobic and racist judgments; according to him, the Indians are not reduced to the level of horse or ass (or even just below it), but somewhere among construction materials, wood, stone, or metal, in any case on the side of inanimate objects. He has this extraordinary formula, which we find difficult to believe is not ironic; but no, it is not: "And so when one wages war with them and comes to hand to hand fighting, one must be very careful not to hit them on the head with the sword, because I have seen many swords broken in this fashion. In addition to being thick, their skulls are very strong" (V, "Preface," see VI, 9). We will not be surprised to learn that Oviedo is in fact a partisan of the "final solution" of the Indian problem, a solution whose responsibility he projects onto the God of the Christians. "God is going to destroy them soon," he proclaims with assurance, and also: "Satan has now been expelled from the island [Hispaniola]; his influence has disappeared now that most of the Indians are dead. . . . Who can deny that the use of gunpowder against pagans is the burning of incense to Our Lord" (ibid.).

The debate between partisans of equality or inequality reaches its apogee, and at the same time finds a concrete incarnation, in the celebrated controversy at Valladolid which, in 1550, sets the scholar and philosopher Ginés de Sepúlveda against the Dominican bishop of Chiapas, Bartolomé de Las Casas. The very existence of this confrontation has something extraordinary about it. Usually such dialogues are established from book to book, and the protagonists do not meet face to face. But it appears that Sepúlveda was denied the right to print his treatise on the just cause of war against the Indians; seeking a judgment of appeal, Sepúlveda insists on a debate before a jury of wise men, jurists, and theologians; Las Casas offers to defend the contrary point of view in this oratorical duel. We have difficulty imagining the spirit that permits theological conflicts to be regulated by such dialogues. Moreover, the conflict will not be settled: after having heard long speeches (in particular that of Las Casas, which lasts five *days*), the exhausted judges separate and indeed reach no final decision; the balance nonetheless tends toward Las Casas's side, for Sepúlveda does not receive authorization to publish his book.

Sepúlveda bases his arguments on an ideological tradition on which other defenders of the inegalitarian thesis also draw to make their points. We may number among such authors the one from whom this thesis claims—with some justice—to derive: Aristotle. Sepúlveda has translated the *Politics* into Latin, he is one of the foremost specialists in Aristotelian thought of his time; and is it not Aristotle, precisely in the *Politics*, who establishes the famous distinction between those who are born masters and those born slaves? "Those, therefore, who are as much inferior to others as are the body to the soul and beasts to men, are by nature slaves. . . . He is by nature slave who . . . shares in reason to the extent of apprehending it without possessing it" (Aristotle, 1254b). Another text to which contemporary reference is made is a treatise *De regimine*, attributed at the time to Aquinas but actually written by Ptolomeus of Lucca, who adds to the assertion of inequality an already hoary explanation, yet one that is destined to enjoy a great future: the reason for this inequality must be sought in the influence of the climate (and in that of the stars).

Sepúlveda believes that hierarchy, not equality, is the natural state of human society. But the only hierarchic relation he knows is that of a simple superiority/inferiority; hence there are no differences of nature, but only different degrees in one and the same scale of values, even if the relation can be infinitely repeated. His dialogue *Democrates Alter*, the very one for which he failed to obtain an *imprimatur*, clearly sets forth his views on the matter. Inspired by the specific principles and assertions he finds in Aristotle's *Politics*, he declares all hierarchies, despite their formal differences, to be based on one and the same principle: "the domination of perfection over imperfection, of force over weakness, of eminent virtue over vice" (p. 20). We have the impression that this is self-evident, that it is an "analytic statement"; the next moment, Sepúlveda, still in an Aristotelian spirit, gives examples of this natural superiority: the body must be subject to the soul, matter to form, children to parents, women to men, and slaves (tautologically defined as inferior beings) to masters. It is only a step to justifying a war of conquest against the Indians: "In wisdom, skill, virtue and humanity, these people are as inferior to the Spaniards as children are to adults and women to men; there is as great a difference between them as there is between savagery and forbearance, between violence and moderation, almost—I am inclined to say—as between monkeys and men" (ibid., p. 33; the last part of the sentence is missing in certain manuscripts).

All the oppositions that constitute Sepúlveda's mental universe ultimately have the same content; and we might rewrite the above assertions as an endless chain of proportions.

$$\frac{\text{Indians}}{\text{Spaniards}} = \frac{\text{children (sons)}}{\text{adults (fathers)}} = \frac{\text{women (wives)}}{\text{men (husbands)}} = \frac{\text{animals (monkeys)}}{\text{human beings}} =$$

$$\frac{\text{savagery}}{\text{forbearance}} = \frac{\text{violence}}{\text{moderation}} = \frac{\text{matter}}{\text{form}} = \frac{\text{body}}{\text{soul}} = \frac{\text{appetite}}{\text{reason}} = \frac{\text{evil}}{\text{good}}$$

Not all the partisans of inequality share so schematic a concept; we see that Sepúlveda groups all hierarchy and all difference around the simple opposition of good and bad—i.e., that he finally abides by the principle of identity (rather than by that of difference). But the reading of this chain of oppositions is no less instructive. First of all, let us set aside the oppositions whose assertion of the superiority of the second term over the first proceeds from tautology: evil/good; those that boast of this or that behavior (forbearance, moderation); finally, those based on a clear biological difference: animals/men or children/adults. There remain two series of oppositions: those based on the body/soul pair and those that set in opposition certain parts of the world's population whose difference is evident but whose superiority or inferiority is problematic: Indians/Spaniards, women/men. It is of course revealing to find the Indians identified with women, which makes an easy transition from internal to external *other* (since it is always a Spanish man who is speaking); moreover we recall that the Indians were making a symmetrical and converse distribution: the Spaniards were identified with women, by reason of their speech, in the observations of the Aztec warriors. It is futile to speculate whether the image of woman has been projected on the foreigner or the foreigner's features on woman: both have always been there, and what matters is their solidarity, not the anteriority of one or the other. That such oppositions are made equivalent with the group relating to the body and the soul is also revealing: above all, *the other* is our body itself; whence, too, the identification of the Indians, as of women, to animals, creatures which, though animate, have no soul.

All the differences are reduced, for Sepúlveda, to what is not one at all: superiority/inferiority, good and evil. Now let us see what his arguments for a just war consist of. Four reasons make a war legitimate (as set forth in his Valladolid speech, but the same arguments are to be found in *Democrates Alter*):

1. To subject by force of arms men whose natural condition is such that they should obey others, if they refuse such obedience and no other recourse remains.

2. To banish the portentous crime of eating human flesh, which is a special offense to nature, and to stop the worship of demons instead of God, which above all else provokes His wrath, together with the monstrous rite of sacrificing men.

3. To save from grave perils the numerous innocent mortals whom these barbarians immolated every year placating their gods with human hearts.

4. War on the infidels is justified because it opens the way to the propagation of Christian religion and eases the task of the missionaries.

We can say that this line of argument unites four descriptive propositions as to the Indians' nature to a postulate that is also a moral imperative. These propositions: the Indians have a slave's nature; they practice cannibalism; they make human sacrifices; they are ignorant of the Christian religion. The postulate imperative: one has the right or even the duty to impose the good on others. We should perhaps specify here that one makes one's own decision as to what is good or evil; one has the right to impose on others what one considers as the good, without concern as to whether or not this is also the good from the other's point of view. This postulate therefore implies a projection of the subject speaking about the universe, an identification of *my* values with *the* values.

We cannot judge the descriptive propositions and the imperative postulate in the same way. The propositions, which concern empirical reality, may be contested or completed; as a matter of fact, they are not far from the truth in this particular case. It is incontestable that the Aztecs are not Christians, that they practice cannibalism and human sacrifice. Even the proposition concerning the natural tendency to obedience is not altogether lacking in veracity, though its formulation is of course tendentious: it is certain that the Indians do not have the same relation to power that the Spaniards do—that, precisely, the simple opposition of superiority/inferiority counts less for them than integration into society's general hierarchy.

The same is not at all true of the imperative postulate, which does not derive from verification and from more-or-less, but from faith and finality: the principle is the very basis of the ideology at work in Sepúlveda's reasoning, and therefore cannot be debated (but only rejected or accepted). This is the postulate he has in mind when he advances the following argument: "As Saint Augustine says in epistle 75, the loss of a single soul dead without baptism exceeds in gravity the death of countless victims, even were they innocent" (*Democrates*, p. 79). Such is the "classical" conception: there exists an absolute value, which here is baptism, inherent in the Christian religion; acquisition of this value weighs more heavily than what the individual regards as his supreme good, i.e., life itself. This is because the individual's life and death are, precisely, a personal good, whereas the religious ideal is an absolute, or more exactly, a social good. The difference between the common, transindividual value and the personal value is so great that it permits an inverse quantitative variation in the terms to which these values are attached: the salvation of one justifies the death of thousands.

Anticipating what follows, we can remark here that Las Casas, as a coherent and systematic adversary of Sepúlveda, will manage to reject precisely this principle, whereby he may be betraying not Christianity in particular but the essence of religion in general, since the latter consists in the affirmation of transindividual values; thus he abandons the "classical" position in order to announce that of the "moderns." He writes: "It would be a great disorder and a mortal sin to toss a child into a well in order to baptize it and save its soul, if thereby it died" (Las Casas, quoted in Friede and Keen). Not only is the death of thousands of persons not justified by the salvation of one, the death of

just one here outweighs his salvation. The personal value—life, death
—has prevailed over the social value.

To what degree does Sepúlveda's ideological context permit him to
perceive the specific features of the Indian society? In a text written
after the Valladolid controversy (but related to it in spirit), "Concerning the kingdom and the king's duties," he writes, "The greatest
philosophers declare that such wars may be undertaken by a very
civilized nation against uncivilized people who are more barbarous than
can be imagined, for they are absolutely lacking in any knowledge of
letters, do not know the use of money, generally go about naked, even
the women, and carry burdens on their shoulders and backs like beasts
for great distances. Moreover here is the proof of their savage life, like
that of wild beasts: their execrable and prodigious immolations of
human victims to demons; the fact of devouring human flesh; of bury-
ing alive the chieftains' wives with their dead husband and other similar
crimes" (I, 4–5).

The portrait Sepúlveda draws here is of the greatest interest, as
much for each feature composing it as for their combination. Sepúlveda
is sensitive to differences, he even seeks them out; he therefore collects
certain of the most striking characteristics of the Indian societies. It is
curious to observe that in doing so he repeats certain idealizing descriptions of the Indians (absence of writing, of money, of garments), while
inverting their signs. What is it that causes precisely these features to
be united? Sepúlveda does not say, but we may suppose that their
connection is no accident. The presence of oral traditions instead of
written laws, of images instead of writing, indicates that a different role
has devolved, on either side, upon presence and absence in general:
writing, in opposition to spoken language, permits the absence of
speakers; in opposition to the image, it permits the absence of the
object designated, including even its form; the necessary memorization
of laws and traditions imposed by the absence of writing determines,
as we have seen, the predominance of ritual over improvisation. The
same is more or less true of the absence of money, that universal
equivalent which dispenses with the necessity of juxtaposing the actual
goods to be exchanged. The absence of garments, if asserted, would
indicate on the one hand that the body always remains present, never
being hidden from sight, and on the other that there is no difference
between private situation and public, intimate and social—i.e., the
nonrecognition of the singular status of the third person. Finally, the

lack of beasts of burden is to be set on the same level as the absence of tools: it is incumbent on the human body to perform certain tasks instead of attributing this function to an auxiliary, animate or not— to the physical person rather than to an intermediary.

Hence, we may ask what is the underlying characteristic of the society responsible for these differences, and thereby return to the reflection sketched apropos symbolic behavior: we had observed that such discourse depended "excessively" on its referent (the famous incapacity to lie or dissimulate) and that there was a certain inadequacy in the Aztecs' conception of the other. It is toward the same inadequacy that Sepúlveda's other "proofs" point: cannibalism, human sacrifice, immolation of the widow all imply that the other's human status is not fully recognized as at once like oneself and different. Now, the touchstone of alterity is not the present and immediate second person singular but the absent or distant third person singular. In the features noted by Sepúlveda we also find a difference in the place assumed by absence (if absence can assume a place): oral exchange, the lack of money and garments as of beasts of burden all imply a predominance of presence over absence, of the immediate over the mediatized. It is precisely here that we can see how the theme of the perception of the other and that of symbolic (or semiotic) behavior intersect—themes that simultaneously concern me throughout this investigation: at a certain level of abstraction, the two become identified. Language exists only by means of the other, not only because one always addresses someone but also insofar as it permits evoking the absent third person; unlike animals, men know citation. But the very existence of this other is measured by the space the symbolic system reserves for him: such space is not the same, to evoke only one massive and by now familiar example, before and after the advent of writing (in the narrow sense). So that any investigation of alterity is necessarily semiotic, and reciprocally, semiotics cannot be conceived outside the relation to the other.

It would be interesting to relate the features of Aztec mentality thus observed to what a form of sacrifice described by Durán teaches us about the functioning of the symbolic: "Forty days before the feast the people dressed a man as a representation of the idol with his same adornments, so that this live Indian slave should be an image of the idol. Once he had been purified, they honored and glorified him during the forty days, exhibiting him in public, as if he had been the god himself. . . . After the god impersonators had been sacrificed, all of them were skinned very rapidly. . . . When the heart had been removed and offered to the east, the skinners (whose task it was) cast the dead body down and split it from the nape of the neck to the heel, skinning it as a lamb. The skin came off complete. . . . Other men donned the skins immediately and then took the names of the gods who had been impersonated. Over the skins they wore the garments and insignia of the same divinities, each man bearing the name of the god and considering himself divine" (I, 9; see fig. 10).

In a first phase, then, the prisoner literally becomes the god: he receives the god's name, appearance, insignia, and treatment; for in order to absorb the god, his representative must be sacrificed and consumed. Yet it is men who have determined this identification, and they do not forget this, since they begin again every year. At the same time they act as if they were confusing the representative with what he represents: what begins as a representation ends as a participation and identification; the distance necessary to the symbolic functioning seems to be lacking. Then, in order to identify themselves with a being or with one of his properties (women are often flayed in rites concerning fertility), they literally get into his skin. One thinks of the practice of masks which can be made to resemble an individual. But the mask, precisely, resembles without participating in the person it represents. Here the object of the representation remains present, in appearance at least (the skin); what symbolizes is not really separated from what it symbolizes. We have the impression that a figurative expression has been taken literally, that we are encountering a presence where we expected to find an absence; curiously, we ourselves have the expression "to get into someone else's skin" without its origin being, for all that, a rite of human flaying.

This discussion of the characteristics of the Aztecs' symbolic conduct leads me to observe not only the difference between two forms of symbolization, but also the superiority of one over the other; or rather and more precisely, to turn from typological description to discuss a developing schema. Do I thereby adopt purely and simply the inegalitarian position? I do not believe so. There exists a realm in which development and progress are beyond doubt; this is the realm of technology. It is incontestable that a bronze or iron ax cuts better than one of wood or stone; that the use of the wheel reduces the physical effort required. Now these technological inventions themselves are not born of nothing: they are conditioned (without being directly determined)

Fig. 10 The use of flayed skins.

by the evolution of the symbolic apparatus proper to man, an evolution we can also observe in certain social behavior. There is a "technology" of symbolism, which is as capable of evolution as the technology of tools, and, in this perspective, the Spaniards are more "advanced" than the Aztecs (or to generalize: societies possessing writing are more advanced than societies without writing), even if we are here concerned only with a difference of degree.

But to return to Sepúlveda. It would be tempting to see in his text the seeds of an ethnological description of the Indians, facilitated by the attention he pays to differences. But we must immediately add that since this difference is always reduced to an inferiority, it loses much of its interest—not only because Sepúlveda's curiosity about the Indians is too slight, once "inferiority" is shown, for him to question the reasons for the differences; nor simply because his vocabulary is filled with value judgments ("uncivilized," "barbarians," "wild beasts") rather than seeking to be descriptive; but also because his anti-Indian prejudice vitiates the information on which his demonstration is based. Sepúlveda is content to draw his information from Oviedo, already violently anti-Indian, and never takes nuance or circumstance into account. Why blame the Indians for not having beasts of burden (rather than simply observing the fact), when horse and donkey, cow and camel are unknown on the American continent: what animals could the Indians use? The Spaniards themselves do not manage to solve the problem with any great speed, and we have seen that the number of victims among the bearers only increased after the conquest. The absence of garments, observed by Columbus in the Caribbean, did not of course characterize the inhabitants of Mexico, whose refined manners, as we have seen, were admired by Cortés and his companions. The question of money, like that of writing, is also more complex. Sepúlveda's facts, then, are distorted by his value judgments, by the identification of difference with inferiority; nevertheless, his portrait of the Indians is not lacking in interest.

If Sepúlveda's hierarchic conception could be placed under Aristotle's sponsorship, Las Casas's egalitarian conception deserves to be presented, as was already done at the time, as derived from the teachings of Christ. Las Casas himself says, in his speech at Valladolid: "Aristotle, farewell! From Christ, the eternal truth, we have the commandment 'You must love your neighbor as yourself.' . . . Although he was a profound philosopher, Aristotle was not worthy to be captured in the chase so that he could come to God through knowledge of true faith" (*Apologia,* 3).

It is not that Christianity is unaware of oppositions or inequalities; but the fundamental opposition here is the one between believer and unbeliever, Christian and non-Christian; yet each man *can* become a Christian: the differences of nature do not correspond to the differences of fact. The same is not at all true in the master-slave opposition derived from Aristotle: the slave is an intrinsically inferior being, since he lacks, at least to some degree, the use of reason, which affords the very definition of man and which cannot be acquired as faith can be acquired. The hierarchy is irreducible in this segment of the Greco-Roman tradition, as equality is an unshakable principle of the Christian tradition; these two constitutive elements of Western civilization, here simplified to extremes, are in direct confrontation at Valladolid. The sponsorship each of them claims has, of course, a mostly emblematic value: we do not expect to see justice rendered to the complexities of Christian doctrine or to the subtleties of Aristotelian philosophy.

Nor is Las Casas the only one to defend the Indians' rights and to declare that the Indians cannot be reduced to slavery; as a matter of fact, the majority of the official documents from the royal house make the same claim. We have seen the sovereigns deny Columbus the right to sell the Indians as slaves, and Isabella's famous testament confirms that they must suffer no wrongs as to their persons. An order of Charles V, dated 1530, is particularly explicit: "No one must dare to enslave any Indian neither in war nor in peace time, nor must he keep any Indian enslaved on the pretext of having acquired him through a just war, or repurchase, or purchase, or barter, or any other means or pretext whatsoever, even if these Indians be considered as slaves by the natives of the islands and mainland themselves." The New Laws of 1542, concerning the government of the Spanish colonies, will be written in the same spirit (and will provoke a veritable hue and cry from the colonists and conquistadors of America).

Simularly, in the papal bull of 1537, Paul III declares: "The Truth . . . said, in sending preachers of the faith to fulfill the function of this predication: 'Go and make disciples of all nations.' He said 'all' without distinction, since all are capable of receiving the discipline of the faith. . . . Acknowledging that the Indians as true men not only are capable of receiving the Christian faith but, as we have been informed, eagerly hurry to it . . . we command that the aforesaid Indians and all other nations which come to the knowledge of Christians in the future must not be deprived of their freedom and the ownership of their property." This declaration derives from fundamental Christian principles: God created man in His image; to offend man is to offend God Himself.

Las Casas therefore adopts this position and gives it a more general expression, positing equality as the basis of all human policy: "The natural laws and rules and rights of men are common to all nations, Christian and gentile, and whatever their sect, law, state, color and condition, without any difference." He even goes one step further, which consists not only in declaring an abstract equality, but in specifying that he means an equality between *ourselves* and *the others*, Spaniards and Indians; whence the frequency, in his writings, of such formulas as: "All the Indians to be found here are to be held as free: for in truth so they are, by the same right as I myself am free" ("Letter to Prince Philip," 20, 4, 1544). He can make his argument particularly concrete by resorting to a comparison which puts the Indians in the place of the Spaniards: "If Moors or Turks had come with the same injunction [*Requerimiento*] declaring Mohammed the ruler of the world, were they [the Spaniards] to believe it?" (*Historia*, III, 58).

But this very declaration of the equality of men is made in the name of a specific religion, Christianity, though without this specificity being acknowledged. Hence, there is a potential danger of seeing not only the Indians' human nature asserted but also their Christian "nature." "The natural laws and rules and rights of men," Las Casas said; but who decides what is natural with regard to laws and rights? Is it not specifically the Christian religion? Since Christianity is universalist, it implies an essential non-difference on the part of all men. We see the danger of the identification in this text of Saint John Chrysostom, quoted and defended at Valladolid: "Just as there is no natural difference in the creation of man, so there is no difference in the call to salvation of all men, barbarous or wise, since God's grace can correct the minds of barbarians, so that they have a reasonable understanding" (*Apologia*, 42).

Here biological identity already involves a kind of cultural identity (in the eyes of religion): all men are called by the God of the Christians, and it is a Christian who determines the meaning of the word "save." In a first phase, then, Las Casas observes that from the doctrinal point of view, the Christian religion *can* be adopted by all. "Our Christian religion is suited to all the nations of the world, and it is open to all in the same fashion; and taking from none its freedom nor sovereignty, it puts none in a state of servitude, on the excuse of a distinction between free men and serfs by nature" (discourse presented before the king in 1520; *Historia*, III, 149). But immediately after he declares that all nations *are* fated to the Christian religion, thereby taking the step separating potentiality from action: "There was never created a generation nor lineage nor people nor language among human beings . . . and still less since the Incarnation and the Passion of the Redeemer . . . that cannot be counted among the predestined, which is to say among the members of the mystic body of Jesus Christ, which, as says Saint Paul, is the Church" (*Historia*, I, "Prologue"). "The Christian religion is granted to different peoples as the universal way to salvation, so that they may leave behind their various sects" (ibid. I, 1).

And it is as an empirical observation that Las Casas declares, and tirelessly repeats, that the Indians already possess Christian traits, and that they aspire to have their "wild" Christianity be recognized: "At no other time and in no other people has there been seen such capacity, such predisposition, and such facility for conversion. . . . Nowhere in the world are there countries more docile and less resistant, or more apt and better disposed than these to receive the yoke of Our Lord" ("Letter to the Council of the Indies," 20, 1, 1531). "The Indians are of such gentleness and decency, that they are more than the other nations of the entire world, supremely fitted and prepared to abandon the worship of idols and to accept, province by province and people by people, the word of God and the preaching of the truth" (*Apologia*, 1).

According to Las Casas, the Indians' most characteristic feature is their resemblance to Christians. . . . What else do we find in his portrait? The Indians are provided with Christian virtues, they are obedient and peaceful. Here are a few phrases taken from various works, written at different moments of his career: "These peoples, considered in general, are by their nature all gentleness, humility and poverty, without weapons or defenses nor the least ingenuity, patient and enduring as none other in the world" (*Historia*, I, "Prologue"). "Very obedient and of great virtue, and by nature peaceful" (*Relación*, "Of the Kingdoms . . ."). "They are, for the greater part, of a peaceful, gentle, harmless nature" ("Letter to Carranza," August 1555).

Las Casas's perception of the Indians is no more nuanced than that of Columbus when the latter believed in the "noble savage," and Las

Casas virtually admits that he is projecting his ideal on them: "The Lucayos . . . lived . . . as in the Golden Age, a life of which poets and historians have sung such praise," he writes, or again, apropos one Indian: "To me he looked like our father Adam before the Fall (*Historia*, II, 44 and 45). This monotony of adjectives is all the more striking in that we are reading here descriptions not only written at various times but describing populations equally distinct and even remote from each other, from Florida to Peru; yet they are all and invariably "gentle and peace-loving." Las Casas notices as much on occasion, but without lingering over the fact: "Their rites and customs differ, but they all have in common the traits of simplicity, peacefulness, gentleness, humility, generosity, and of all the sons of Adam, they are without exception the most patient. In addition, they are eminently ready to be brought to the knowledge of their Creator and to the Faith" (*Historia*, I, 76). Another description in the Preface to the *Relación* is quite as revealing in this regard: "And of all the infinite universe of humanity, these people are the most guileless, the most devoid of wickedness and duplicity, the most obedient and faithful to their native masters and to the Spanish Christians whom they serve. They are by nature the most humble, patient, and peaceable, holding no grudges, free from embroilments, neither excitable nor quarrelsome. These people are the most devoid of rancors, hatreds or desire for vengeance of any people in the world." It is striking to see how Las Casas is led to describe the Indians in terms which are almost entirely negative or privative: they are *without* defects, *neither* thus *nor* so. . . .

Further, what is asserted positively is merely a psychological state (once again, as with Columbus): good, calm, patient; never a cultural or social configuration which might permit the understanding of differences. Nor, indeed, any behavior that is initially inexplicable: why do the Indians so humbly obey the Spaniards depicted as cruel monsters? Why are they so readily defeated by adversaries so few in number? The only explanation that can occur to Las Casas is because they behave as veritable Christians. For example, he notices a certain indifference on the part of the Indians to material goods, which causes them not to be eager to work and grow rich. Some Spaniards have accounted for this indifference by asserting that the Indians are by nature lazy; Las Casas retorts: "In comparison with our own fervent and indefatigable desire to accumulate wealth and temporal goods, on account of our innate ambition and our insatiable cupidity, these people, I grant, may be taxed with idleness or indolence; but not according to natural reason, the divine law and the evangelical perfection which praise and approve that man be content with no more than what is necessary" (*Historia*, III, 10). Thus Las Casas's first impression, an accurate one, is neutralized because he is convinced of the universality of the Christian spirit: if these people are indifferent to wealth, it is because they have a Christian morality.

His *Apologética Historia* contains, it is true, a mass of information, collected either by himself or by the missionaries and concerning the Indians' material and spiritual life. But as the very title of the work reveals, history here becomes apologia: for Las Casas, the essential is that none of the Indians' customs or practices prove that they are inferior beings; he approaches each phenomenon with certain evaluative categories, and the result of the confrontation is determined in advance: if Las Casas's book has a value as an ethnographic document today, it is certainly in spite of the author. We must acknowledge that the portrait of the Indians to be drawn from Las Casas's works is rather poorer than that left us by Sepúlveda: as a matter of fact, we learn nothing of the Indians. If it is incontestable that the prejudice of superiority is an obstacle in the road to knowledge, we must also admit that the prejudice of equality is a still greater one, for it consists in identifying the other purely and simply with one's own "ego ideal" (or with oneself).

Las Casas sees every conflict, and in particular that of the Spaniards and the Indians, in terms of a unique—and entirely Spanish—opposition: believing/unbelieving. The originality of his position proceeds from the fact that he attributes the "valued" pole to the other, and the rejected pole to "us" (the Spaniards). But this inverted distribution of values, incontestable proof of his generosity of spirit, does not lessen the schematism of his vision. We see this especially in the analogies to which Las Casas resorts in order to describe the confrontation of Indians and Spaniards. For instance, he will systematically utilize the evangelical comparison between apostles and lambs, infidels and wolves or lions, etc.; we recall that the conquistadors themselves employed this comparison, though without giving it its Christian meaning. "Into this sheepfold, into this land of meek outcasts, there came some Spaniards who immediately behaved like ravening wild beasts, wolves, tigers, or lions that had been starved for many days" (*Relación*, Preface).

Similarly, he will identify the Indians with the Hebrews, the Spaniards with Pharaoh, the Indians with the Christians, the Spaniards with the Moors. "The government [of the Indies] is much more unjust and cruel than the rule by which Pharaoh of Egypt oppressed the Jews" ("Memorial to the Council of the Indies," 1565). "The wars have been worse than those of the Turks and the Moors against the Christian peoples" ("Discourse at Valladolid," 12); we may note in passing that Las Casas never shows the slightest tenderness toward the Muslims, doubtless because the latter cannot be identified as "unwitting" Christians; and when he demonstrates in his *Apologia* that it is not legitimate to treat the Indians as "barbarians" simply because they are different, he does not forget to condemn "Turks and Moors, the veritable barbarian outcasts of the nations."

As for the Spaniards in America, they are ultimately identified with the Devil: "Consider whether it is accurate to call such Christians devils and whether it would be any worse to allocate the Indians to devils from hell rather than to allocate them to the kind of Christians who are in the Indies" (Las Casas, *Relación*, "Granada"). He will oppose the conquistadors, he says again, "until Satan is expelled from the Indies" ("Letter to Prince Philip," 9, 11, 1545). This sentence has a familiar ring: it is the racist historian Oviedo who also hoped that "Satan would be expelled from the islands"; we have merely changed Satans—Indian here, Spaniard there—but the conceptualization remains the same. Thus, at the same time that he misperceives the Indians, Las Casas fails to know the Spaniards. The latter are not, it is true, Christians like himself (or like his ideal); but one does not apprehend the transformation that has occurred in the Spanish mentality if one merely presents it as a manifestation of the devil—i.e., by retaining the very frame of reference that has been called into question. The Spaniards, for whom the notion of chance has replaced that of fate, have a new way of living their religion (or of living without religion); this explains to a degree how they build their transatlantic empire so easily, how they contribute to the subjection of a great part of the world to Europe: is this not the source of their capacity for adaptation and improvisation? But Las Casas chooses to ignore this way of experiencing religion and here behaves as a theologian, not as a historian.

Indeed, Las Casas is content to maintain an egocentric position with regard to time as well as space. If he admits that there are differences between Spaniards and Indians that would function to the latter's disadvantage, he does so in order to reduce them immediately by evolutionary scheme: they *(over there)* are *now* even as we *(here)* were *once* (of course he is not the first to propose such a schema). Originally all nations were crude and barbarous (Las Casas is not willing to acknowledge a specifically modern barbarism); with time they will achieve civilization (our own, it is understood). "We have no reason to be surprised at the defects, at the uncivilized and excessive customs which we may encounter among the Indian nations, nor to despise them for this. For most if not all the nations of the world have been even more perverted, irrational and depraved, and shown even less caution and wisdom in their manner of government and in their exercise of moral virtues. We ourselves have been much worse in the times of our ancestors and in the length and breadth of our span, as much by the excess and confusion of manners as by our vices and bestial customs" (*Apologética Historia*, III, 263).

Here again there is an incontestable generosity on the part of Las Casas, who refuses to despise others simply because they are different. But he goes one step further and adds: moreover, they are not (or will not be) different. The postulate of equality involves the assertion of identity, and the second great figure of alterity, even if it is incontestably more attractive, leads to a knowledge of the other even less valid than the first.

Enslavement, Colonialism, and Communication

Las Casas loves the Indians. And is a Christian. For him, these two traits are linked: he loves the Indians precisely *because* he is a Christian, and his love *illustrates* his faith. Yet such solidarity is not a matter of course. As we have seen, precisely because he was a Christian, his perception of the Indians was poor. Can we really love someone if we know little or nothing of his identity; if we see, in place of that identity, a projection of ourselves or of our ideals? We know that such a thing is quite possible, even frequent, in personal relations; but what happens in cultural confrontations? Doesn't one culture risk trying to transform the other in its own name, and therefore risk subjugating it as well? How much is such love worth?

Las Casas's first major treatise devoted to the Indians' cause is entitled *On the one way to draw all peoples to the true religion*. This title distills all the ambivalence of his position. This "one way" is of course peaceful persuasion; Las Casas's work is a polemic against the conquistadors who claim to justify their wars of conquest by the goal pursued, which is evangelization. Las Casas rejects such violence; but at the same time, for him there is only one "true" religion: his own. And this "truth" is not only personal (Las Casas does not consider religion true *for him*), but universal; it is valid for everyone, which is why he himself does not renounce the evangelizing project. Yet is there not already a violence in the conviction that one possesses the truth oneself, whereas this is not the case for others, and that one must furthermore impose that truth on those others?

Las Casas's life is rich in actions in the Indians' favor. But with the exception of those of his last years, to which we shall return in the following chapter, all are marked by one form or another of this same ambiguity. Before his actual "conversion" to the Indians' cause, he is full of kindness and humanity in their regard; and yet the limits of his intervention very soon appear. We recall the Caonao massacre, of which he had been a witness, as chaplain to Narvaez's troops; what can he do to relieve the sufferings of the Indians massacred? Here is what he himself tells us: "And just as the young man came down, a Spaniard who was there drew a cutlass or half sword and gives him a cut through the loins, so that his intestines fall out. . . . The Indian, moaning, takes his intestines in his hands and comes fleeing out of the house. He encounters the cleric [Las Casas] . . . and the cleric tells him some things about the faith, as much as the time and anguish permitted, explaining to him that if he wished to be baptized he would go to heaven to live with God. The poor creature, weeping and showing pain as if he were burning in flames, said yes, and with this the cleric baptized him. He then fell dead on the ground" (*Historia*, III, 29).

To a believer, of course, it is not a matter of indifference to know that a soul is going to paradise (being baptized) or to hell; by performing this action Las Casas is certainly moved by love of his neighbor. Yet there is something ludicrous about this baptism *in extremis*, and Las Casas himself has said as much on other occasions. The concern for a conversion here assumes a preposterous quality, and the remedy is really not proportional to the difficulty. The benefit the Indians derive from Christianization is then quite meager, as is also illustrated by this anecdote reported by Bernal Díaz: "Jesus permitted the cacique to become a Christian: the monk baptized him, and he asked and was granted by Alvarado that he was not burned at the stake, but hanged." Cuauhtemoc too "died in a somewhat Christian manner": "The Spaniards hanged him from a silk-cotton tree," but "a cross was placed in his hands" (Chimalpahin, 7, 206).

After his "conversion," during which he releases the Indians he owns, Las Casas launches a new enterprise, which is the peaceful colonization of the region of Cumana, in what is today Venezuela: here soldiers are replaced by priests, Dominicans and Franciscans, and farmer-colonists brought from Spain; certainly this is colonization on the spiritual as well as the material level, but it is to be conducted gently. The expedition is a failure: Las Casas finds himself forced to make more and more concessions to the Spaniards accompanying him; moreover the Indians do not turn out to be so docile as he had hoped. The venture ends in bloodshed. Las Casas escapes alive and is not discouraged. Some fifteen years later, he undertakes pacification of a particularly tumultuous region in Guatemala which will be called Vera Paz. Once again, priests are to replace soldiers; once again the result is to be the same colonization, even better than if soldiers were carrying it out: Las Casas promises that the profits of the crown will increase if his advice is followed. "We declare ourselves ready to pacify them and to reduce them to the service of our lord the king, and to convert them and instruct them in the knowledge of their Creator; after which we shall cause these populations to pay, each year, tributes and services to their Majesties, according to the possibilities granted them by their resources: all for the best advantage of the king of Spain and of these countries" ("Letter to a Dignitary of the Court," 15, 10, 1535). This enterprise succeeds better than the preceding one; but when some years later, the missionaries feel they are in danger, they themselves appeal to the army, which in any case is not far away.

Las Casas's attitude with regard to black slaves might also be brought up in this context. His adversaries, who have always been numerous, interpret it as a proof of his partiality toward the Indians, and therefore a means of rejecting his testimony concerning their destruction. This interpretation is unfair; but it is true that initially Las Casas did not have the same attitude toward Indians and blacks: he consents that the latter, but not the former, be reduced to slavery. We must remember that enslavement of blacks is an acknowledged phenomenon at the time, whereas that of the Indians is beginning before his eyes. But at the period when he is writing the *History of the Indies*, he declares that he no longer makes any distinction between the two groups: "He always considered the Blacks as unjustly and tyrannically reduced to slavery, for the same reasons applied to them and to the Indians" (*Historia*, III, 102). Yet we know that in 1544 he still possessed a black slave (he had released his Indians in 1514), and we still find expressions of this sort in his *History:* "Surely the blindness of those people who first came here and treated the natives as if they were Africans was something to marvel at" (*Historia*, II, 27, p. 132). Without seeing this as a phenomenon destroying the authenticity of his testimony concerning the Indians, we must remark that his attitude toward blacks is unclear. Is this not because his generosity is based on a spirit of identification, on the assertion that the other is like oneself, and that he finds such a statement too preposterous in the case of the blacks?

One thing is sure: Las Casas does not want to put an end to the annexation of the Indians, he merely wants this to be effected by priests rather than by soldiers. This is the content of his letter to the Council of the Indies of January 20, 1531: the conquistadors must be "expelled from these countries and replaced by persons fearing God, of good conscience and great prudence." Las Casas's dream is that of a theocratic state in which the spiritual power governs the temporal (which is a certain way of returning to the Middle Ages). The change he proposes may find its best expression in a comparison which he finds in a letter from the bishop of Santa Marta to the king on May 20, 1541, and which he adopts as his own in the *Relación:* this land must be "wrested from the power of these unnatural fathers and given to a husband who will treat her with the reasonableness she deserves." Las Casas, then, just like Sepúlveda, identifies the colony with a woman; and there is no question of emancipation (of either women or Indians): it suffices to replace the father, who has revealed himself to be cruel, by a husband who it is hoped will be reasonable. Now, in regard to female emancipation, Christian doctrine would be more or less in agreement with Aristotle: woman is as necessary to man as the slave is to the master.

Submission and colonization must be maintained, but conducted differently; it is not only the Indians who stand to gain (by not being tortured and exterminated) but also the king and Spain. Las Casas never fails to develop this second argument alongside the first. We might suppose that in doing so he is not sincere, but simply holds out this carrot to gain a hearing for his remarks; but the thing is of little importance, not only because it is impossible to establish, but also because Las Casas's texts—i.e., what can function publicly—certainly say that there is a material advantage to be derived from colonization. In an audience with old King Ferdinand in 1515, Las Casas tells him that his propositions "are a matter which means much to the royal conscience and estate" (Historia, III, 84). In a memorandum of 1516 he declares: "All will be of great profit to His Highness, whose revenues will increase proportionately." In his letter to the Council of the Indies of January 20, 1531, he claims that following his advice would "furthermore afford great benefits and the promise of an unsuspected prosperity." In a letter from Nicaragua of 1535: the priest "has served the king somewhat better than those who are making him lose vast kingdoms, stripping him of so much wealth, depriving him of such fabulous treasures."

These repeated assertions, however, are not enough to clear Las Casas of all suspicion that he seeks to reject the imperial power, and he must explicitly defend himself against that suspicion, listing in his turn the reasons which make him believe that this power is indeed legitimate; this is notably the case in the *Thirty Propositions* of 1547 and the *Treatise of Proofs* of 1552. In the latter text we read: "The Roman pontiff has doubtless all power over the infidels." "The Apostolic See can therefore select certain territories of these infidels and appoint them to a Christian king." "The king whom the Apostolic See has chosen to exercise the ministry of the faith in the Indies must necessarily be invested with the supreme sovereignty and the perpetual monarchy over the said Indies and be constituted emperor above many kings." Are we not hearing a paraphrase of the *Requerimiento,* even if the local kings here preserve some semblance of power?

The same attitude is adopted in this regard by other defenders of the Indians: we must not make war upon them, we must not reduce them to slavery, not only because we thus inflict sufferings upon the Indians (as upon the conscience of the king) but also because we are improving the finances of Spain. "The Spaniards do not realize," Motolinia writes, "that were it not for the friars, there would be no further servitors, either in their houses or in their fields, for they would have killed them all, as may be observed in Santo Domingo and in other islands where the Indians were exterminated" (III, 1). And Bishop Ramirez de Fuenleal, in a letter to Charles V: "It is good to prevent any Indian from being reduced to slavery, for it is they who must make the territory profitable, and insofar as there will be great number of them, the Spaniards will lack for nothing."

I do not want to suggest, by accumulating such quotations, that Las Casas or the other defenders of the Indians should, or even could, have behaved differently. In any case, the documents we are reading are generally missives addressed to the king, and it is difficult to see the point of suggesting that the latter renounce his realms. On the contrary, by asking for a more humane attitude with regard to the Indians, they do the only thing possible and at all useful; if anyone contributed to the improvement of the Indians' lot, it is certainly Las Casas; the inextinguishable hatred which all the Indians' adversaries, all those loyal to the notion of white supremacy, have vented upon him is a sufficient indication of that. He has achieved this result by using the weapons which best suited him: by writing, with passion. He has left an ineffaceable picture of the destruction of the Indians, and every line devoted to them since—including this one—owes him something. No one else, with such abnegation, has dedicated such enormous energy and a half-century of his life to improving the lot of *others*. But it takes nothing away from the greatness of the figure, quite the contrary, to acknowledge that the ideology "assumed" by Las Casas and by other defenders of the Indians is certainly a colonialist one. It is precisely because we cannot help admiring the man that we must judge his policies lucidly.

The kings of Spain were not deceived. In 1573, under Philip II, definitive ordinances were drawn up concerning "the Indies." At the head of the Council of the Indies, responsible for the tenor of these ordinances, was Juan de Ovanda, who not only knew Las Casas's doctrines but in 1571 brought to the court the text of the famous Valladolid controversy. Here are some extracts from the ordinances:

"Discoveries are not to be called conquests. Since we wish them to be carried out peacefully and charitably, we do not want the use of the term 'conquest' to offer any excuse for the employment of force or the causing of injury to the Indians. . . . They are to gather information about the various tribes, languages and divisions of the Indians in the province and about the lords whom they obey. They are to seek friendship with them through trade and barter, showing them great love and tenderness and giving them objects to which they will take a liking. Without displaying any greed for the possessions of the Indians, they are to establish friendship and cooperation with the lords and nobles who seem most likely to be of assistance in the pacification of the land. . . . In order that the Indians may hear the faith with greater awe and reverence, the preachers should convey the Cross in their hands and should be wearing at least albs or stoles; the Christians are also to be told to listen to the preaching with great respect and veneration, so that by their example the non-believers will be induced to accept instruction. If it seems advisable, the preachers may attract the attention of the non-believers by using music and singers, thereby encouraging them to join in. . . . The preachers should ask for their children under the pretext of teaching them and keep them as hostages; they should also persuade them to build churches where they can teach so that they may be safer. By these and other means are the Indians to be pacified and indoctrinated, but in no way are they to be harmed, for all we seek is their welfare and their conversion."

Reading the text of the Ordinances, we realize that since Palacios Rubios's *Requerimiento* there has been not only Las Casas but also Cortés: the old injunction has been influenced by both. From Las Casas, obviously, comes the concern for mildness. Slavery is banished, as is violence, save in cases of extreme necessity. "Pacification" and subsequent administration are to be practiced with moderation, and taxes are to remain reasonable. The local leaders are to be retained, provided they agree to serve the interests of the crown. Conversion itself is not to be imposed, but only offered; the Indians are to embrace the Christian religion only of their own free will. But it is to the (vague) influence of Cortés that we owe the surprising, and assumed, presence of the discourse of seeming. The text cannot be more explicit on this point: it is not conquests that are to be banished, but the word *conquest;* "pacification" is nothing but another word to designate the same thing, but let us not suppose that this linguistic concern is a futile one. Subsequently, one is to act *under cover* of commerce, by *manifesting* love, and without *showing* greed. For those who cannot understand such language, it is made even clearer that the presents offered must be of little value: it suffices that they please the Indians (this is the tradition of the red cap offered by Columbus). At the same time, evangelization benefits from the staging of the *"son et lumière"* shows Cortés had inaugurated: the rite must be surrounded with all possible solemnity, the priests decked out in their finest vestments, and music too laid under contribution. One remarkable phenomenon: the Spaniards' devotion can no longer be automatically counted on, hence here too semblances must be regulated: the Spaniards are not asked to *be* good Christians but to *appear* to be so.

Despite these obvious influences, the *Requerimiento*'s intention is also not absent, and the total objective is not modified: it is still the submission of these lands to the crown of Spain. And the stick is not forgotten, despite the presence of the carrot: the churches are not only to be splendid but also capable of serving as fortresses. As for the teaching generously offered to the children of the nobles, it is merely a pretext for seizing them and making them serve, if need be, as a means of blackmail (your children in our schools are so many hostages . . .).

Another lesson from Cortés is not forgotten: before dominating, one must be informed. Cortés himself did not fail to make this rule explicit in certain documents dating from after the conquest, for example this memorandum addressed to Charles V in 1537: before conquering a country, he writes, "it must be determined whether it is inhabited, and if so by what kind of peoples, and what religion or rite they have, and upon what they live, and what there is in the land." Here we glimpse the function of the future ethnologist: the exploration of these countries will lead to their (better) exploitation, and we know that Spain is the first colonial power to apply this precept, thanks to the investigations undertaken at the crown's prompting. A new trinity replaces—or rather puts in the background, for he must always remain ready to intervene—the old-style soldier-conquistador: it consists of the scholar, the priest, and the merchant. The first collects information about the condition of the country, the second permits its spiritual annexation, the third makes certain of the profits; they help each other, and all help Spain.

Las Casas and the other defenders of the Indians are not hostile to the Spanish expansion; but they prefer one of its forms to the other. Let us call each of them by a familiar name (even if these names are not quite exact historically): they function within the *colonialist* ideology, against the *enslavement* ideology. Enslavement, in this sense of the word, reduces the other to the status of an object, which is especially manifested in conduct that treats the Indians as less than men: their flesh is used to feed the surviving Indians or even the dogs; they are killed in order to be boiled down for grease, supposed to cure the wounds of the Spaniards: thereby they are identified with animals for the slaughterhouse; all their extremities are cut off, nose, hands, breasts, tongue, sexual organs, thereby transforming them into shapeless trunks, as one might trim a tree; it is suggested that their blood be used to irrigate the fields, as if it were the water of a stream. Las Casas reports that the price of a female slave rises according to whether or not she is pregnant, exactly as in the case of cattle: "This godforsaken man . . . said that he worked as hard as he could to get Indian women with child, for when he sold them as slaves he would be paid more if they were pregnant" (*Relación*, Yucatán).

But this form of human utilization is obviously not the most profitable. If, instead of regarding the other as an object, he were considered as a subject capable of producing objects which one might then possess, the chain would be extended by a link—an intermediary subject—and thereby multiply to infinity the number of objects ultimately possessed. Two additional concerns proceed from this transformation. The first is that the "intermediary" subject must be maintained in precisely this role of subject-producer-of-objects and kept from becoming like ourselves: the goose laying golden eggs loses all interest if it consumes its own products. The army, or the police, will be concerned with this matter. The second is expressed thus: the subject will be all the more productive insofar as he is better cared for. The priests will therefore dispense medical treatment on the one hand, and education on the other (Motolinia and Olarte ingenuously say, in a letter to the Viceroy Luis de Velasco, in 1554: "These poor creatures are not yet sufficiently instructed to pay [new levies] of their own free will"). The body's health and that of the soul will then be ensured by lay specialists, the doctor and the professor.

The efficiency of colonialism is greater than that of enslavement, at least that is what we can observe today. In Spanish America, there is no lack of colonialists of stature: if a Columbus is to be classified in the party of enslavement, figures as different, and as opposed in reality, as Cortés and Las Casas are both to be identified with the colonialist ideology (this kinship is made explicit by the ordinances of 1573). A fresco by Diego Rivera in the National Palace of Mexico shows the elementary image of the relation between the two figures (see fig. 11): on one side Cortés with a sword in one hand and a whip in the other, trampling down the Indians; facing him Las Casas, the Indians' protector, halts Cortés with a cross. It is true that many things separate the two men. Las Casas loves the Indians but does not always understand them; Cortés knows them in his way, even if he does not bear any great "love" toward them; his attitude toward Indian enslavement, as we have been able to note, illustrates his position nicely. Las Casas is against the *repartimiento*, the feudal cession of the Indians to the Spaniards, which Cortés, on the contrary, promotes. We know virtually nothing of the feelings of the Indians of the period toward Las Casas, which, in itself, is already significant. Cortés, on the other hand, is so popular that he makes those in possession of legal power tremble—those representatives of the Spanish emperor who know that the Indians will revolt at a word from Cortés; the members of the second Audience explain the situation thus: "The affection which the Indians have for the Marqués comes from the fact that it is he who has conquered them, and from the fact that in truth he has treated them better than all the rest." And yet Las Casas and Cortés are in agreement on one essential point: the subjugation of America to Spain, the annexation of the Indians to the Christian religion, the preference for colonialism over enslavement.

We may be surprised to see every form of the Spanish presence in America stigmatized by the name "colonialism" which is nowadays an insult. Since the period of the conquest, authors of the pro-Spanish party insist on the benefits the Spaniards contributed to the uncivilized countries, as we frequently encounter such enumerations as these: the Spaniards suppressed human sacrifice, cannibalism, polygamy, homosexuality, and brought Christianity, European clothes, domestic animals, tools. Even if today we do not always see why this or that novelty is superior to this or that ancient practice, and if we judge some of these gifts to have been bought at a very high price, certain indisputably positive points subsist: technological developments, but also, as we have seen, symbolic and cultural advances. Are these, too, the products of colonialism? In other words, is any influence, by the very fact of its externality, detrimental? Raised in this form, the question can receive, it seems to me, only a negative answer. Hence it appears that if colonialism opposes enslavement, it simultaneously opposes that contact with the other which I shall simply call communication. To the triad understand/seize/destroy corresponds this other triad in inverted order: enslavement/colonialism/communication.

Vitoria's principle, according to which free circulation of men, ideas, and goods must be permitted, seems generally accepted today (even if it does not suffice to justify a war). In the name of what would we reserve "America for the Americans"—or Russians inside Russia? Furthermore, did not these Indians themselves come from elsewhere: from the north or even, according to some, from Asia, across the Bering Straits? Can the history of any country be other than the sum of the successive influences it has undergone? If there really existed a people who rejected all change, would such a will illustrate anything but an impulse of hypertrophied death instinct? Gobineau believed that the superior races were the purest; do we not believe today that the richest cultures are the most mixed?

But we also cherish another principle, that of self-determination and noninterference. How to reconcile them with "cross-pollination"? Is it not contradictory to claim the right to influence and also to

Fig. 11 Cortés and Las Casas.

condemn interference? No, though the matter is hardly self-evident and requires explanation. It is not a question of judging the positive or negative content of the influence in question: we could do that only by invoking entirely relative criteria, and even here we would risk never reaching an agreement, matters being so complex. How to measure the impact of Christianization on America? The question seems almost devoid of meaning, so greatly can the answers vary. One small example will make us reflect on the relativity of values; here is an episode reported by Cortés in the course of his expedition to Honduras: "It happened that a Spaniard found an Indian of his company, a native of Mexico, eating a piece of flesh of the body of an Indian he had killed when entering that town, and this Spaniard came to tell me of it, and I had the Indian burned in the presence of that lord, telling him the reason for such a punishment, namely that he had killed and eaten one of his fellow men, which was forbidden by Your Majesty and which I, in Your Royal name, had required and commanded them not to do. And so I had him burned, for I wished to see no one killed" (5).

The Christians are disgusted by cases of cannibalism (see fig. 12). The introduction of Christianity involves their suppression. But, in order to achieve this suppression, men are burned alive! The whole paradox of the death penalty is here: the penal instance accomplishes the very action it condemns—it kills in order to forbid killing. For the Spaniards, this was a way of fighting what they judged to be barbarism; times have changed and we scarcely perceive the difference in "civilization" between being burned alive and eaten dead. Such is the paradox of colonization, even if it is created in the name of values believed to be "higher."

On the other hand it is possible to establish an ethical criterion to judge the form of influences: the essential thing, I should say, is to know whether they are *imposed* or *proposed*. Christianization, like the export of any ideology or technology, can be condemned as soon as it is imposed, by arms or otherwise. A civilization may have features we can say are superior or inferior; but this does not justify their being imposed on others. Even more, to impose one's will on others implies that one does not concede to that other the same humanity one grants to oneself, an implication which precisely characterizes a lower civilization. No one asked the Indians if they wanted the wheel, or looms, or forges; they were obliged to accept them. Here is where the violence resides, and it does not depend on the possible utility of these objects.

Fig. 12 Scene of cannibalism.

But in whose name would we condemn the unarmed preacher, even if his avowed goal is to convert us to his own religion?

Perhaps there is a simplistic utopianism in thus reducing matters to the use of violence, especially since violence, as we know, can take forms that are not really subtler but less obvious: can we say of an ideology or a technology that it is merely proposed when it is carried by every means of communication in existence? No, of course not. Conversely, a thing is not imposed when one can choose another thing instead, and knows one can so choose. The relation of knowledge to power, as we were able to observe on the occasion of the conquest, is not contingent but constitutive. Vitoria, one of the founders of modern international law, was already aware of this. As we have seen, he admitted the existence of just wars, those motivated by the reparation of an injustice. Yet he did not fail to raise the question: how can we determine the just nature of a war? His answer emphasizes the role of information. It is not sufficient that the prince believe it to be just: the prince is too implicated, and a man can be deceived. Nor that the population, even in its entirety, believe so: a people does not have access to state secrets—it is by definition not informed. The cause must be just in itself, and not only for an ever-manipulable public opinion. Such absolute propriety is accessible only to the wise, whose obligation it thereby becomes. "Consultation must be made of men who are honest and wise, capable of speaking freely, without anger or hatred or greed" (Vitoria, *De Jure Belli*, 21, 59). Ignorance is only temporarily an excuse; beyond the moment, it is culpable: "He who has doubts and neglects to seek the truth no longer possesses good faith" (ibid., 29, 84).

When Vitoria applies this general doctrine to the case of wars against the Indians, he does not neglect this concern for information: the Spaniards can complain of the Indians' hostility only if they can prove that the Indians were duly informed of the newcomers' good intentions; the act of providing information is an obligation, as was that of seeking it. Yet Vitoria himself does not perfectly illustrate his own precept—and thereby incarnates the characteristic separation of the modern intellectual, between saying and doing, between the statement's content and the speech-act's meaning. Alongside the "reciprocal" reasons capable of justifying a war, and alongside those attributable to his own ethnocentrism, he also gave others, whose defect is not a lack of reciprocity but an unconcern for information. He admits, for example, that the leaders, or a part of the population, may appeal to foreign powers; the latter's intervention would then constitute a just war. But he does not breathe a word as to the modalities of consulting the population in such a case, and does not envisage the possibility of the leaders' bad faith. Or again, he justifies those interventions made in the name of military alliances; but the example he gives—he takes it from the conquest of Mexico—betrays him: "It is said that the Tlaxcaltecs acted thus toward the Mexicans: they reached an understanding with the Spaniards so that these would help them combat the Mexicans; the Spaniards afterwards received all that could come to them by virtue of the right of war" (*De Indis*, 3, 17, 296). Vitoria proceeds as if the war between Mexicans and Tlaxcaltecs were the fundamental relation, the Spaniards intervening only as the latter's allies. But we know that this is a brutal travesty of the truth; it is Vitoria who is thereby culpable of relying on the approximation of rumor, of the "sayings of those who have been to that country" (ibid., 3, 18, 302), without really "seeking the truth."

Good information is the best means of establishing power, as we have seen in the case of Cortés and the royal ordinances. But the right to information is also inalienable, and there is no legitimacy of power if this right is not respected. Those who are not concerned to know, like those who abstain from informing themselves, are guilty before their society; or, to put the matter in positive terms, the function of information is an essential social function. Yet if information is effective, the distinction between "imposing" and "proposing" will retain its pertinence. We need not be confined within a sterile alternative: either to justify colonial wars (in the name of the superiority of Western civilization), or to reject all interaction with a foreign power in the name of one's own identity. Nonviolent communication exists, and we can defend it as a value. It is what may permit us to act so that the triad: enslavement/colonialism/communication is not merely an instrument of conceptual analysis, but also turns out to correspond to a succession within time.

4. KNOWLEDGE

Typology of Relations to the Other

THERE is a certain paradox in identifying Las Casas's behavior toward the Indians with that of Cortés, and we have had to surround such an assertion with several restrictions; this is because the relation to the other is not constituted in just one dimension. To account for the differences that exist in actuality, we must distinguish among at least three axes, on which we can locate the problematics of alterity. First of all, there is a value judgment (an axiological level): the other is good or bad, I love or do not love him, or, as was more likely to be said at the time, he is my equal or my inferior (for there is usually no question that I am good and that I esteem myself). Secondly, there is the action of *rapprochement* or distancing in relation to the other (a praxeological level): I embrace the other's values, I identify myself with him; or else I identify the other with myself, I impose my own image upon him; between submission to the other and the other's submission, there is also a third term, which is neutrality, or indifference. Thirdly, I know or am ignorant of the other's identity (this would be the epistemic level); of course, there is no absolute here, but an endless gradation between the lower or higher states of knowledge.

There exist, of course, relations and affinities between these three levels, but no rigorous *implication;* hence, we cannot reduce them to one another, nor anticipate one starting from the other. Las Casas knows the Indians less well than Cortés, and he loves them more; but they meet in their common policy of assimilation. Knowledge does not imply love, nor the converse; and neither of the two implies, nor is implied by, identification with the other. Conquest, love, and knowledge are autonomous and, in a sense, elementary forms of conduct (discovery, as we have seen, has more to do with lands than with men; with regard to men, Columbus's attitude can be described in altogether negative terms: he does not love, does not know, and does not identify himself).

We shall not confuse this delimitation of axes with the diversity to be observed in one and the same axis. Las Casas has provided us an example of love for the Indians; but in reality he himself already illustrates more than one attitude; and to do him justice, we must now complete his portrait. This is because Las Casas has undergone a series of crises, or transformations, which have led him to take up a series of related yet distinct positions in the course of his long life (1484–1566). He releases the Indians he owns in 1514, but becomes a Dominican only in 1522–23, and this second conversion is as important as the first. It is still another transformation that will concern us now: the one that takes place toward the end of his life, after his final return from Mexico, and also after the failure of several of his undertakings; we might take the year of the Valladolid debate, 1550, as our point of reference (but as a matter of fact there is not a distinct "conversion" here). Las Casas's attitude toward the Indians, the love he bears them, are not the same before and after this date.

The change seems to have occurred following his reflections on the human sacrifices performed by the Aztecs. The existence of these rites was the most convincing argument for the Indians' inferiority advanced by the party represented by Sepúlveda; it was, moreover, incontestable (even if no agreement was reached with regard to quantity; see figs. 13 and 14). It is not difficult, even several centuries later, for us to imagine the reactions; we cannot help wincing when we read the descriptions taken down from their informants by the Spanish monks of the period.

Are not such practices striking proof of savagery, and hence of the inferiority of peoples among whom they occur? Such was the argument Las Casas had to refute. He goes about it in his *Apologia* written in Latin, presented to the Valladolid judges, and in several chapters of the *Apologética Historia*, which must have been written at the same time. His reasoning on this subject deserves to be followed in some detail. In a first phase, Las Casas asserts that even if cannibalism and human sacrifice are in themselves condemnable, it does not thereby follow that we must declare war on those who practice them: such a remedy risks being worse than the disease. To this he adds the respect, which Las

Fig. 13 Sacrifice by extraction of the heart.

Fig. 14 Sacrifice by fire.

Casas supposes common to Indians and Spaniards, for the laws of the land: if the law imposes sacrifice, one acts as a good citizen by performing it, and the individual cannot be blamed for doing so. But he then takes a further step: the condemnation itself will be made problematical. For this purpose Las Casas employs two types of argument, which lead to two assertions.

The first argument concerns the order of facts, and it will be supported by historical comparisons. Las Casas wants to make human sacrifice less strange, less exceptional for his reader, and he reminds us that this sacrifice is not entirely absent from the Christian religion itself. "It can be persuasively argued from the fact that God commanded Abraham to sacrifice to Him his only son Isaac, that it is not altogether detestable to sacrifice human beings to God" (*Apologia*, 37). In the same way, Jephthah found himself compelled to sacrifice his daughter (Judges, 11:31 ff). Were not all firstborn sons promised to God? To those who object that these examples come from the Old Testament, Las Casas would point out that after all Jesus had been sacrificed by God the Father, and that the first Christians were also obliged to accept death if they did not wish to abandon their faith; such, apparently, was the Divine Will. In a comparable manner, Las Casas had already reconciled his reader to the notion of cannibalism by telling him of cases in which Spaniards, driven by necessity, had eaten in one case the liver, in another the thigh of one of their compatriots.

The second argument (which comes first in Las Casas's discussion) is even more ambitious: it seeks to prove that human sacrifice is acceptable not only de facto but also de jure. Thereby Las Casas is led to presuppose a new definition of religious feeling, and it is here that his reasoning is especially interesting. The argument is drawn from "natural reason," from a priori considerations as to the nature of man. Las Casas appeals to four "evidences":

1. Every human being has an intuitive knowledge of God—i.e., of "that than which there is nothing better or greater" (*Apologia*, 35).

2. Men worship God according to their capacities and in their fashion, always trying to do the best they can.

3. The greatest proof one can give of one's love for God consists of offering Him what is most precious to oneself, human life itself. This is the heart of the argument, and here is how Las Casas expresses

himself: "The greatest way to worship is to offer Him sacrifice. This is the unique way by which we show Him to whom we offer our sacrifice that we are subject to Him and grateful to Him. Furthermore, nature teaches that it is just to offer God, whose debtors we admit we are for so many reasons, those things that are precious and excellent, because of the surpassing excellence of His majesty. But, according to human judgment and truth, nothing in nature is greater or more valuable than the life of man, or man himself. Therefore nature itself dictates and teaches those who do not have faith, grace or doctrine, who live within the limitations of the light of nature, that, in spite of every contrary positive law, they ought to sacrifice human victims to the true God or to the false god who is thought to be true, so that by offering a supremely precious thing they might be more grateful for the many favors they have received" (ibid., 36).

4. Hence, sacrifice exists by the force of natural law, and its forms will be established by human laws, notably in regard to the nature of the object sacrificed.

Thanks to this series of arguments, Las Casas ends by adopting a new position, introducing what we might call perspectivism into the heart of religion. We will have noted how he takes precautions to remind us that the god of the Indians, though not the "true God," is nonetheless considered such by them, and that it is from this point that we should proceed: "the true God or the false god who is thought to be true" (ibid., 36); "the true God or the reputed god, if the latter is taken for the true God" (ibid., 35); "to the true God or the one whom they mistakenly thought is the true God" (ibid., 35). . . . But to acknowledge that their god is true for them—is that not to take a first step toward another acknowledgment, i.e., that our God is true for us —and only for us? What then remains common and universal is no longer the God of the Christian religion, to whom all should accede, but the very idea of divinity, of what is above us; the religious rather than religion. The presupposed part of his reasoning is also its most radical element (rather than what he says about sacrifice itself): it is really surprising to see "perspectivism" introduced into a field that so poorly lends itself to it.

Religious feeling is not defined by a universal and absolute content but by its orientation, and is measured by its intensity; so that even if the Christian God is in Himself an idea superior to what is expressed through Tezcatlipoca (as is believed by the Christian Las Casas), the Aztecs can be superior to the Christians with regard to religious feeling, and in fact they are so. The very notion of religion emerges utterly transformed: "The nations who offered human sacrifices to their gods thereby showed, as deluded idolators, the high idea they had of the excellence of divinity, of the value of their gods, and how noble and high was their veneration of divinity. They consequently demonstrated that they possessed, better than other nations, natural reflection, rectitude of speech, and the judgment of reason; they employed their understanding better than the others. And in religious feeling they exceeded all the other nations, for the latter are the most religious nations in the world who, for the good of their peoples, offer their own children as sacrifices" (*Apologética Historia*, III, 183). At the heart of the Christian tradition, only the martyrs of the first period, according to Las Casas, could be compared to the Aztec believers.

Hence, it is by confronting the most troublesome argument that Las Casas is led to modify his position and to illustrate thereby a new variant of the love for one's neighbor, for the Other—a love that is no longer assimilationist but, so to speak, distributive: each has his own values; the comparison can be made only among certain relations—of each human being to *his* god—and no longer among substances: there are only formal universals. Even as he asserts the existence of one God, Las Casas does not a priori privilege the Christian path to that God. Equality is no longer bought at the price of identity; it is not an absolute value that we are concerned with: each man has the right to approach god by the path that suits him. There is no longer a true God (ours), but a coexistence of possible universes: if someone considers it as true. . . . Las Casas has surreptitiously abandoned theology and practices here a kind of religious anthropology which, in his context, is indeed a reversal, for it certainly seems that the man who assumes a discourse on religion takes the first step toward the abandonment of religious discourse itself.

It will be even easier for him to apply this principle to the general case of alterity, and hence to show the relativity of the notion of "barbarism" (indeed he seems to be the first person to do so in the modern period): each of us is the other's barbarian, to become such a thing, one need only speak a language of which that other is ignorant: it is merely babble to his ears. "A man will be called a barbarian in comparison with another man because he is strange in his ways of speaking and because he pronounces the other's language badly. . . . According to Strabo, Book XIV, this was the main reason the Greeks called other peoples barbarians, that is, because they pronounced the Greek language improperly. But from this point of view, there is no man or race which is not barbarian in relation to another man or another race. As Saint Paul says of himself and of others in Corinthians I, 14:10–11: 'There are, it may be, so many kinds of voices in the world, and none of them is without signification. Therefore if I know not the meaning of the voice, I shall be unto him that speaketh a barbarian, and he that speaketh shall be a barbarian unto me.' Thus, just as we consider the peoples of the Indies barbarians, they judge us to be the same, because they do not understand us" (ibid., III, 254). Las Casas's radicalism denies him any middle way: either he asserts, as in the previous phase, the existence of a single true religion, which ineluctably leads him to assimilate the Indians to a previous (and hence inferior) phase of the Europeans' evolution; or else, as in his old age, he accepts the coexistence of ideals and values, and rejects any nonrelative meaning of the word *barbarian*, hence all evolution.

By asserting equality to the detriment of hierarchy, Las Casas returns to a classical Christian theme, as is suggested by the reference to Saint Paul, also quoted in the *Apologia*, and by this other quotation from Matthew: "Therefore all things whatsoever ye would that men should do to you, do ye even so to them" (7:12). "This is a thing," Las Casas comments, "that every man knows, grasps, and understands by the natural light that has been imparted to our minds" (*Apologia*, I). We have already encountered this theme of Christian egalitarianism, and at the same time we have seen how ambiguous it remained. All writers of this period laid claim to the spirit of Christianity. It is in the name of Christian morality that Catholics (and, for instance, the early Las Casas) regard the Indians as their equals, hence as like themselves, and try to assimilate them, to identify them with themselves. With the same references present to their minds Protestants, on the contrary, emphasize the differences and isolate their community from that of the natives, when they find themselves in contact (curiously, this position somewhat suggests that of Sepúlveda). In both cases, the other's identity is denied: either on the level of existence, as in the case of the Catholics; or on that of values, as in that of the Protestants; and it is absurd to ask which of the two parties goes farther down the path to the other's destruction. But it is still within Christian doctrine that the later Las Casas discovers that higher form of egalitarianism we are calling perspectivism, in which each man is put in relation to his own values, rather than being faced with a single ideal.

At the same time we must not forget the paradoxical character of this union of terms, "an egalitarianizing religion," which explains the complexity of Las Casas's position. This same paradox is illustrated by another approximately contemporary episode in the history of ideologies and of men: the debate on the finitude or the infinity of the world, and consequently on the existence of a hierarchy internal to the world. In his treatise in dialogue form, *De l'infinito universo e mondi*, written in 1584, Giordano Bruno, a Dominican like Las Casas, brings two conceptions into confrontation. One, which asserts the finite character of the world and its necessary hierarchy, is defended by the Aristotelian (whose name is not Sepúlveda); the other is Bruno's own. Just as Las Casas (and Saint Paul before him) had asserted the relativity of the positions from which human affairs are to be judged, Bruno does so for physical space, and rejects the existence of any privileged position. "Thus the earth no more than any other world is at the centre; and no points constitute definite determined poles of space for our earth, just as she herself is not a definite and determined pole to any other point of the ether or of the world space, and the same is true of all other bodies. From various points of view these may all be regarded either as centres, or as points on the circumference, as poles, or zeniths, and so forth. Thus the earth is not the center of the Universe; she is central only in relation to our own surrounding space." "For all who posit a body of infinite size ascribe to it neither centre nor boundary" (2).

Not only is the earth not the center of the universe, but no physical point is so; the very notion of center has a meaning only in relation to a particular point of view: center and periphery are notions as relative as those of civilization and barbarism (and even more so). "There is in the universe neither centre nor circumference, but, if you will, the whole is central, and every point also may be regarded as part of a circumference to some other central point" (5).

But the Inquisition, which had been indulgent with regard to Las Casas (not to mention Saint Paul!), does not accept Bruno's assertion: already excluded from the Dominican order when he writes these sentences, he will shortly thereafter be arrested, condemned for heresy, and burned publicly in 1600, in that last year of the century which had seen Las Casas's various combats. In his egalitarianism, his discourse, like Las Casas's, is both Christian and antireligious: but it is the former element that will be emphasized by Las Casas's judges, and the latter by Bruno's. This is perhaps because Las Casas's assertion bears on the world of men, for which, after all, different interpretations are conceivable; whereas Bruno's concerns the whole universe, which includes God —or, precisely, does not include Him, which comes down to sacrilege.

The fact remains that here is a phenomenon worthy of astonishment: no objection is made to Las Casas's strictly political endeavors, at the end of his life. Not that they are accepted as such, of course, but they are simply ignored; it is difficult to imagine, moreover, how such projects could be granted even a rudiment of realization, so utopian are they and so little account do they take of the interests engaged in the enterprise. The solution Las Casas favors is to preserve the ancient states, with their kings and governors; to preach the Gospel in them, but without the support of arms; if these local kings seek to form a kind of federation presided over by the king of Spain, to accept it; to profit by their wealth only if they propose such a thing themselves: "Supposing that the kings and natural lords of the Indians grant the King of Castile their rights over the mines of gold, silver, precious stones, salt and other resources" ("Letter to Fray Bartolomé Carranza de Miranda," August 1555). In other words, Las Casas suggests to the king of Spain that he renounce his transatlantic possessions, no more and no less. And the only war he envisages would be the one waged by the king against the Spanish conquistadors (for Las Casas suspects that the latter will not be willing to renounce their holdings of their own free will): "The means which offers fewest disadvantages, and the true remedy to all these evils, the one which in my opinion (and I believe in it as I believe in God) the kings of Castile, by divine precept, are obliged to apply, including by war if it cannot be done peacefully, and were they to risk therein all the temporal goods which they possess in the Indies, is to deliver the Indians from the diabolic power to which they are subject, to restore their first liberty to them, and to re-establish in their sovereignties all their kings and natural lords" (ibid.).

Thus Las Casas's "distributive" and "perspectivist" justice leads him to modify another element of his position: renouncing, in practice, the desire to assimilate the Indians, he chooses the neutral path: the Indians will decide their own future for themselves.

Now let us examine some actions in the perspective of the second axis we have set up to describe relations to the other, the axis of identification or assimilation. Vasco de Quiroga offers an original example of this latter. He is a member of the Second Audience of Mexico, i.e., belongs to the administrative government; later he becomes bishop of Michoacán. In many respects he resembles other lay or religious humanists who will try, in Mexico, to protect the Indians against the conquistadors' excesses; but he stands apart from them on one point: his attitude is assimilationist, but the ideal to which he seeks to assimilate the Indians is not incarnated by himself or by contemporary Spain; he assimilates them, in short, to a third party. Vasco de Quiroga has a mind formed by his reading: of the Christian Scriptures first of all, but also of Lucian's famous *Saturnales*, which detail the myth of the golden age; finally, and above all, of Thomas More's *Utopia*. In short, Vasco de Quiroga asserts that the Spaniards belong to a decadent phase of history, whereas the Indians resemble the first apostles and the characters of Lucian's poem (even if elsewhere Vasco de Quiroga is just as likely to censure their faults): "They have the same customs and manners, the same quality, simplicity, goodness, obedience and humility, the same festivities, games, pleasures, drinking, idling, pastimes, and nudity, and lacked any but the poorest of household goods nor had any desire for better, and had the same clothing, footwear and food, all such as was provided free by the fertility of the soil and almost without labor, care or seeking on their part" ("Informacion en derecho," pp. 81ff).

Here we can see that Vasco de Quiroga, despite his experience "in the field," had not taken his knowledge of the Indians very far: like Columbus or like Las Casas, relying on a few superficial resemblances, he sees them not as they are but as he would like them to be, a variant of Lucian's characters. However, matters are somewhat more complex, for this idealizing vision stops halfway: the Indians are indeed an incarnation of Vasco de Quiroga's idyllic vision, but they are far from perfection. Thus it is he who, by a deliberate action taken upon them, will transform this promise into an ideal society. This is why, unlike Las Casas, it is not to the king that he will make his representations but to the Indians themselves. To this effect he will resort to the teachings of a sage: a social thinker, Thomas More, has already found, in his *Utopia*, the ideal forms suitable to the life of such persons; significantly, More himself had been inspired by the first enthusiastic accounts of the New World (we have here a fascinating play of mirrors, in which the misunderstandings of interpretation motivate the transformation of society). All that remains to be done is to promote this project into a reality. Vasco de Quiroga will organize two villages according to utopian prescriptions—one near Mexico City, the other in Michoacán, both called Santa Fe—which illustrate both his philanthropic spirit and the threatening principles of the utopian state. The basic social unit is the extended family, consisting of ten or twelve adult couples related to one another, under the orders of a *padre de familia;* the *padres* in their turn elect the village chief. There are no servants and labor is obligatory, for men as for women, but cannot exceed six hours a day. All must alternate work in the fields with artisanal work at home; the profits of their production are to be divided equitably, according to the needs of each. Medical care, apprenticeship (spiritual as well as manual) are free and obligatory; luxury objects and activities are prohibited, and it is even forbidden to wear dyed clothes. The village "hospitals" are the only owners of goods, and they have the right to expel wrongdoers —the refractory, the drunk, or the idle (it is true that reality will not warrant such a program).

Vasco de Quiroga has no doubt as to the superiority of this mode of life, and believes that all means are justified to achieve it: thus he will be—with Sepúlveda and against Las Casas—a defender of "just wars" against the Indians and of the distribution of the Indians into feudal *encomiendas.* This will not keep him, on the other hand, from acting as a veritable defender of the Indians against the claims of the Spanish colonists, and it is certain that his villages enjoy a great popularity among the Indians.

Vasco de Quiroga illustrates an unconditional though original assimilationism. Examples of the converse conduct—of identification with Indian culture and society—are much rarer (whereas cases of identification in the other direction abound: La Malinche was one). The purest example is that of Gonzalo Guerrero. After being shipwrecked off the coast of Mexico in 1511, he lands, with several other Spaniards, on the Yucatán coast. His companions die, all except Aguilar, Cortés's future interpreter, who is sold as a slave in the interior. The bishop of Yucatán, Diego de Landa, tells the rest of the story: "Since he understood the language Guerrero went to Chectemal, which is the Salamanca of Yucatán, and there he was received by a lord named Nachancan, who placed him in command of the affairs of war. He was very skilled at this and many times defeated his masters' enemies; he also showed the Indians how to fight, teaching them how to build fortresses and bastions. In this manner, and by behaving like an Indian, he built up a great reputation for himself, and they married him to a very high-ranking lady by whom he had children. For this reason he, unlike Aguilar, never made any attempt to escape. On the contrary, he tattooed his body, grew his hair long, and pierced his ears, so as to wear earrings like the Indians; and it is possible that he also became an idolater like them" (3).

Here we are faced with a complete identification: Guerrero has adopted the Indians' language and customs, religion and manners. Hence we must not be surprised that he refuses to rejoin Cortés's troops when the latter lands in Yucatán, and that he gives as the reason for this refusal, according to Bernal Díaz, his very integration into the Indian culture: "They look on me as a *cacique* here, and a captain in time of war. Go, and God's blessings be with you. But my face is tattooed and my ears are pierced. What would the Spaniards say if they saw me like this? And look how handsome these children of mine are!" (27) It is believed that Guerrero did not even abide by this position of neutrality and reserve, but that he fought against the conquistadors' armies at the head of the Yucatán forces; he was killed, according to Oviedo (II, 32, 2), in 1528, by Montejo's lieutenant, Alonso de Avila, in a battle against the cacique of Chectemal.

Curious in that it illustrates one of the possible variants in relation to the other, Guerrero's case does not have much historical and political importance (in this, too, he is quite the contrary of La Malinche): his example was not followed and it is clear today that it could not be, for in no way did it correspond to the relation of forces on the scene. It is only three hundred years later, upon the independence of Mexico, that we shall see—but in entirely different circumstances—certain Creoles siding with the Indians against the Spaniards.

A more interesting, because more complex, example in the submission of/to the Indians is that of the conquistador Albar Nuñez Cabeza de Vaca. His fate is extraordinary. He sets out for Florida in an expedition headed by Panfilo de Narvaez, whom we have already encountered in other circumstances. Shipwreck, disastrous ventures, calamities of all kinds: the result is that Cabeza de Vaca and several of his companions find themselves obliged to live among the Indians, and to live like them. They then undertake a long journey (on foot), reaching Mexico City only eight years after their arrival in Florida. Cabeza de Vaca returns to Spain only to leave again some years later, this time as leader of a new expedition to what is now Paraguay. This venture ends badly too, but for other reasons: in conflict with his subordinates, Cabeza de Vaca is stripped of his power and possessions and sent back in chains to Spain. A long trial follows, which also goes against him; but he leaves two accounts, one devoted to each of his journeys.

In his judgments of the Indians, Cabeza de Vaca does not present any great originality: his position is quite close to that of Las Casas (of before 1550). He esteems them and wishes them no harm; if there is to be evangelization, it must be conducted without violence: "Clearly, to bring all these people to Christianity and subjection to Your Imperial Majesty, they must be won by kindness, the only certain way" (I, 32). He makes this reflection when he is alone among the Indians; but as governor of Río de la Plata he has not forgotten the lesson and tries to put it into effect in his relations with the Indians; this is doubtless one of the reasons for the conflict with the other Spaniards. But this "kindness" nonetheless does not make him forget the goal he seeks, and he declares in all simplicity, during the Florida voyage: "These are the most obedient people we had found anywhere, also in general the best looking" (I, 30), or again: "The people are well disposed, serving such Christians as are their friends with great good will" (I, 34). As a matter of fact he does not exclude a recourse to arms, and reports in detail the Indians' war methods, "to impart a knowledge of usages and artifices, which would be of value to those who might sometime in the future find themselves among these people" (I, 25); "these people" were subsequently exterminated without leaving a trace. In short, he is never far from the *Requerimiento*, which promises peace in cases where the Indians agree to submit, and war if they refuse (see, for instance, I, 35).

Cabeza de Vaca differs from Las Casas not only in that, like Vasco de Quiroga, he acts on the Indians rather than at the Spanish court, but also by his precise and direct knowledge of their way of life. His narrative contains a remarkable description of the countries and peoples he discovers, precious details concerning the Indians' material and spiritual culture. This is no accident; on several occasions he makes his concern explicit: when he chooses a route, "We chose this course to find out more about the country, so that should God our Lord please to lead any one of us to the land of Christians, we might carry information of it with us" (I, 28); when he reports a technique, it is "because their method of cooking is so novel and strange, I must describe it" (I,

30); if he is interested in any practice, it is "to indulge the curiosity of human beings about each other" (I, 25).

But it is obviously on the level of a (potential) identification that Cabeza de Vaca's example is most interesting. In order to survive, he is obliged to carry on two trades; the first is that of a peddler: for nearly six years, he travels back and forth between the interior and the coast, carrying objects indispensable to either place: food, medicaments, seashells, animal hides, reeds for arrows, glue. "This occupation suited me; I could travel where I wished, was not obliged to work, and was not a slave. Wherever I went, the Indians treated me honorably and gave me food, because they liked my commodities. . . . This served my principal purpose, which all the while was to determine an eventual road out of the country" (I, 16).

His second trade is more interesting still: he becomes a healer or, if you will, a shaman. This is not a deliberate choice; but after certain vicissitudes, the Indians decide that Cabeza de Vaca and his Christian companions can cure the sick, and ask them to intervene. At first the Spaniards resist, declaring themselves to be incompetent; but since the Indians then cut off their food supply, they finally consent. The practices they perform have a double inspiration: on the one hand, they observe the native healers and imitate them: they must lay on hands, breathe on the sick, bleed, and cauterize them with coals. Then, for greater security, they recite Christian prayers. "Our method was to bless the sick, breathe upon them, recite a *Pater Noster* and *Ave Maria*, and pray earnestly to God our Lord for their recovery" (I, 15). According to Cabeza de Vaca's narrative, these interventions are always crowned with success, and he even manages, on one occasion, to resuscitate a dead man.

Cabeza de Vaca adopts the trades of the natives, dresses as they do (or goes naked like them), eats what they eat. Yet the identification is never complete: there is a "European" justification which makes the peddler's trade agreeable to him, and there are Christian prayers in his healer's arts. At no moment does he forget his own cultural identity, and this resolution sustains him in the most difficult ordeals: "My only solace in these labors was to think of the sufferings of our Redeemer, Jesus Christ, and the blood He shed for me. How much worse must have been His torment from the thorns than mine were here!" (I, 22). Nor does he ever forget his goal, which is to escape and rejoin his own people: "I can say for myself that I had always trusted His Providence and that He would lead me out of my captivity; I constantly expressed this to my companions" (I, 22). Despite his extreme integration into Indian society, he experiences an equally extreme joy at meeting other Spaniards: "This was a day of as great joy as we ever knew" (I, 17). The very fact of writing a narrative of his life clearly indicates his solidarity with European culture.

Hence Cabeza de Vaca is nothing like a Guerrero, and we cannot imagine him leading Indian armies against the Spaniards or taking an Indian wife and begetting half-caste children. Further, as soon as he regains "civilization" (Spanish civilization, to be sure) in Mexico, he boards a ship to return to Spain; he will never return to Florida, Texas, or northern Mexico. And yet this extended sojourn does not fail to leave certain traces upon him, as we notice particularly in the narrative of the end of his journey. He has reached the first Spanish posts, accompanied by friendly Indians; he encourages these people to renounce any hostile action, and assures them that the Christians will do them no harm. But this was to underestimate the latter's greed and their desire to acquire slaves; hence Cabeza de Vaca finds himself deceived by his own coreligionists. "We sought to ensure the freedom of the Indians, and at the moment when we believed we had achieved it, the contrary occurred. They [the Christians] had in fact determined to attack the Indians whom we had sent away reassured as to their peaceful intentions. They took us through forests and wastes so we would not communicate with the natives and would neither see nor learn of their crafty scheme. Thus we often misjudge the motives of men; we thought we had effected the Indians' liberty where the Christians were but poising to pounce. For two days we wandered lost in the woods without water or trail. Seven of our men perished and a great number of friendly Indians, whom the Christians had with them, did not reach the place where there was water, which we found the second night" (I, 34). Here Cabeza de Vaca's mental universe seems to vacillate, his uncertainty as to the referents of his personal pronouns contributing to the effect; there are no longer two parties, we (the Christians) and they (the Indians), but indeed three: the Christians, the Indians, and "we." But who is this "we," external to both worlds, though having experienced them both from within?

Alongside this blurring of identity, we also observe, as might be expected, partial identifications which are much better controlled. Notably those of the Franciscan monks who, without ever renouncing their religious ideal or their evangelizing goal, readily adopt the Indians' way of life; as a matter of fact, the one serves the other: the initial movement of identification facilitates the assimilation in depth. "When the president of the second Audience asked them the reason why they liked these friars better than the others, the Indians answered 'because these go about poorly dressed and barefoot just like us; they eat what we eat, they settle among us, and their intercourse with us is gentle' " (Motolinia, III, 4). We find the same image in the *Dialogues* between Christian and Indian priests, narrated by the ancient Mexicans: the first word the latter put in the Franciscans' mouths is an assertion of resemblance: "Let us not disconcert you as to something, take care lest you see us as something superior, indeed, we are only your peers, likewise we are only common people, furthermore, we are men, such as you are, we are surely not gods. We are also inhabitants of the earth, we also drink, we also eat, we also die of cold, we are also overwhelmed by heat, we are also mortal, we also can be destroyed" (I, 28–36).

Someone like Cabeza de Vaca goes quite far along the path of identification, and he knows his Indians very well. But as has been said, there is no relation of implication between these two features. Proof of this would be afforded, if we needed such a thing, by the example of Diego de Landa. This Franciscan owes his fame to a double gesture, decisive for our knowledge of Mayan history. He is, on the one hand, the author of the *Relación de las cosas de Yucatán,* the most important document we have concerning the Mayan past; on the other hand, he is the instigator of several public autos-da-fé in which all the Mayan books in existence at the time will be burned, as Landa reports in the course of his own *Relación:* "We found a great number of these books in Indian characters, and because they contained nothing but superstition and the Devil's falsehoods, we burned them all; and this they felt most bitterly and it caused them great grief" (41).

As a matter of fact, this paradox of a man who both burns and writes books is not a real one: it vanishes if we note that Landa rejects the slightest identification with the Indians and demands on the contrary their assimilation to the Christian religion, but at the same time he is interested in knowing about these Indians. There is in fact a succession in his actions. Landa had sojourned in Yucatán from 1549 to 1562, the year of the auto-da-fé described. His actions, which include not only the destruction of books but also certain punishments for

Indian "heretics" imprisoned, flogged, and even executed on his orders, caused him to be recalled to Spain for prosecution (he justified his use of torture with regard to the Indians by claiming that otherwise it would have been impossible to obtain any information whatever). He was initially sentenced by the Council of the Indies, but subsequently acquitted by a special commission and sent back to Yucatán, this time with the more important powers of a bishop. It is while he was in Spain, in 1566, that he wrote his book, in part to defend himself against the accusations brought against him. We see here the complete separation of the two functions: the assimilator acts in Yucatán; the scholar writes books in Spain.

Other religious figures of the period have combined these two features: at the same time that they seek to convert the Indians to the Christian religion, they also describe the Indians' history, their customs, their religion, and thereby contribute to a knowledge of them; but none of these figures commits the excesses of a Landa, and all regret that the manuscripts were burned. They form one of the two major groups of authors to whom we owe what knowledge we now have concerning ancient Mexico; among them are representatives of the various religious orders, Franciscans, Dominicans, Jesuits. The other group is constituted by Indian or half-caste authors who have learned Spanish or else use the Latin alphabet to write in Nahuatl: these are Muñoz Camargo, Alva Ixtlilxochitl, Bautista Pomar, Alvarado Tezozomoc, and others (certain texts are anonymous). Together they produce an incomparable group of documents, richer than those we possess concerning any other traditional society.

Two exceptional figures dominate the group of works devoted to the Indians, and deserve to be examined in greater detail: they are Diego Durán and Bernardino de Sahagún.

Durán, or the Hybridization of Cultures

W<small>E FIND</small> a doubling of personality achieved in a much more complex way by the author of one of the most successful descriptions of the pre-Columbian world, the Dominican Diego Durán. Born in Spain around 1537, unlike many other leading figures of this period he comes to live in Mexico at the age of five or six, and hence will be "formed" in the New World. The result of this experience will be an understanding of Indian culture from within unequaled in the sixteenth century. Shortly before his death (in 1588), Durán will write between 1576 and 1581 a *Historia de las Indias de Nueva España y Islas de la Tierra Firme* (an incoherent title doubtless added to his book by someone else), the first two parts dealing with the Aztecs' religion and the third with their history. These works will not be published until the nineteenth century.

Durán's ambivalence is more complex both because his life does not consist of alternate sojourns in Spain and in Mexico, and because his knowledge of Indian culture is much more intimate; his is also a much more dramatic position. On the one hand, there is the convinced Christian, the committed evangelizer; this person has decided that the conversion of the Indians requires a better knowledge of their ancient religion. More precisely, Durán links the two following inferences: to impose the Christian religion, all trace of the pagan one must be uprooted; to eliminate paganism successfully, it must first of all be known thoroughly. "[The Indians] will never find God until the roots have been torn out, together with that which smacks of the ancestral religion. If we are trying earnestly to remove the memory of Amalech, we shall never succeed until we fully understand the ancient religion" (I, "Introduction"). Durán's entire explicit motivation is in these two implications, which he never tires of repeating throughout his work on the Aztec religion, from (literally) the first paragraph of the first part to the last of the second; he sees this as the sole reason which has led him to undertake such a labor: "My entire purpose was and is that of warning our priests of the mysteries and idolatrous practices of these people, so that they may be aware of and wakeful for some survivals of ancient heathen beliefs which might still linger" (I, 19).

For the idolatries to be uprooted, they must first be recognizable: Durán has no doubt on this score. Yet the clergy of the period, those assuming responsibility for evangelization, are ignorant. Priests are content with a superficial knowledge of the language (two expressions are enough for them, Durán complains; "what is your name for that?" and "it will come" I, 8); yet without possessing the language thoroughly, the culture cannot be understood, and one will be seduced into fallacious interpretations, guided by those two perfidious counselors, analogy and wishful thinking. Durán tells how a certain form of tonsure linked to pagan practices was taken for homage to the monks because it resembled their own: "I have tried to believe their explanation, given in such holy simplicity, and I must persuade myself that it is [the result of] extreme ignorance on their part and lack of understanding of the language of the Indians" (I, 5). This is why Durán blames those who, like Diego de Landa or Juan de Zumarraga, first bishop of Mexico, have burned the ancient books: they have made the work of evangelization still more difficult: "Those who with fervent zeal (though with little prudence) in the beginning burned and destroyed all the ancient Indian pictographic documents were mistaken. They left us without a light to guide us—to the point that the Indians worship idols in our presence, and we understand nothing of what goes on in their dances, in their marketplaces, in their bath-houses, in the songs they chant (when they lament their ancient gods and lords), in their repasts and banquets; these things mean nothing to us" (I, "Introduction").

There is a dispute here, and some—who had heard of Durán's labors—did not hesitate to blame him for contributing to a result precisely contrary to the one to which he aspired: that is, wakening the old superstitions by producing so detailed an inventory of them. Durán replies that the vestiges of the old religion are indeed present everywhere (but invisible to the ignorant), and that the Indians have no need of his labors in order to encounter them. Yet if such had been the case, "I would be the first to cast these things into the fire, so that such an abominable religion would fall into oblivion" (R, 411). Hence he is not against the principle of the autos-da-fé, but simply doubts that they are the appropriate means to combat paganism: more is lost by them, perhaps, than is gained. This is why he persists in his work with such passion: "Once my book is published, no one will be able to feign ignorance" (I, 19).

Yet once the idolatry is known, one must not rest until it is altogether eliminated: such is Durán's second point, which is interesting precisely for its radical character. Conversion must be total: no individual, no fraction of the individual, no practice, however trivial it may seem, must escape. One must not be content, he says, with an all too frequent acceptance of the external rites of Christianity, "as monkeys would perform them" (I, 17): "We salve our consciences with the appearance of 'Christians' which the Indians feign for us" (I, 8). Nor must one rejoice over the conversion of the majority: a single black sheep can infect the entire flock. "Though not all the people follow these customs, it is enough that there is a single man with the ancient ideas in a village to do much harm" (I, 3). And above all, one must not assume that it is enough to abide by the essentials: the slightest reminiscence of the old religion can entirely pervert the new (and only true) worship. "Let [God's servant] not consider them things of little concern! If he does not fight against them, reprehend them, showing wrath and grief over them, the natives become accustomed [to our lenience] and to things of more weight and gravity . . . Some will say that these things are of little importance. But I say that it is a subtle form of idolatry, besides being an ancient custom" (I, 7). "If any recollection of the ancient religion exists among the natives, it is necessary that it be uprooted" (I, 17).

In for a penny, in for a pound: anyone who allows the slightest trace of paganism to subsist betrays the very spirit of the Christian religion. "Let [our ministers] in their laxity and negligence, in their idleness and recreation, not permit the Indians to practice even small things, such as the shearing of the children's heads, the feathering with plumes of wild fowl, nor the smearing of rubber upon their heads or on their foreheads, nor the smearing with pitch, nor the anointing with holy bitumen" (I, 5). In his zeal, Durán tracks down every vestige of idolatry, even in the Indians' dreams. "[The natives] should be examined [in confession] regarding what they dream; in all of this there may be reminiscences of pagan times. In dealing with these things it would be good to ask them [in confession] 'What do you dream?' and not try to skim over it like a cat walking on hot coals. Our preaching should be dedicated to condemning and abominating all this" (I, 13).

What angers Durán more than anything else is that the Indians manage to insert segments of their old religion into the very heart of Christian religious practices. Syncretism is a sacrilege, and it is in this specific battle that Durán's work is to serve: "This is our principal weapon: to warn them [the clergy] of the confusion that may exist between our own feasts and those [of the Indians]. These, pretending to celebrate the festivities of our God and of the Saints, insert, mix, and celebrate those of their gods when they fall on the same day. And they introduce their ancient rites in our ceremonies" (I, 2). If on a certain Christian holiday the Indians dance in a certain way, look closely, that is a way of worshiping their gods, under the very noses of the Spanish priests. If a certain chant is combined with the office for the dead, it is still the demons who are being celebrated. If flowers and ears of corn are offered for the Nativity of Our Lady, it is because through her an ancient pagan goddess is being addressed. "On such days I have heard chants in honor of God and of the Saint during the festivities, mixed with the ancient metaphors which only the devil, their teacher, understands" (II, 3). Durán even wonders if those who attend mass in the Cathedral of Mexico do not do so in reality to be able to worship the old gods, because their stone images have been used to build this Christian temple: the columns of the cathedral are actually standing on the plumed serpent!

If religious syncretism is the most scandalous form of the survival of idolatries, other forms are no less reprehensible, and the danger lurks in their very multiplicity. In a strongly hierarchized, codified, and ritualized society like that of the Aztecs, everything is linked, somehow, to religion: Durán is not mistaken after all. Though he may take pleasure in certain theatrical performances which occur in the city, he nonetheless perceives their pagan character: "All these native farces were highly amusing and pleasant, but were not acted out without pagan meaning" (I, 6). To go to the market, to give banquets, to eat such and such food (for example barkless dogs), to get drunk, to take baths: all these actions have a religious signification and must be eliminated! And Durán, who will not burn books because he doubts the effectiveness of such a gesture, does not hesitate to destroy objects whose more or less remote connection with the ancient worship he perceives: "I myself have torn down some bath-houses in order to cause fear, especially because these were bath-houses built in the ancient times" (I, 19). Some objected that these were only customs and not superstitions, or decorations and not pagan images; one Indian said to him on one occasion, in reply to his reproaches, that "this practice was not due to ancient belief, but was simply their way of doing things" (I, 20); occasionally, and reluctantly, Durán accepts this argument, but in his heart of hearts he prefers the radical consequences of his intransigent position: if the whole of Aztec culture is impregnated with the old religious values, then let it vanish from the face of the earth. "Heathenism and idolatry are present everywhere: in sowing, in reaping, in storing grain, even in plowing the earth and in building houses; in wakes and funerals, in weddings and births . . ." (I, "Introduction"). "I would like to see all ancient customs disappear and fall into oblivion" (I, 20): all!

On this point, Durán is not expressing the opinion of all Spanish priests in Mexico; he takes one side in a conflict which sets two policies in opposition with regard to the Indians, by and large that of the Dominicans against that of the Franciscans. The Dominicans are rigorists: faith is not to be bargained for, conversion must be total, even if this implies a transformation of every aspect of the converts' lives. The Franciscans are closer to what we should call realists: either they are actually unaware of the survivals of idolatry among the Indians or they have decided to pay no attention to them; in either case they recoil before the enormity of the task (total conversion), and adapt themselves to the present situation, however imperfect. This policy, which will be the one to prevail, turns out to be effective; but it is true that Mexican Christianity still bears the traces of syncretism.

Durán of course chooses the rigorist party, and addresses bitter reproaches to his adversaries: "There have been friars who have stated that it is not necessary to force the people to observe the feasts that fall within the week, but I consider this improper and wrong since they are Christians and should know better" (I, 17). A holy wrath seethes in his imprecations when he demands that severe punishments be inflicted on his colleagues, as guilty in his eyes as the heretics, since they do not maintain the purity of his religion. "The faults [of our clergy] which I have described should be judged as cases for the Inquisition, and ministers who behave in this manner should be suspended perpetually" (I, 4). But the other side exclaims just as loudly, and Durán complains of the injunctions by which he is forced to abide, compelling him to ignore the old idolatries; no doubt this is one of the reasons why Durán's work remained unpublished and virtually unread for three hundred years.

This is one aspect of Durán: a rigid, intransigent Christian, defender of religious purity. Hence it is with some surprise that we find him quite willing to indulge in analogy and comparison in order to make the Mexican realities intelligible to his presumably European reader; of course there is nothing reprehensible in this, but for someone who makes a profession of the vigilant maintenance of differences, he certainly sees many resemblances: traitors are punished the same way in both cultures, and the punishments involve the same feeling of shame; the tribe takes the name of its leader, the family that of its head, exactly as among us. They subdivide the country into regions, as in Spain, and their religious hierarchy resembles our own. Their priests' vestments resemble our chasubles; their dances, our saraband. They have the same sayings and the same kind of epic narratives. When they play games, they speak and blaspheme exactly as Spaniards do, and moreover their game *alquerque* is astonishingly like chess: in both countries the pieces are black and white. . . .

Some of these analogies strike us as rather forced; but the reader's surprise turns into stupefaction when he discovers that Durán's comparisons are especially abundant in the religious realm! It is no longer the Indians who are more or less consciously trying to mingle pagan elements with Christian rites; it is Durán himself who discovers, in the heart of the ancient pagan rites as they were practiced before the conquest, certain Christian elements, whose number ends by becoming disconcerting. "The ancient beliefs are still so numerous, so complex, so similar to our own in many cases, that one overlays the other. . . . [They] always had their own sacraments and a divine cult which in many ways coincides with our own religion, as we shall see during the course of this work" (I, "Introduction").

And indeed we see astounding things! Perhaps we supposed that Easter was a specifically Christian feast? But for the feast of Tezcatlipoca, the temple is covered with flowers as with us on Maundy Thursday. And the offerings to Tlaloc are "exactly" like those we make on Good Friday. As for the new fire, lit every fifty-two years, it is like the candles lit at Easter. . . . The sacrifice in honor of Chicomecoatl reminds him of another Christian feast: "It almost seemed Christmas Eve" (I, 14), because the crowd keeps watch over the fires late into the night! Durán has no difficulty, moreover, in discovering the essential rites of the Christian religion "exactly" reproduced in the Aztec ritual: the great drum beaten at sunset is like the bells of the *Ave Maria;* the Aztec purification by water is like confession; penances are the same in both religions, and also the mendicant priests. Or rather, no, the Aztec ablutions are like baptism: water is used in both: "The water was held to be the purifier of sin. In this the Indians were not too far from the truth, since in the substance of the water God placed the Sacrament of Baptism by which we are cleansed of original sin" (I, 19). And if all this does not suffice, it will be discovered that Tezcatlipoca—who has many incarnations, reduced for this occasion to three—is nothing but a version of the Trinity: "[The people] revered the Father, the Son, and the Holy Ghost, and called them Tota, Topiltzin and Yolometl. These words mean Our Father, Our Son, and the Heart of Both, honoring each one separately and all three as a unity. Here we see evidence that these people knew something about the Trinity" (I, 8).

What we see above all is that Durán manages to discover resemblances where the very idolaters he is attacking had never dared seek them: according to him, one could merely obey the ancient religion, with a few modifications, since it is the same as the new one! Durán called in the Inquisition to pronounce anathema upon those who mingled the two rites, or even upon those professionals of Christian worship who were not sufficiently severe with regard to the Aztec; but what judgment would have been brought against him if it had been known that confession and baptism, Christmas and Easter, and even the Trinity were in his eyes no different from the rites and conceptions of the Aztec pagans? What seemed to Durán the greatest infamy— religious syncretism—characterized his own outlook.

For so many resemblances, there are only two possible explanations. According to the first, which Durán prefers, if the Aztec rites so powerfully suggest those of the Christians, it is because the Aztecs had already received, in a more remote past, a Christian teaching: "I interrogated the Indians regarding their ancient preachers. . . . In reality they were Catholic. When I realized the knowledge the Indians had regarding the Beatitudes of Eternal Rest and the holy life that must be lived on earth in order to obtain these things, I was amazed. However, all of this was mixed with their idolatry, bloody and abominable, and it tarnished the good. I simply mention these things because I believe there actually was an evangelist in this land who left the natives this information" (I, 9).

Durán does not stop at this general assertion but specifies his belief: the preacher in question was Saint Thomas, and his memory is preserved in the Aztec narratives under the features of Topiltzin, which is merely another name for Quetzalcoatl. The reason for this identification is another resemblance discerned by Durán: "Since the natives were also God's creatures, rational and capable of salvation, He cannot have left them without a preacher of the Gospel. And if this is true, that preacher was Topiltzin, who came to this land. According to the story, he was a sculptor who carved admirable images in stone. We read that the glorious apostle Saint Thomas was a master craftsman in the same art" (I, 1). Durán would have been delighted to find somewhat more tangible proofs of the evangelizer's sojourn than these analogies; sometimes he has the impression he is about to discover them, but at the last moment they slip between his fingers. He is told of a cross carved into the mountainside; unfortunately no one remembers where it is to be found. He also hears that the Indians in one village possessed a book written in characters they did not understand. He hurries there, only to learn that the book was burned some years before: "I was sorry to hear this, because the manuscript could have shed light on our suspicion that it might have been the Holy Gospel in Hebrew. Vehemently I reprehended those who had had the book burned" (I, 1). This lack of final proof does not keep Durán from choosing this title for the chapter devoted to Quetzalcoatl: "Which treats of the god known as Quetzalcoatl, deity of the Cholultecs, highly venerated and held in awe by them. [He was the] father of the Toltecs and of the Spaniards, inasmuch as he predicted the coming of the latter" (I, 6).

Thus Quetzalcoatl was the common father of the Toltecs and the Spaniards! Sometimes however a terrible doubt seizes Durán's mind, and makes him see that another explanation of all these resemblances is quite as likely. "In many cases the Christian religion and the heathen ways found a common ground. And though I am convinced (owing to many agreements I have discovered which give me reason to believe thus) that in this land there were preachers [of Christianity], [my arguments] are not well enough established to permit us to use them as definitive proofs. . . . One cannot give a definite opinion. On the other hand, one *can* say that the devil had persuaded and instructed them, stealing from and imitating the Divine Cult so that *he* be honored as a god; for everything was a mixture of a thousand heathen beliefs, deceits and imperfections" (I, 16). "Either (as I have stated) our Holy Christian Religion was known in this land, or the devil our cursed adversary forced the Indians to imitate the ceremonies of the Christian Catholic religion in his own service and cult, being thus adored and served" (I, 3).

What a dreadful choice! One is flung from one extreme to the other: either an especially perfidious diabolical ruse, or else an exceptional divine grace. . . . Durán does not withstand the tension of such doubts for long, and at the period when he is writing his history—in 1580–81—he has made his decision: the Aztecs are none other than one of the lost tribes of Israel. The first chapter of his history opens with this assertion: "Because of their nature we could almost affirm that they are Jews and Hebrew people, and I believe that I would not be committing a great error if I were to state this fact, considering their way of life, their ceremonies, their rites and superstitions, their omens and false dealings, so related to and characteristic of those of the Jews" (III, 1). The proofs of this common origin are still no more than analogies: both make a long journey, multiply greatly, have had a prophet, have known earthquakes, have received the divine manna, derive from the meeting of heaven and earth, and know human sacrifice (for Durán a resemblance can be explained only by circulation). And if in his book on religion Durán alternated comparisons with the Christians and comparisons with the Jews, in his history he discusses practically nothing but resemblances between Aztec rites and Jewish rites.

Most likely Durán himself came from a family of converted Jews. We may see this as the reason for the zeal with which he attaches himself to resemblances while neglecting differences: he must have already, and more or less consciously, performed an activity of this sort in an effort to reconcile the two religions, Jewish and Christian. Perhaps he was already predisposed toward cultural hybridization; in any case, the confrontation he represents between the Indian civilization and the European makes him the most accomplished cultural hybrid of the sixteenth century.

The meeting of these two divergent civilizations and the necessity of their coexistence can only introduce disparity into the very heart of every subject, whether Spaniard or Aztec. Durán is chiefly sensitive to the mutation the Indians are undergoing. At the end of the war of conquest, during the siege of Mexico, he already shows the division reigning among the Aztecs: "The land was troubled and divided against itself. Some wished to make peace with the Spaniards, while others wanted war. Some wished to destroy the strangers and were preparing their warlike equipment and building walls and dikes. But others remained passive, asking only for peace, quiet, and the preservation of their lives and possessions" (III, 76). Fifty years later, in the period when he is writing his books, the division is still as strong, even if its object is no longer military but religious; the Indians know this too. Durán tells how he had discovered an Indian persisting in his pagan practices: "I reprehended him for the foolish thing he had done, and he answered, 'Father, do not be astonished; we are still *nepantla.*' Although I understood what that metaphorical word means, that is to say 'in the middle,' I insisted that he tell me which 'in the middle' he referred to. The native told me that since the people were not yet well rooted in the Faith, I should not marvel at the fact that they were neither fish nor fowl; they were governed by neither one religion nor the other. Or, better said, they believed in God and also followed their ancient heathen rites and customs" (III, 3). But the Spaniards, too, cannot escape this confrontation unscathed, and Durán unwittingly draws what is also his own portrait, or rather, writes the allegory of his destiny.

His own hybridization is manifested in several ways. The most obvious, but perhaps the most superficial as well, is that he shares in the Indians' way of life, their privations, their difficulties; this was, according to him, the lot of many missionaries: "They have become beasts with the beasts, Indians with the Indians, barbarians with the barbarians, men estranged from our own ways, nation, and order." But this is the price that must be paid in order to understand: "Those who speak as outsiders, those who have never wished to take part in these affairs, understand little about such things" (II, 3). In this life, he will accept and even adopt certain kinds of conduct whose idolatrous character he suspects, either because he prefers to let the doubt remain, as in the case of those probably religious chants for which he cannot repress his admiration: "I have heard these lays sung many a time at public dances, and even though they were in honor of their native lords,

I was elated to hear such high praise and notable feats . . . I have seen these [songs] danced occasionally with religious chants, and they are so sad that I was filled with melancholy and woe" (I, 21); or because he despairs of changing his flock, as when he discovers that the flowers replacing the candles in a Christian ceremony are in reality a reminiscence of Tezcatlipoca: "I see these things, but I am silent, since I realize that everyone feigns ignorance. So I pick up my staff of flowers like the rest and walk along" (I, 4).

Other forms of cultural hybridization are less conscious and indeed more important. First of all, Durán is one of the rare individuals who really understand both cultures—or, if you will, who is capable of translating the signs of the one into the signs of the other; thereby his work is the summit of sixteenth-century Spanish scholarship with regard to the Indians. He himself has left testimony as to the difficulties encountered by the practice of translation. "All the native lays are interwoven with such obscure metaphors that there is hardly a man who can understand them unless they are studied in a very special way and explained so as to penetrate their meaning. For this reason I have intentionally set myself to listen with much attention to what is sung; and while the words and terms of the metaphors seem nonsense to me, afterward, having discussed and conferred [with the natives, I can see that] they seem to be admirable sentences, both in the divine things composed today and in the worldly songs" (I, 21). Here we see how knowledge involves a value judgment: having understood, Durán cannot help admiring the Aztec texts, although they concern divine—i.e., idolatrous—matters.

The result of this understanding is the inestimable Durán's text on the Aztec religion—inestimable because it is virtually the only one which is not content to describe from outside, even with good will and attention, but which at least attempts to understand the motive of the actions described. "His [Tezcatlipoca's] head was encircled with a band of burnished gold, ending in a golden ear painted with fumes or puffs of smoke": that is the description, valuable of course, but in itself incomprehensible. The explanation, or rather the current association, follows immediately after: "This meant that he listened to the prayers and requests of wretches and sinners" (I, 4). Or again: "When the priest killed these two noblewomen, as an exception [to the usual custom], to indicate that they died virgins, their legs were crossed one upon the other and their hands extended, as was the custom" (I, 16):

the indication of purpose permits an understanding of the orientation of the Aztecs' symbolic evocations. Perhaps everything is not accurate in Durán's speculations, but at least he has the virtue of looking for the answers.

Another fascinating manifestation of cultural hybridization can be perceived in the development of the point of view from which Durán's work is written. In his book on religion, as we have seen, the two points of view, Aztec and Spanish, are distinguished, even if corruptions occur from one to the other; Durán's ultimate syncretism nonetheless jeopardized any distinct attributions. The historical work, posterior to the religious one, is even more complex in this regard. At first glance though, Durán's intention is simple enough: that of a translator, in the most limited sense of the word. He has before his eyes, he tells us, a manuscript written in Nahuatl which he is turning into Spanish, sporadically comparing it with other sources or illuminating certain obscure passages for the Spanish reader; this is the famous and enigmatic "Cronica X" (so-called by today's specialists), a splendid epic fresco of Aztec history whose original is unknown to us but which has also served as the point of departure for the books of Tezozomoc and Tovar. "My only intention in this work is to translate the story from the Aztec language, Nahuatl, into Spanish" (III, 18). He does not fail to indicate, when necessary, the difference between his own point of view and that of the Aztec account: "All of this seemed incredible to me, but the *Chronicle* has forced me to put it down and I have found confirmation of it in other written and painted manuscripts. Otherwise I would not dare to write these things, since I would be called a liar. He who translates a history is only obliged to reproduce in a new language what he finds written in the foreign tongue, and this is what I have done" (III, 44). His goal is not truth, for which he himself would be responsible, but fidelity to a different voice; the text he provides is not only a translation but also a citation: Durán is not the author of the sentences we read. "I must tell the truth according to the stories and traditions of the Indians" (III, 74): this is obviously something different from telling the mere truth.

But this project is not sustained throughout the book. When Durán says: "I wish to return to my subject, as my topic is the Aztec nation, its great deeds, and its tragic end" (III, 77), he makes no further mention of an intermediary subject between himself and the history of the Aztecs: he himself has become the narrator. He goes even further in another comparison: "The king had stone statues carved of them [the members of his family], in order to perpetuate their memory, and he had the historians and painters inscribe their lives and deeds with fine brushes and bright colors in the books. In this way their fame would grow and magnify like the brightness of the sun throughout all the nations. In the same way I have wished in this my history to preserve the fame and memory of those heroes, so that their honor may last as long as my work lasts and may be an example for all those who love virtue. Let their memory be a blessing, since such men are the loved ones of God, similar to the saints in Paradise" (III, 11).

We seem to be dreaming: far from taking up his position as a humble translator, even one seconded by an "annotator," Durán claims for himself the historian's function, which is to perpetuate the glory of his heroes. And he will do so in the same fashion as the carved or painted images left by the Aztecs themselves—save that he sees these heroes in the image of the saints of the Christian paradise, which was not to be the case of the Aztec painters. Durán has completely identified himself with the Aztec point of view—and yet not, for he never jeopardizes his own Christian faith; the last sentence of his history reads: "I will conclude this work by honoring and glorifying Our God and Lord and His Blessed Mother the Sovereign Virgin Mary, subjecting the book to the correction of the Holy Catholic Church, Our Mother, whose son I am, and under whose protection I promise to live and die as a true and faithful Christian" (III, 78). Neither Spaniard nor Aztec, Durán is, like La Malinche, one of the first Mexicans. The author of the original historical narrative ("Cronica X") must have been an Aztec; Durán's reader, necessarily, a Spaniard; Durán himself is that being who permits the transition from one to the other, and is himself the most remarkable of his own works.

In the account of the conquest the fusion of points of view appears most clearly. As a matter of fact, with regard to earlier history, Durán could rely on only one type of testimony, the traditional narratives, and these incarnated a consistent point of view. Yet with regard to the conquest, the Aztec point of view itself is no longer entirely coherent. Initially, the narrative shows us Montezuma as an ideal king, in the tradition of the portraits of the earlier kings: "He was a mature man, pious, virtuous, generous and of an invincible spirit. He was blessed with all the virtues that can be found in a good ruler and his decisions had always been correct, especially in matters of war" (III, 52). But such a judgment is problematic, for it no longer permits us to understand *from inside* the reasons for the Aztec empire's collapse. As we have seen, nothing is more intolerable to the Aztecs' historical mentality than this event totally exterior to their own history. Hence we must find in the latter sufficient reasons for Montezuma's failure; this will be, according to the Aztec chronicler, his excessive pride: "Soon he will see what is to come upon him, and this will happen because he has wanted to be adored more than God himself" (III, 66). "His pride has blinded him. . . . The God of All Created Things is angered, and he himself has sought the evils that are to come upon him" (III, 67). In a comparable fashion, the Tovar manuscript, derived from the same "Cronica X" and written in a similar spirit, includes an illustration that attributes the hybridization to the Emperor Montezuma himself (see fig. 15): the latter is shown with the features of a bearded man of European aspect, although provided with the attributes of an Aztec leader; such a figure obviously prepares the transition between Aztecs and Spaniards, and thereby renders it less shocking.

These sentences, in Durán's history, although probably deriving from the original chronicler, already reveal a certain Christian influence. But if the Aztec chronicler begins by speaking of his compatriots as "they," Durán will do as much with the Spaniards! Both writers are alienated from their original milieu; the resulting narrative of their common efforts is therefore inextricably ambivalent. Gradually, the difference between the two is erased, and Durán begins directly to assume the discourse he utters. This is why he gradually introduces other sources of knowledge (thereby abandoning his ideal of fidelity and focusing on that of truth), notably the conquistadors' accounts.

Doing so obliges him to compare these different sources, for they are often in disagreement, and to choose among the various versions of an event the one to which he can affix his own caveat: "This seems difficult to believe, since I have never met a Spaniard who will concede this point. But as all of them deny other things which have always been obvious, and remain silent about them in their histories, writings, and narrations, I am sure they would also deny and omit this" (III, 74). "My *Chronicle* says no such thing; if I record this event it is only because I have heard certain trustworthy persons speak of it. . . . My reasons for believing the latter rather than the former are based upon the description given to me by the friar who had been a conqueror" (III, 74). "Even though the *Chronicle* does not speak of this, I do not

Fig. 15 Portrait of Montezuma II.

believe that the virtue of our Spaniards was so great that they insisted that these women persevere in their chastity, modesty, and seclusion" (III, 75).

Thus the history of the conquest as told by Durán differs noticeably from the native accounts of the same facts, and is to be located somewhere halfway between them and a Spanish history like Gomara's. Durán has eliminated all the misunderstandings that might persist in the Aztec narratives; he indicates the conquistadors' motives as they might seem to a Spaniard of the period. The narrative of the massacre Alvarado perpetrates in the temple of Mexico is exemplary in this regard, and is explicitly assumed by Durán. Here is a brief extract from it: "The Aztec priests brought out a large heavy beam and sent it rolling down the steps. But it is said that it stuck on the topmost steps, and its flight was arrested. This was held to be a miraculous thing, and so it was, since divine mercy did not wish those who had committed that wicked and cruel massacre [i.e., the Spaniards] to go straight to hell, but was desirous of giving them the opportunity to do penance. However, not realizing the mercy of God in liberating them from this great peril, they ascended, killed all the priests and cast the idol of Huitzilopochtli down the steps" (III, 75).

In this scene, in which the Spanish soldiers attack Huitzilopochtli's temple and overturn the idols, Durán sees the intervention of divine mercy—but not at all where we might expect it: God has saved the Spaniards only so that they can expiate their sins; it was rejecting this mercy to overturn the idol and to kill its priests. It is only a step to taking Huitzilopochtli for God's prophet or a Christian saint; Durán's point of view remains both Indian and Christian. And in this, Durán is not at all like any of the groups in which he participates: neither Spaniards nor Aztecs of the conquest period could think as he does. Having acceded to the status of cultural hybrid, Durán, without realizing it, has had to abandon the status of mediator and interpreter, which he had chosen for himself. Asserting his own hybrid identity in confronting the beings he is trying to describe, he no longer succeeds in his project of comprehension, since he attributes to his characters thoughts and intentions which belong only to himself and to the other cultural hybrids of his time. The mastery of knowledge leads to a rapprochement with the object observed; but this very rapprochement serves as an obstacle to the process of knowledge.

We will not be surprised to see that Durán's judgment of the

Indians and their culture is profoundly ambiguous, not to say contradictory. It is clear that he regards them as neither noble savages nor brutes lacking in reason; but he is not certain how to reconcile the results of his observations: the Indians possess an admirable social organization, but their history contains only cruelties and violence; they are remarkably intelligent men, yet they remain blind in their pagan faith. Thus Durán finally decides not to decide, but to maintain, in all honesty, the ambivalence of his sentiments. "In part these people were well organized and polished, but on the other hand they were tyrannical and cruel, filled with the shadows of retributions and death" (I, "Introduction"). "Every time I stop to consider the childlike things on which these people based and founded their faith, I am filled with wonder at the ignorance which blinded them—a people who were not ignorant or brutish but skillful and wise in all worldly things, especially the elite among them" (I, 12). As for the Spaniards, on the other hand, Durán has certainly decided: he misses no opportunity to condemn those who preach the faith sword in hand; his position here is not very different from that of Las Casas, another Dominican, even if his expressions are less virulent. This puts Durán in great perplexity when he must evaluate everything that has resulted from the conquest. "It was in the year One Reed [of the Aztec calendar] that the Spaniards arrived in this land. The benefit for the souls of the natives was a great and blissful thing, because they received our Faith, which has multiplied and continued to multiply. [But] when did the natives suffer more than in that year?" (II, 1).

On the axiological level as on the praxiological, Durán remains a divided being: a Christian converted to "Indianism" who converts the Indians to Christianity. . . . No ambiguity, however, on the epistemological level: here Durán's success is incontestable. Yet this was not his explicit project: "I could tell of many other diversions, farces, and mockery, and jesting games and representations of those people. But this is not the purpose of my account, since I am only desirous of exposing the evil that existed then so that today, if some of it is suspected or felt, it may be remedied and pulled up by the roots, as it should be" (II, 8). It is our good fortune that this utilitarian project has been supplanted by another, doubtless deriving from the fact that Durán was, in his own words, "always curious and fond of asking questions" (I, 8). Thus he will remain for us an exemplary figure of what he himself calls "the desire to know" (I, 14).

Sahagún
and His Work

Bernardino de Sahagún was born in Spain in 1499; as a young man he studied at the University of Salamanca, then joined the Franciscan order. He arrived in Mexico in 1529, and remained there till his death in 1590. His career is devoid of any extraordinary event: it is the life of a man of letters. We are told that he was so handsome as a youth that the Franciscans were reluctant to let him appear in public, and that until his death he scrupulously observed his order's rituals and the obligations that derived from them. "He was gentle, humble and meek, decorous in his speech and affable with everyone," writes his contemporary and companion Geronimo de Mendieta (V, 1, 41).

Sahagún's activity, rather like a modern intellectual's, follows two main directions: teaching and writing. Sahagún is, originally, a grammarian or "linguist"; once he arrives in Mexico he learns Nahuatl, in this following the example of priests who had preceded him, such as Olmos and Motolinia. This fact is in itself already significant: usually it is the conquered who learns the conqueror's language. It is no accident that the first interpreters are Indians: those whom Columbus has taken back to Spain, those who come from islands already occupied by the Spaniards ("Julian" and "Melchior"), or La Malinche, given to the Spaniards as a slave. On the Spanish side, too, one learns the language when one is in a position of inferiority: thus Aguilar or Guerrero, forced to live among the Mayas, or later Cabeza de Vaca. We cannot imagine Columbus or Cortés learning the language of those they subjugate, and even Las Casas never masters a native language. The Franciscans and other priests from Spain are the first to learn the language of the conquered, and though this gesture is based on evident interests (to serve the propagation of the Christian religion), it is no less pregnant with meaning: even if it is only to identify the other with oneself, one begins by identifying oneself, at least in part, with the other. Conflicting ideological implications of this action are already perceived at the time, since, in an uncompleted letter to the pope in 1566, Las Casas reports that "certain unworthy persons present themselves before Your Holiness and disparage the bishops who learn the language of their flocks"; the very superiors of the Augustine, Dominican, and Franciscan orders in Mexico ask the Inquisition, in a petition dated September 16, 1579, to forbid the Bible to be translated into the native languages.

Sahagún, then, learns Nahuatl thoroughly and becomes a professor of (Latin) grammar in the Franciscan seminary of Tlateloco at its founding in 1536. This seminary is meant for the Mexican elite, it recruits its students among the sons of the former nobility; the level of studies rapidly becomes a superior one. Sahagún himself reports later on: "The Spaniards and the monks of other orders who learned of this laughed heartily and mocked us, considering it as beyond doubt that no one would be able to teach grammar to people who possessed so few aptitudes. But after we had worked with them for two or three years, they were able to penetrate into every subject which concerns grammar, and speaking, understanding and writing in Latin, even to the point of composing heroic verses" (X, 27).

We may muse upon this rapid development of minds: toward 1540, scarcely twenty years after the siege of Mexico City by Cortés, the Mexican noblemen's sons are composing heroic verses in Latin! What is also remarkable is that the instruction is reciprocal: at the same time that he introduces the young Mexicans into the subtleties of Latin grammar, Sahagún himself takes advantage of this contact to perfect his knowledge of Nahuatl language and culture; as he says: "Since they are already instructed in the Latin language, they teach us the properties of the words and of their own ways of speaking, as well as the incongruous things which we say in our sermons or which we put into our teaching. They correct us in all this, and nothing of what is to be translated into their language can be cleared of errors if it is not examined first by them" (ibid.).

The rapid advances of the Mexican students provoke as much hostility in the surrounding society as the monks' interest in the other's culture. A certain Geronimo Lopez, after visiting the seminary of Tlatelolco, writes to Charles V: "It is good that they should know the catechism, but to know how to read and write is as dangerous as to approach the devil"; and Sahagún explains: "When the lay brothers and the priests were convinced that the Indians were making progress and were capable of doing still more, they began to give over and to raise many objections with the goal of preventing the matter from going any further. . . . They were saying that since these people were not to take orders, what good would it do to teach them grammar? For thus they were in danger of becoming heretics, and it was also said that by reading the Holy Scriptures they would realize that the ancient patriarchs had several wives at once, even as they themselves were in the custom of having" (ibid.). Language has always been the companion of empire; the Spaniards fear that in losing supremacy over the former realm, they may lose it over the latter as well.

The second direction in which Sahagún's efforts are oriented is writing, and here he obviously draws on the knowledge acquired during his teaching. He is the author of numerous works, some of which are lost, but all of which partake of an intermediary role between the two cultures, a role he had chosen for himself: either they present the Christian culture to the Indians, or else they record and describe Nahuatl culture for the Spaniards' benefit. This activity of Sahagún's also encounters various obstacles. It is almost a miracle that his texts, especially his *History*, have been preserved to the present day. He is constantly at the mercy of his hierarchical superior, who can encourage him as well as render his endeavor impossible. At a given moment, on the excuse that the enterprise is too costly, his funds are cut off: "The author was obliged to dismiss his copyists, and to write everything out in his own hand. Now, since he was over seventy years of age and his hand trembled, he could write nothing, and the above-mentioned ban could not be raised for over five years" (II, "Prologue"). "I have not been able to do better," he writes elsewhere, "for lack of assistance and protection" (I, "To the Honest Reader"). Geronimo de Mendieta writes these bitter sentences in his regard: "This wretched monk had so little luck, apropos of his numerous writings, that these same eleven books of which I speak were cunningly taken from him by a governor of the region, who sent them to Spain to a chronicler seeking writings on the Indies, which will no doubt be made into wrapping papers for grocers. As for those of his labors which remained among us, he could print only certain hymns intended for the Indians for the festivals of Our Lord and His Saints" (V,1,41). The other texts will be published in the nineteenth and twentieth centuries.

Sahagún's most important work is the *Historia general de las cosas de Nueva España.* The project derives, as in Durán's case, from religious and proselytizing considerations: to facilitate the expansion of Christianity, Sahagún proposes to describe in detail the ancient religion of the Mexicans. Here is how he accounts for it himself: "It is in order to obey the orders of my *prelado mayor* that I have taken it upon myself to describe in the Mexican language what seems to me to be the most useful to dogma, to culture, and to the permanence of Christianity among the natives of New Spain, and what would be, at the same time, most likely to serve as a prop to the ministers and collaborators who instruct them" (II, "Prologue"). The ways of the future converts must be known, just as in order to cure a sickness the patient must be known; this is the comparison Sahagún employs on another occasion: "The physician cannot accurately prescribe remedies to his patient if he does not first know the humors and the causes from which the sickness proceeds . . . the preachers and the confessors are the physicians of the soul, and in order to cure certain spiritual sicknesses, they must know these remedies and these sicknesses. . . . The sins of idolatry, its rites, its superstitions and omens, its abuses and ceremonies have not altogether disappeared. In order to preach against these things, and in order to know if they still exist, it is necessary to learn how such people employed them in the era of their idolatry" (I, "Prologue"). Durán himself had said: "Fields of grass and fruit trees do not prosper on uncultivated rocky soil, covered with brambles and brush, unless all roots and stumps are torn out" (I, "Introduction"). The Indians are this soil, and these passive bodies, which must receive the virile and civilized insemination of the Christian religion.

This attitude, moreover, follows the Christian tradition: "Saint Augustine did not believe it would be a vain or superfluous affair to treat of the fabulous theology of the Gentiles, in the sixth book of the *City of God;* because, as he himself says, the fables and vain fictions of which the Gentiles made use, on the subject of their false gods, once being known, it would become easier to make them understand that these were no gods at all and that, from their essence, nothing useful could proceed for beings endowed with reason" (III, "Prologue"). This project is in accord with many other actions undertaken by Sahagún throughout his life: the writing of Christian texts in Nahuatl or the participation in the practice of evangelization.

But alongside this declared motive there exists another, and the copresence of the two goals will be responsible for the complexity of Sahagún's work: this is the desire to know and to preserve Nahuatl culture. This second project receives an initial realization before the first one. As a matter of fact, around 1547, Sahagún has collected a group of ritual discourses, the *huehuetlatolli*, a kind of applied moral philosophy of the Aztecs, and in 1550 he begins recording the native accounts of the conquest; whereas the first project of the *History* begins to take shape in 1558, when Sahagún is in Tepepulco. But here what is most important is that this second project, the knowledge of the culture of the ancient Mexicans, determines the method he will use in writing his work, which in its turn is responsible for the text as we have it today.

Indeed, the dominant concern that presides over the work's construction will be less the search for the best means of converting the Indians than fidelity to the object described; knowledge will prevail over pragmatic interests even more powerfully than in Durán. This is what leads Sahagún to his most important decisions: this text will be composed from information gathered from the witnesses most worthy of belief; and in order to guarantee their truthfulness this information will remain cited in the language of the informants: the *History* will be written in Nahuatl. In a second phase, Sahagún decides to add a free translation, and to have the whole thing illustrated. The result is a work of great structural complexity, in which three mediums continually interweave—Nahuatl, Spanish, and drawings.

Hence he must first choose his informants and make certain, by frequent verifications, of the accuracy of their accounts. Sahagún, who is one of the first in Western history to resort to this practice, acquits himself of his task with exemplary scrupulosity. During his stay in Tepepulco, in 1558–60, he convenes several dignitaries of the city: "I set forth before them what I was intending to do, and I begged them to furnish me with several skillful and experienced persons with whom I could discuss the matter, and who would be likely to satisfy me in all that I might ask of them" (II, "Prologue"). The dignitaries retire and return the next day with a list of twelve old men particularly expert in matters of ancient history. Sahagún for his part summons his four best students from the seminary of Tlatelolco. "During nearly two years I often discussed matters with these dignitaries and these grammarians, equally men of condition, in accordance with the plan I had made. They produced drawings of what constituted the subjects of our meetings (for such was the writing they employed of old), and the grammarians formulated these drawings in their own language, writing even upon the drawings themselves" (ibid.).

Sahagún returns to Tlatelolco in 1561, remaining there until 1565; the initial operation is repeated: the dignitaries select the specialists, he surrounds himself with his best students: "For over a year, confined in the seminary, we corrected, we wrote, we completed all that I had already written in Tepepulco, and of it we made a fair copy" (ibid.). It is at this moment that the essentials of the definitive text are constituted. Finally, by 1565, he is in Mexico City, and the entire work is once again revised; it is now divided into twelve books, including in its plan the previously collected material on moral philosophy (which becomes Book VI) and on the conquest (Book XII). "Here, for three years, I revised, by myself, several times over, my writings, and made certain corrections upon them; I divided them into twelve books, and each of the books into chapters and paragraphs. . . . The Mexicans corrected and added many things to my twelve books, while we were concerned to put them in final form" (ibid.). Throughout his labor Sahagún consults, along with his informants, the ancient codices in which the history of the Mexicans is consigned to images, and has these explained to him; his attitude toward them is the converse of that of Diego de Landa, and identical to that of Diego Durán. He reports the existence of the autos-da-fé, but adds: "A great number of those [works] which remained hidden were preserved, and these we have examined. Many of them are kept even today, and it is thanks to them that we have been able to understand their traditions" (X, 27).

Once the Nahuatl text is definitively established, Sahagún decides to *add* a translation. This decision is at least as important as the first (to find the best specialists and to verify their assertions). To appreciate the originality of Sahagún's work, let us compare it with that of his contemporaries, equally interested in Mexican history and having the same recourse (for they could not proceed otherwise) to informants and codices (hence setting aside such compilations as Las Casas's *Apologética Historia* and José de Acosta's *Historia natural y moral de las Indias*). A Motolinia has of course heard speeches; but his *History* is written from his own point of view, and the language of the other intervenes only in the form of brief citations, invariably accompanied by a remark like "This is the Indian manner of speaking, as are other expressions used in this book which do not agree with the Spanish usage" (III, 14). The rest of the time, then, we have a "free indirect style," a mixture of discourse whose ingredients are impossible to isolate with any precision: the content comes from informants, the point of view from Motolinia; but how are we to know where one stops and the other begins?

The case of Durán is more complex. His book is taken, he says, "from traditions and paintings, and from consulting the old people" (II, 1), and he carefully describes each source; he is scrupulous about their selection but does not commit himself, like Sahagún, to complex procedures. For his history, he also uses the Nahuatl "Cronica X," which is no longer a pictographic codex. As we have seen, he sometimes perceives his task as that of a translator; but in reality it is not a question of a simple translation: Durán himself often indicates that he is making cuts, or that he is abandoning his chronicle for the sake of information taken from witnesses or other manuscripts; he regularly furnishes the reasons that make him select one version or another. Occasionally he also refers to his own experience as a child brought up in Mexico; the result is that his book, as we have seen, allows us to hear a voice whose multiplicity is internal to it.

Moreover Durán, like other translator-compilers, practices another kind of intervention which we might describe as annotation (though the remarks figure within the text and not outside it). In order to observe this practice, let us take another example, that of Father Martín de Jesús de Coruña, presumed translator of the *Relación de Michoacán*, who offers certain explanations of idiomatic or metaphorical expressions: " 'I shall marry you,' they say, and their present intention is copulation because this is the way they speak their language" (III, 15; we may wonder if this is a way of speaking that characterizes the Tarascans exclusively); certain indications as to ways of speaking: "It should be understood that the narrator always attributed the wars and accomplishment of great deeds to his god Curicaveri, telling no more about the lords" (II, 2); additional information that makes the narrative intelligible, explaining intentions by the description of customs: "This was according to the usual custom, for when these people take a captive who is to be sacrificed, they dance with him and say that the dance is to express sorrow for him and make him arrive in heaven quickly" (II, 34); lastly, certain indications as to what has happened since the period of the narrative: "Later, a Spaniard exhumed his ashes and found very little gold, because it was at the beginning of the conquest" (II, 31).

But there are also other interventions made by this Father Coruña, which turn his text into the free indirect style, instead of remaining within the direct style. He designates the speaking subject by "they," "them," "people," and never "we"; he precedes certain assertions by modalizing formulations such as "people believe" (III,1); sometimes he introduces comparisons which cannot come from his informants: "They do not mingle lineages as do the Jews" (III,11); and even certain details whose authenticity appears problematic: "She stopped at the door, crossed herself . . ." (II,15). These interventions do not eliminate the documentary value of a text like the *Relación de Michoacán*, but they show the limits of the translation's fidelity, limits that would have been done away with if we had, alongside the translation, the original text.

Sahagún, for his part, chooses the path of total fidelity, since he reproduces the very speeches that are made to him, and to them *adds* his translation, rather than *replacing* them by it (Olmos is one of the rare figures in Mexico to have preceded him on this path). This translation, moreover, no longer needs to be literal (but were those of the others literal? We can never know), its function is different from that of the Nahuatl text; it therefore omits certain developments and adds others. The dialogue of voices here becomes all the subtler. This total fidelity, let us note right away, does not signify total authenticity; but total authenticity is by definition impossible, not for metaphysical reasons but because it is the Spaniards who have brought writing. Even when we have the Nahuatl text, we can no longer separate what is an expression of the Mexican point of view from what is said to please, or on the contrary to displease, the Spaniards: the latter are the recipients of *all* these texts, yet the recipient is almost as responsible for the content of a discourse as its author.

Finally the manuscript will be illustrated; those who produce the drawings are Mexicans, but they have already undergone the powerful influence of European art, so that the drawing itself is a site of confrontation between two systems of representation, a dialogue superimposed upon that of languages and viewpoints constituting the text. In all, the creation (which I have not described here in all its details) of this exceptional work, the *Historia general de Nueva España*, occupies Sahagún for nearly forty years.

The result of these efforts is an inestimable encyclopedia of the spiritual and material life of the Aztecs before the conquest, the detailed portrait of a society that differed very notably from our (Western) societies and which was doomed to perish forever in a very short while. It corresponds to the ambition that Sahagún acknowledged, "not to leave in obscurity the affairs of the natives of New Spain" (I, "Prologue"), and warrants applying one of his comparisons not only to the words, as Sahagún desired, but also to the things the words designate: "This work is comparable to a net, which would be intended to bring up into the daylight all the words of this language with their own and their metaphorical meanings, all the ways of speaking and most of the traditions, good or bad" (ibid.).

But if this encyclopedia has been appreciated at its true worth since its publication and serves as a basis of all studies of the Aztec world, less attention has been paid to the fact that here is also a book, an object, or rather an action, which deserves to be analyzed as such; now it is from precisely this point of view that Sahagún interests us here, in the context of this investigation of relations to the other, and of the place in them occupied by knowledge. We might see Durán and Sahagún as two opposing forms of a relation, somewhat as one used to describe the opposition of our classic and romantic: interpenetration of contraries in the former, separation in the latter; and it is certain that if Sahagún is more faithful to the Indians' discourse, Durán is closer to the Indians themselves and understands them better. But in reality the difference between the two is less distinct, for Sahagún's *History*, in its turn, is the site of the interaction of two voices (leaving aside that of the drawings); but that interaction takes less visible forms, and its analysis requires a closer observation.

1. It would of course be naive to imagine that the informants' voice is the only one we hear in the Nahuatl text, and only Sahagún's in the Spanish text: not only, as is obvious, are the informants responsible for the major part of the Spanish text itself, but also, as we shall see, Sahagún is present, though more discreetly, in the Nahuatl text. But there exist passages that are absent in one version or the other, and the latter are directly pertinent to our question. The most obvious of Sahagún's interventions in the Spanish text are the various prologues, notes, prefaces or digressions which assume a framing

function: they ensure the transition between the present text and the environing world. Yet these prefaces do not have the same object as the main text: they are a metatext, they bear on the book rather than on the Aztecs, and comparison is therefore not always illuminating. On several occasions, however, Sahagún intervenes in the matter, as in the Appendix of Book I or at the end of Chapter 20, Book II. The first time, after describing the Aztec pantheon, Sahagún adds a refutation, preceded by this apostrophe: "You, inhabitants of this New Spain, Mexicans, Tlaxcaltecs, inhabitants of the country of Michoacán, and all other Indians of these Western Indies, know that you have lived in the great darkness of idolatry and faithlessness, in which your ancestors have left you, as is proved clearly by your writings, your drawings, and the idolatrous rites in which you have lived until this day. Now listen with care . . ." And Sahagún faithfully transcribes (in Latin) four chapters of the Bible concerning idolatry and its deadly effects. Then comes the refutation proper. He is here addressing his informants themselves, speaking in his own name; then comes a new apostrophe, this time "to the reader"; and finally some "Expostulations of the Author" addressed to no one in particular, if not to God, in which Sahagún expresses his regret at seeing the Mexicans stray into the ways of error.

The second intervention, equally isolated by the title "Expostulation of the Author," follows the description of a child sacrifice. "I do not believe there can be a heart so hard as not to be touched and softened by tears, horror and fear, in hearing of a cruelty so inhuman, worse than bestial and diabolical, such as we have just presented above." In this case the "expostulation" serves chiefly to seek a justification, a defense of the Mexicans who might, after such an account, be judged unfavorably. "The cause of this cruel blinding, of which these wretched children were the object, must not be so much imputed to the cruelty of their fathers, who were shedding abundant tears and indulging in such practices with pain in their hearts; we must impute it to the infinitely cruel hatred of our ancient enemy Satan" (II,20).

What is remarkable in these interventions is not only that they are so rare (I may remind the reader that the Spanish text of Sahagún's work takes up nearly seven hundred pages), but also that they are so clearly separated from the remainder: here, Sahagún juxtaposes his voice with that of his informants, without the possibility of any confusion between their voices. On the other hand he abandons any value judgment in the descriptions of the Aztec rites themselves, presented exclusively from the Indians' viewpoint. Let us take as an example the description of a human sacrifice and notice how the different authors of the period preserve or influence the Indian viewpoint expressed in the account. Here, first of all, is Motolinia:

"On this stone they laid the unhappy wretches on their backs to sacrifice them. The chest was arched up and very tense, because their hands and feet were tied. The principal priest of the idols, or his lieutenant, who were the ones who usually performed the sacrifice . . . rapidly and with great force cut upon the tense chest with a cruel flint knife and quickly cut out the heart. . . . The priest who performed this evil deed then struck the heart against the outer part of the threshold of the altar, leaving a bloodstain there. . . . Let no one think that any of those whom they sacrificed by killing them and cutting out their hearts or by any other form of death, were voluntary victims. On the contrary, they were sacrificed by force, bitterly mourning their death and suffering frightfully" (I,6).

"Cruel," "evil," "unhappy wretches," "suffering frightfully": it is obvious that Motolinia, who possesses a native account but does not quote it, introduces his own point of view into the text, sprinkling it with terms that express the position shared by Motolinia and his eventual reader; Motolinia anticipates and in a sense makes explicit the latter's reaction. The two voices are never on an equal footing, each expressing itself in its turn: one of the two (Motolinia's) includes and integrates the other, which no longer addresses the reader directly, but only through Motolinia, who remains the sole subject, in the full sense of the word.

Now let us take a similar scene described by Durán: "The victim, carrying the bag of gifts to the sun together with the staff and shield, slowly began to climb the steps of the pyramid. In this ascent he represented the course of the sun from east to west. As soon as he reached the summit and stood in the center of the great Sun Stone, which represented noon, the sacrificers approached the captive and opened his chest. Once the heart had been wrenched out, it was offered to the sun and blood sprinkled toward the solar deity. Imitating the descent of the sun in the west, the corpse was toppled down the steps of the pyramid" (III,23).

No more "cruel," no more "evil," no more "miserable wretches": Durán transcribes this account in a detached tone, avoiding any value judgment (which he will not fail to produce on other occasions). But instead, a new vocabulary, absent from Motolinia's account, has appeared: that of interpretation. The slave *represents* the sun, the center of the stone is here to indicate noon, the falling body *represents* the setting sun. . . . Durán, as we have seen, understands the rites of which he speaks, or more exactly knows the associations that habitually accompany them; and he lets his reader share what he knows.

Sahagún's style is still different: "Their masters pulled them up and dragged them by the hair to the sacrificial stone where they were to die. Having brought them to the sacrificial stone, which was a stone of three hands in height, or a little more, and two in width, or almost, they threw them upon it, on their backs, and five [priests] seized them —two by the legs, two by the arms, and one by the head; and then came the priest who was to kill him. And he struck him with a flint [knife], held in both hands and made in the manner of a large lance-head, between the breasts. And into the gash which he made, he thrust his hand, and tore from [the victim] his heart, and then he offered it to the sun and cast it into a gourd vessel. After having torn their hearts from them and poured the blood into a gourd vessel, this the master of the slain man himself received, they started the body rolling down the pyramid steps" (III,2).

It is as if we were suddenly reading a page from some *nouveau roman:* this description is the contrary of those by Durán or Motolinia: no value judgment, but no interpretation either; we are reading pure description. Sahagún seems to be practicing the literary technique of *estrangements:* he describes everything from outside, accumulating technical details, whence the abundance of measurements: "three hands in height, or a little more," etc.

But it would be a mistake to suppose that Sahagún is giving us the uncontaminated narrative of the Indians, whereas Motolinia and Durán imposed on it the imprint of their own personality, or of their culture; in other words, that monophony is replacing dyphony. It is more than certain that the Indians did not speak the way Sahagún does: his text has the resonance of an ethnographical investigation with all its scrupulous interrogations (which are ultimately somewhat beside the point, for what is grasped is the form but not the meaning). The Indians had no need to express themselves in this way among themselves; such discourse is powerfully determined by the identity of their interlocutor. Moreover, Sahagún's text affords us proof of this: the extract we have just read has no counterpart in Nahuatl; it is written by Sahagún himself, in Spanish, from testimonies collected in another chapter (II, 21); here we find the elements of the rite but none of the technical details. Then is this final version of the rite the zero degree of intervention? We may doubt this, not because the missionaries acquitted themselves badly of their ethnographic labors, but because the very notion of zero degree is perhaps illusory. Discourse, as has been said, is fatally determined by the identity of its interlocutor; now, the latter is, in every case, a Spaniard, a foreigner, an outsider. We can go further and, without being able to observe it, be sure that among themselves the Aztecs did not speak the same way when addressing a child, a new initiate, or a wise old man; nor did priest and warrior speak in the same fashion.

2. Another very circumscribed intervention of Sahagún's occurs in the titles of certain chapters, in particular of Book I. These titles constitute an attempt, though indeed quite a timid one, even if Sahagún undertook to repeat it several times, to establish a series of equivalences between the Aztec and Roman gods: "7. The goddess they called Chicomecoatl. This is another Ceres." "11. The goddess of water, whom they called Chalchiuhtlicue; this is another Juno." "12. The goddess of carnal things, whom they called Tlazolteotl, another Venus," etc. In the "Prologue" to Book I, Sahagún proposes an analogy concerning the cities and their inhabitants: "This famous and great city of Tula, so rich and fine, so wise and brave, ultimately suffered the wretched fate of Troy. . . . The city of Mexico is another Venice [on account of the canals] and they themselves are new Venetians, by their knowledge and their civility. . . . The Tlaxcaltecs seem to have succeeded the Carthaginians." This kind of comparison is indeed very widespread in writings of the period (I shall return to it); what is striking here is the limited role it assumes, both numerically and in the space granted to it: again, outside the actual text describing the Aztec universe (these analogies do not figure in the Nahuatl version), in the frame (titles, prefaces) rather than in the picture. Once more, we cannot be mistaken as to the source of the voice; the intervention is frank, not dissimulated but actually exhibited.

These two forms of interaction, "expostulations" and analogies, clearly separate the two discourses. But other forms will incarnate increasingly complex interpenetrations of the two voices.

3. When it comes to describing a sacrifice, Sahagún does not add,

in the translation, any term implying a moral judgment. But in speaking of the Aztec pantheon, he finds himself facing a difficult choice: whatever the term used, a value judgment is inevitable: he compromises himself as much by translating "god" as "devil," or "priest" as "necromancer": the first term already legitimates, the second condemns; neither is neutral. How to avoid this situation? Sahagún's solution consists in not opting for one of the two terms, but in alternating them; in short, erecting absence of system into a system, thereby neutralizing the two terms—in principle bearers of opposing moral judgments—which now become synonyms. For example, a title in Appendix 3 of Book II announces a "Relation of the ceremonies which were performed to honor the demon," and the title of Appendix 4 is "Relations of the differences between the ministers responsible for the service of the gods." The first chapter of the third book inverts the order: the title says "Of the origin of the gods," and the first sentence: "Here is what the old native knew and told us of the birth and origin of the devil called Huitzilopochtli." In the "Prologue" to the entire work, Sahagún establishes the same neutrality by a controlled *lapsus:* "I have written twelve books on the divine matters or, more properly, idolatrous ones. . . ." We can imagine that it is his informants who think "god" and Sahagún who thinks "devil." But in collecting both terms in his own discourse, he inflects that discourse in the direction of his informants, though without entirely embracing their position: thanks to their alternation, the terms lose their qualitative nuances.

In another title, we find a different testimony to the actual ambivalence of Sahagún's position: "This is the prayer of the grand satrap, in which are to be found numerous subtleties" (VI, 5). Perhaps, as some have asserted, Sahagún, here resembling Durán, admires the Aztecs' natural world (here, their language) and condemns their supernatural world (their idols); the fact is that here we have another example where the informant's voice is heard within Sahagún's, transforming it. In other texts by Sahagún, Christian sermons addressed to the Mexicans and written in Nahuatl, we observe another interference: Sahagún in his turn uses certain stylistic devices of Aztec prose (parallelisms, metaphors).

4. If the informant's voices were present in Sahagún's discourse, Sahagún's voice in its turn steeps their discourse. This is not a question of the direct interventions that, as we have seen, are clearly indicated and delimited; but of a presence both more diffuse and more massive.

This is because Sahagún works according to a plan he has established following his first contacts with the Aztec culture but also in terms of his idea of what a civilization can be. We know from Sahagún himself that he makes use of a questionnaire, and we cannot overestimate this fact. The questionnaires have unfortunately not survived, but they have been reconstituted, thanks to the ingenuity of today's investigators. For example, the description of the Aztec gods in Book I reveals that all the chapters (and hence all the answers) obey a specific order, which corresponds to the following questions: 1. What are the titles, attributes, and characteristics of this god? 2. What are his powers? 3. What are the rites performed in his honor? 4. What is his appearance? Sahagún therefore imposes his conceptual framework on the Aztec lore, and the latter seems to afford an organization which in reality derives from the questionnaire. It is true that, within each book, we perceive a transformation: the beginning always follows a strict order, whereas the sequel includes more and more digressions and deviations from this schema; Sahagún has had the good sense to preserve the latter, and the share left to improvisation somewhat compensates for the questionnaire's effect. But this effect keeps Sahagún from understanding, for example, the nature of the supreme divinity (one of whose names is Tezcatlipoca), since such a divinity is invisible and intangible, is its own origin, creator of history but itself without history; Sahagún expects the Aztec gods to resemble the Roman gods, not the God of the Christians! In certain cases, the result is frankly negative, as in Book VII, which deals with the Indians' "natural astrology"; here Sahagún does not understand the answers, which are based on a cosmic conception entirely different from his own, and apparently returns again and again to his questionnaires.

Not only do the questionnaires impose a European organization on American knowledge, and sometimes keep the relevant information from passing through, they also determine the themes to be treated, by excluding certain others. To take one massive example (though there are many others to choose from), we learn very little concerning the Aztecs' sexual life from Sahagún's book. Perhaps this information was dismissed by the informants themselves; perhaps, unconsciously, by Sahagún; we cannot know, but we have the impression that the acts of cruelty already present in Christian mythology do not excessively shock the Spanish investigator, and that he transcribes them quite faithfully, whereas sexuality finds no place at all.

It is rather amusing to see that the book's first editors, in the nineteenth century, imposed an entirely conscious censorship with regard to the rare—and to them scabrous—passages containing references to sexuality: at the time there no longer existed prohibitions concerning religion (generally speaking), hence there no longer existed sacrileges or blasphemies; on the other hand, decorum had increased, and everything seemed to suggest an obscenity. In his 1880 Preface, the French translator feels obliged to justify at great length "these contrasts between purity of the soul and liberties in the expression of thought" on the part of the Spanish monks of the sixteenth century, and ultimately puts the responsibility for this situation on the natives, whose remarks, during confession, have corrupted the good monks' ears —"now, need I say in what vile filth the Indians' first confessors were obliged to conduct extended conversations, day after day" (Preface, p. xiii). Thus the translator in his turn praises himself for his courage, which enables him to furnish the entirety of Sahagún's text, although from time to time he permits himself a few corrections: "Thus the translator, following Bustamente [the first editor of the Spanish text] believes he is warranted in suppressing a scabrous passage which the delicacy of the French language would make intolerable for the reader" (p. 430); as a matter of fact, the passage is preserved in a note, in Spanish—apparently a less delicate language. Or again: "The chapter which follows includes certain scabrous passages excusable only by the naiveté of the language initially employed, and by Sahagún's resolution to render everything with exactitude. . . . I shall follow the text absolutely in my translation, without making other changes than to replace by the word *nudity* the more realistic word which Sahagún chose to use in order not to depart from what his old men said to him in the Nahuatl tongue" (p. 210). The Spanish text actually says, quite simply: *miembro genital* (III, 5): must we, in fact, assign responsibility for this expression to the Aztec elders? Let us rejoice that Sahagún was not so prudish as his editors three hundred years later! The fact remains that in all this he is responsible for the Nahuatl text itself, and not only for the Spanish version of it; the original even bears traces of Sahagún's religious convictions, his education, and his social allegiances.

5. If we now shift to the macrostructural level, after these observations on the microstructure, we find the same kind of "interference" of one voice with the other. The choice of themes treated, for example, lets us hear the informants' voices within Sahagún's. We recall that

Sahagún's explicit project was to facilitate the evangelization of the Indians by the study of their religion. But barely a third of the book corresponds to this idea. Whatever Sahagún's initial intention, it is clear that the wealth of materials available to him has convinced him to replace his initial project by another, and that he has sought to constitute an encyclopedic description, in which the affairs of men or even of nature take up as much space as the divine or the supernatural; this transformation has every likelihood of being due to the influence of his native informants. Whatever can be the Christian utility of a description like this of the water serpent (see fig. 16)?

"And when it has caught no one, when it has drowned no one, it also hunts people. It digs a small pit at the water's edge; it forms it like a basin. And there in the watery cavern it catches crag fish, the bearded ones, any kind of fish. It removes all, quickly bringing them up in its teeth; it places them in the sandy basin which has been dug. . . . When it comes to the surface it looks all around, turns about repeatedly . . . then it deposits the fish in the earth basin and once again enters the water and submerges there, remaining submerged. And someone daring, someone drunk, while the serpent has submerged, then runs up. He gathers up the fish, he puts them in the folds of his cape. During a favorable moment he will run off. And when the serpent has emerged, it can see that its fish have indeed been taken. It rises up on its tail, looks about repeatedly. No matter where the man goes it can see him. And it follows him as if flying, sliding over the grass or the bushes. When it reaches the man bearing fish on his back, then it coils itself around him many times. And its tail, since it is really forked, it inserts in each of his nostrils, or in his anus. Then the serpent squeezes the one who had robbed him and kills him there" (XI, 4, 3).

Here Sahagún transcribes and translates what he is told, without any concern for the place such information occupies in relation to his initial project.

6. At the same time, the general plan remains Sahagún's: a scholastic *summa* which proceeds from the highest (God) to the lowest (stones). The numerous corrections and additions have somewhat obscured this plan; but if we keep to the main outlines, we can reconstruct it as follows: Books I, II, and III deal with the gods; books IV, V, and VII, with astrology and divination, i.e., with relations between gods and men; Books VIII, IX, and X are devoted to human affairs; finally, book XI concerns animals, plants, and minerals. Two books, corresponding

Fig. 16 The fabulous serpent.

to materials previously collected, have no real place in this plan: Book VI, a collection of ritual discourses, and book XIII, the narrative of the conquest. Not only does this plan correspond better to Sahagún's mind than to that of his informants, but the very existence of such an encyclopedic project, with its subdivisions into books and into chapters, has no corresponding entity in Aztec culture. Though Sahagún's work is not very common even in the European tradition, it certainly belongs to that tradition, regardless of the fact that its content comes from informants. We might say that, starting from the *discourses* of the Aztecs, Sahagún has produced a *book;* yet the book is, in this context, a European category. And yet the initial objective is inverted: Sahagún had started from the notion of utilizing the Indians' knowledge in order to contribute to the propagation of the Europeans' culture; he has ended by putting his own knowledge in the service of the preservation of the native culture.

There are, of course, other forms of interpenetration of the two voices to be accounted for; but these are sufficient to attest to the complexity of the speaker, the subject in the *Historia general de las cosas de Nueva España;* or, we might just as well say, to the distance between the ideology professed by Sahagún and that which is imputable to the author of the book. This also appears in the reflections he supplies in the margins of the central argument. Not that Sahagún doubts his faith or abandons his mission. But he finds himself led to distinguish, in the manner of Las Casas or of Durán, between the idea of religion and its object: if the Christians' God is superior, the Indians' religious feeling is stronger. "With regard to religion and the worship of their gods, I believe there have never been in the world idolators with greater tendencies to revere their gods than the Indians of New Spain, though at the price of so many sacrifices" (I, "Prologue"). The replacement of Aztec society by Spanish society is therefore a two-edged sword; and after having carefully weighed the pros and cons, Sahagún decides, more forcefully than Durán, that the final result is negative. "Since all these [idolatrous] practices ceased upon the Spaniards' arrival, who made it their task to trample on all customs and on all ways of governing themselves the natives possessed, with the claim to reduce them to living as in Spain, as much in the divine practices as in human affairs, by the mere fact of considering them as idolaters and barbarians, we destroyed all their ancient government. . . . But now we see that this new organization renders men vicious, produces in them very bad inclinations and worse undertakings which render them hateful to God and for man as well, not counting the grievous diseases and the shortening of human life" (X, 27).

Sahagún thus sees clearly that social values form an interpenetrating whole: idols cannot be toppled without thereby toppling the society itself; and even from the Christian point of view, what has been constructed in its place is inferior to what was originally there. "If it is true that they attested to still greater aptitudes in times gone by, either in the administration of public affairs or in the service of their gods, it is because they lived under a system in closer relationship with their aspirations and their needs" (ibid.). Sahagún formulates no revolutionary conclusion; but the implication of his reasoning is surely that Christianization has on the whole brought more harm than good, and that it would have been better if it had not taken place at all. In reality, his dream, as in the case of other Franciscans, is instead the creation of an ideal new state: Mexican (hence independent of Spain) and Christian at the same time, a kingdom of God upon earth. But he knows that this dream is not close to coming true, and therefore contents himself with collecting and noting the negative aspects of the present state. This position, however, combined with the importance he grants to Mexican culture, brings down upon his work the outright condemnation of the authorities; not only are his funds cut off, as we have seen, but a royal edict signed by Philip II, dated 1577, forbids taking note of this work and, a fortiori, contributing to its circulation.

In everyday practice as well, the presence of the brothers has, according to Sahagún, an ambiguous effect. The new religion leads to new ways, yet these provoked a reaction still farther from the Christian spirit than the old religion was. Sahagún quite humorlessly describes the excesses which attend on the education of the young: "In the fashion of their former habits . . . we accustomed them to get up in the middle of the night and to sing the matins of Our Lady; at dawn, we made them recite the Hours; we even taught them to flagellate themselves during the night and to occupy their minds with mental prayer. But, since they did not devote themselves to the physical labors of past times, as their condition of lively sensuality requires, and since moreover they ate much better food than they were accustomed in their former State, and consequent upon the gentleness and the compassion which was the custom among us, they began to feel sensual impulses and to give themselves up to lascivious practices" (ibid.). And in this fashion the Good Lord leads us to the devil!

Once again, there is no question of asserting that Sahagún has sided with the Indians. Other passages of his book show him entirely firm in his Christian convictions, and all the documents we possess testify that, to the end of his life, he remained preoccupied by the Christianization of the Mexicans more than by anything else. But we can see to what point his work is the product of the interaction of two voices, two cultures, two points of view, even if this interaction is less evident than in Durán. This is why we can only reject the views of certain contemporary specialists who dismiss this exceptional work and, neglecting all interaction, declare that the informants alone are responsible for the Nahuatl text of the book, and Sahagún alone for the Spanish text; who make, in other words, two books out of a work which derives its major interest from the very fact that it is *one!* A dialogue is not the addition of two monologues, whatever else it may be. And we can only hope for the imminent publication of a complete or critical edition which will permit us to read and to appreciate at its true worth this unique monument of human thought.

How are we to locate Sahagún in the typology of relations to the other? On the level of value judgments, he adheres to the Christian doctrine of the equality of all men. "In truth, with regard to government, they yield in nothing, if we except certain tyrannical violences, to other nations who have laid great claims to civility" (I, "Prologue"). "What is certain is that all these peoples are our brothers, proceeding from Adam's stock even as we ourselves; they are our neighbors whom we must love as ourselves" (ibid.).

But this position of principle does not lead him to an assertion of identity, nor to an idealization of the Indians, in the fashion of Las Casas; the Indians have virtues and defects, just like the Spaniards, but in a different distribution. He complains on occasion of various features of their character which seem to him regrettable; he accounts for these, however, not by a natural inferiority (as Sepúlveda would have done) but by the different conditions in which they live, notably climatic conditions; the change is considerable. After describing their idleness and hypocrisy, he notes: "I am not too surprised by the defects and foolishness which we find among the natives of this country, for the Spaniards who live there and still more those born there also acquire such wicked inclinations. . . . I believe that this is due to the climate or to the constellations of this country" (X, 27). One detail nicely illustrates the difference between Las Casas and Sahagún: for Las Casas, it will be remembered, all the Indians give evidence of the same qualities—there is no difference among peoples, not to mention individuals; Sahagún, for his part, refers to his individual informants by their own names.

On the level of behavior, Sahagún also occupies a specific position: he does not to any degree renounce his way of life or his identity (there is nothing of a Guerrero about him); yet he learns the other's language and culture in depth, devotes his life to this task, and ends, as we have seen, by sharing certain values of those who at the start were the object of his studies.

But it is obviously on the epistemic level, the level of knowledge, that Sahagún's example is most interesting. It is initially the quantitative aspect that strikes him: the amount of what he knows is enormous and exceeds all others (Durán comes closest to him). More difficult to formulate is the qualitative nature of this knowledge. Sahagún contributes an impressive mass of materials, but does not interpret them—i.e., does not translate them into the categories of another culture (his own), thereby revealing the latter's relativity. This is the task to which today's ethnologists will apply themselves—starting from his own investigations. Insofar, we might even say, as his work or that of other learned monks who were his contemporaries contained germs of the ethnological attitude, he was unacceptable to his period: indeed it is striking that books by Motolinia, Olmos, Las Casas (*Apologética Historia*), Sahagún, Durán, Tovar, and Mendieta were not published before the nineteenth century, or are even lost. Sahagún himself takes only one timid step in this ethnological direction, as we have seen: his comparisons between the Aztec and Roman pantheons. Las Casas will go much further down the comparatist path in his *Apologética Historia*, and others will follow him. But the comparatist attitude is not actually the ethnologist's. The comparatist puts certain *objects*, all of which are external to him, on the same level, and he himself remains the sole *subject*. The comparison, in Sahagún as in Las Casas, affects the gods of *others*: of the Aztecs, of the Romans, of the Greeks; it does not put the Other on the same level as oneself, and does not call into question one's own categories. The ethnologist, on the other hand, contributes to the reciprocal illumination of one culture by another, to "making us look into the other's face," according to the splendid phrase already devised in the sixteenth century by Urbain Chauveton: we know the other by the self, but also the self by the other.

Sahagún is not an ethnologist, whatever his modern admirers may say. And unlike Las Casas, he is not fundamentally a comparatist; his work rather relates to ethnography, to the collecting of documents, that indispensable premise of ethnological work. The dialogue of cultures is, in him, fortuitous and unconscious, it is an uncontrolled *slippage*, it is not (and cannot be) erected into a method. He is even a declared enemy of the hybridization of cultures; the fact that it is easy to identify the Virgin Mary with the Aztec goddess Tonantzin is for him the consequence of a "satanic invention" (XI, 12, Appendix 7), and he never tires of putting his coreligionists on guard against any easy enthusiasm provoked by the coincidences between the two religions, or by the rapidity with which the Indians embrace Christianity. His intention is to juxtapose voices rather than to make them interpenetrate: either it is the natives who tell their "idolatries" or it is Holy Writ copied out into his own book—one of these voices tells the truth, the other lies. And yet we see here the first sketches of a future dialogue, the unformed embryos that herald our present.

EPILOGUE

Las Casas's Prophecy

At the very end of his life, Las Casas writes in his will: "I believe that because of these impious, criminal and ignominious deeds perpetrated so unjustly, tyrannically and barbarously, God will vent upon Spain His wrath and His fury, for nearly all of Spain has shared in the bloody wealth usurped at the cost of so much ruin and slaughter."

These words, half prophecy and half curse, establish the collective responsibility of the Spaniards—and not merely of the conquistadors—for all time to come and not merely the present. And they announce that the crime will be punished, that the sin will be expiated.

We are in a good position today to decide if Las Casas saw matters clearly or not. We can make a slight correction to the extent of his prophecy and replace Spain by "Western Europe": even if Spain takes the lead in the movement of colonization and destruction of the other, Spain is not alone: Portugal, France, England, Holland will follow close after, Belgium, Italy, and Germany will try to catch up. And if in matters of destruction the Spaniards do more than the other European nations, it is not because the latter have not tried to equal and to exceed them. Let us read, then: "God will vent upon Europe His wrath and His fury," if that can make us feel more directly concerned.

Has the prophecy come true? Each of us will answer this question according to his own judgment. For myself, conscious though I am of how arbitrary any estimation of the present is likely to be when the collective memory has not yet performed its sifting function, and hence of the ideological choice implied here, I prefer to assume my vision of events openly, without disguising it as a description of events themselves. Doing so, I choose in the present circumstances the elements that seem to me most characteristic, that consequently contain—or should contain—the future in germ. Inevitably, these remarks will remain quite elliptical.

Certainly many events of recent history seem to bear Las Casas out. Slavery has been abolished for a hundred years, and old-style *(à l'espagnole)* colonialism for about twenty. Many acts of revenge have been and are still taken against citizens of the former colonial powers, whose sole personal crime is that of belonging to the nation in question; the English, the Americans, the French are thus often held to be collectively responsible for their former colonized peoples. I do not know if we are to regard this as the effect of divine wrath and fury, but I think that two reactions are inevitable for anyone familiar with the exemplary history of the conquest of America: first of all, that such retaliatory actions never succeed in righting the balance of the crimes perpetrated by the Europeans (and because of that, such actions can be absolved); next, that such actions merely reproduce the worst of what the Europeans have already accomplished, and nothing is more distressing than to see history repeating itself—even when it is a matter of the history of destruction. That Europe should in her turn be colonized by the peoples of Africa, of Asia, or of Latin America (we are far from this, I know) would perhaps be a "sweet revenge," but cannot be considered my ideal.

A Mayan woman died, devoured by dogs. Her story, reduced to a few lines, concentrates one of the extreme versions of the relation to the other. Her husband, of whom she is the "internal other," already leaves her no possibility of asserting herself as a free subject: fearing to be killed in war, he seeks to ward off the danger by depriving the woman of her will; but war will not be only an affair among men: even when her husband is dead, the wife must continue to belong to him. When the Spanish conquistador appears, this woman is no more than the site where the desires and wills of two men meet. To kill men, to rape women: these are at once proof that a man wields power and his reward. The wife chooses to obey her husband and the rules of her own society; she puts all that remains of her personal will into defending the violence of which she has been the object. But, in fact, a cultural exteriority will determine the outcome of this little drama: she is not raped, as a Spanish woman might have been in time of war; she is thrown to the dogs because she is both an unconsenting woman and an Indian woman. Never was the fate of the other more tragic.

I am writing this book to prevent this story and a thousand others like it from being forgotten. I believe in the necessity of "seeking the truth" and in the obligation of making it known; I know that the function of information exists, and that the effect of information can be powerful. My hope is not that Mayan women will now have European men thrown to the dogs (an absurd supposition, obviously), but that we remember what can happen if we do not succeed in discovering the other.

For the other remains to be discovered. The fact is worthy of astonishment, for man is never alone, and would not be what he is without his social dimension. And yet this is the call: for the newborn child, *his* world is *the* world, and growth is an apprenticeship in exteriority and sociality; we might say, somewhat cavalierly, that human life is confined between these two extremes, one where the *I* invades the world, and one where the world ultimately absorbs the *I* in the form of a corpse or of ashes. And just as the discovery of the other knows several degrees, from the other-as-object, identified with the surrounding world, to the other-as-subject, equal to the *I* but different from it, with an infinity of intermediary nuances, we can indeed live our lives without ever achieving a full discovery of the other (supposing that such a discovery can be made). Each of us must begin it over again in turn; the previous experiments do not relieve us of our responsibility, but they can teach us the effects of misreading the facts.

Yet even if the discovery of the other must be assumed by each individual and eternally recommenced, it also has a history, forms that are socially and culturally determined. The history of the conquest of America makes me believe that a great change occurred—or, rather, was revealed—at the dawn of the sixteenth century, say between Columbus and Cortés; a similar difference (not similar in details, of course) can be observed between Montezuma and Cortés; this difference functions, then, in time as in space, and if I have lingered over the spatial contrast more than the temporal one, it is because the latter is blurred by countless transitions whereas the former, with the help of an ocean, has all the necessary distinctness. Since the period of the conquest, for almost three hundred and fifty years, Western Europe has tried to assimilate the other, to do away with an exterior alterity, and has in great part succeeded. Its way of life and its values have spread around the world; as Columbus wished, the colonized peoples have adopted our customs and have put on clothes.

This extraordinary success is chiefly due to one specific feature of Western civilization which for a long time was regarded as a feature of man himself, its development and prosperity among Europeans thereby becoming proof of their natural superiority: it is, paradoxically, Europeans' capacity to understand the other. Cortés affords us a splendid example of this, and he was conscious of the degree to which the art of adaptation and of improvisation governed his behavior. Schematically this behavior is organized into two phases. The first is that of interest in the other, at the cost of a certain empathy or temporary identification. Cortés slips into the other's skin, but in a metaphoric and no longer a literal fashion: the difference is considerable. Thereby he ensures himself an understanding of the other's language and a knowledge of the other's political organization (whence his interest in the Aztecs' internal dissension, and he even masters the emission of messages in an appropriate code: hence he manages to pass himself off as Quetzalcoatl returned to earth. But in so doing he has never abandoned his feeling of superiority; it is even his very capacity to understand the other that confirms him in that feeling. Then comes the second phase, during which he is not content to reassert his own identity (which he has never really abandoned), but proceeds to assimilate the Indians to his own world. In the same way, it will be recalled, the Franciscan monks adopted the Indians' ways (clothes, food) to convert them more effectively to the Christian religion. The Europeans exhibit remarkable qualities of flexibility and improvisation which permit them all the better to impose their own way of life. Of course, this capacity of simultaneous adaptation and absorption is not at all a universal value and with it brings its converse, which is much less appreciated. Egalitarianism, of which one version is characteristic of the (Western) Christian religion as well as of the ideology of modern capitalist states, also serves colonial expansion: here is another, somewhat surprising lesson of our exemplary history.

At the same time that it was tending to obliterate the strangeness of the external other, Western civilization found an interior other. From the classical age to the end of romanticism (i.e., down to our own day), writers and moralists have continued to discover that the person is not *one*—or is even nothing—that *Je est un autre*, or a simple echo chamber, a hall of mirrors. We no longer believe in wild men in the forests, but we have discovered the beast in man, "that mysterious thing in the soul, which seems to acknowledge no human jurisdiction but in spite of the individual's own innocent self, will still dream horrid dreams, and mutter unmentionable thoughts" (Melville, *Pierre*, IV, 2). The instauration of the unconscious can be considered as the culminating point of this discovery of the other in oneself.

I believe that this period of European history is, in its turn, coming to an end today. The representatives of Western civilization no longer believe so naively in its superiority, and the movement of assimilation is running down in that quarter, even if the recent or ancient nations of the Third World still want to live like the Europeans. On the ideological level, at least, we are trying to combine what we regard as the better parts of both terms of the alternative; we want *equality* without its compelling us to accept identity; but also *difference* without its degenerating into superiority/inferiority. We aspire to reap the benefits of the egalitarian model *and* of the hierarchic model; we aspire to rediscover the meaning of the social without losing the quality of the individual. The Russian socialist Alexander Herzen wrote in the middle of the nineteenth century: "To understand the extent, reality, and sacred nature of the rights of the person without destroying society, without fracturing it into atoms: such is the most difficult social goal." We are still telling ourselves the same thing today.

To experience difference in equality is easier said than done. Yet several figures of my exemplary history came close to it, in various ways. On the axiological level, a Las Casas managed in his old age to love and esteem the Indians as a function not of his own ideal, but of theirs: this is a nonunifying love, one might even say a "neutral" one, to use the word as Blanchot and Barthes do. On the level of action, of the assimilation of the other or of identification with him, a Cabeza de Vaca also reached a neutral point, not because he was indifferent to the two cultures but because he had experienced them both from within —thereby, he no longer had anything but "the others" around him; without becoming an Indian, Cabeza de Vaca was no longer quite a Spaniard. His experience symbolizes and heralds that of the modern exile, which in its turn personifies a tendency characteristic of our society: a being who has lost his country without thereby acquiring another, who lives in a double exteriority. It is the exiled person who today best incarnates, though warping it from its original meaning, the ideal of Hugh of St. Victor, who formulated it this way in the twelfth century: "The man who finds his country sweet is only a raw beginner; the man for whom each country is as his own is already strong; but only the man for whom the whole world is as a foreign country is perfect" (I myself, a Bulgarian living in France, borrow this quotation from Edward Said, a Palestinian living in the United States, who himself found it in Erich Auerbach, a German exiled in Turkey).

Finally, on the level of knowledge, a Durán and a Sahagún heralded, without fully achieving, the dialogue of cultures that characterizes our age and which is incarnated by ethnology, at once the child of colonialism and the proof of its death throes: a dialogue in which no one has the last word, in which neither voice is reduced to the status of a simple object, and in which we gain advantage from our externality to the other. Durán and Sahagún are ambiguous symbols, for theirs are medieval minds; perhaps it is this very exteriority to the culture of their time that is responsible for their modernity. Through these different examples one characteristic is asserted: a new exotopy (to speak in Bakhtine's fashion), an affirmation of the other's exteriority which goes hand in hand with the recognition of the other as subject. Here perhaps is not only a new way of experiencing alterity, but also a characteristic feature of our time, as individualism (or autotelism) was for the period whose end we are now beginning to discern.

That is what an optimist like Levinas would propose: "Our period is not defined by the triumph of technology for technology's sake, as it is not defined by art for art's sake, as it is not defined by nihilism. It is action for a world to come, transcendence of its period—transcendence of self which calls for epiphany of the Other."

Does this book itself illustrate this new attitude toward the other, through my relation with the authors and figures of the sixteenth century? I can testify only to my intentions, not to the effect that they produce. I have tried to avoid two extremes. The first is the temptation to reproduce the voices of these figures "as they really are"; to try to do away with my own presence "for the other's sake." The second is to subjugate the other to myself, to make him into a marionette of which I pull the strings. Between the two, I have sought not a terrain of compromise but the path of dialogue. I question, I transpose, I interpret these texts; but also I let them speak (whence so many quotations) and defend themselves. From Columbus to Sahagún, these figures did not speak the same language as the one I speak; but one does not let the other live merely by leaving him intact, any more than by obliterating his voice entirely. I have tried to see them, both close and distant, as forming one of the interlocutors of our dialogue.

But our age is also defined by a "caricature" experience of these very features; such a thing is no doubt inevitable. This experience often camouflages the new feature by its very abundance, and sometimes even precedes it, the parody not requiring a model. "Neutral" love, *Las Casas's* "distributive" justice, are parodied and drained of meaning in a generalized relativism where anything goes, so long as one chooses the right point of view; perspectivism leads to indifference and to the renunciation of all values. The discovery the "I" makes of the "others" inhabiting it is accompanied by the more alarming assertion of the disappearance of the "I" into the "we" characteristic of all totalitarian regimes. Exile is fruitful if one belongs to both cultures at once, without identifying oneself with either; but if a whole society consists of exiles, the dialogue of cultures ceases: it is replaced by eclecticism and comparatism, by the capacity to love everything a little, of flaccidly sympathizing with each option without ever embracing any. Heterology, which makes the difference of voices heard, is necessary; polylogy is insipid. Lastly, the anthropologist's position is fruitful; much less so is that of the tourist whose curiosity about strange ways takes him to Bali or Bahia, but who confines the experience of the heterogeneous within the space of his paid vacations. It is true that, unlike the anthropologist, he pays for his trip out of his own pocket.

The exemplary history of the conquest of America teaches us that Western civilization has conquered, among other reasons, because of its superiority in human communication; but also that this superiority has been asserted at the cost of communication with the world. Having emerged from the colonialist period, we vaguely experience the need to evaluate such communication with the world; here again, the parody seems to precede the serious version. The American hippies of the sixties, in their refusal to adopt the ideal of their country, which was bombing Vietnam, tried to rediscover the life of the noble savage. A little like the Indians of Sepúlveda's description, they tried to do without money, to forget books and writing, to show indifference to clothes and renounce the use of machines—to do their own thing. But such communities were obviously doomed to failure, since they pasted these "primitive" features on an altogether modern individualist mentality. Any "Club Med" allows us to experience this plunge into the primitive (absence of money, of books, and ultimately of clothes) without calling into question the continuity of our "civilized" existence; we know the formula's commercial success. Returns to various ancient or new religions are countless; they testify to the power of the impulse but cannot, I believe, incarnate it: the return to the past is impossible. We know we no longer want the morality (or the amorality) of "everything is permitted," for we have experienced its consequences; but we must find new prohibitions, or a new motivation for the old ones if we are to perceive their meaning. The capacity for improvisation and for instantaneous identification seeks to balance itself by a valorization of ritual and identity; but we may doubt that a return to the soil will suffice.

In reporting and analyzing the history of the conquest of America, I have been led to two apparently contradictory conclusions. In order to speak of forms and kinds of communication, I have first of all adopted a typological perspective: the Indians favor exchanges with the world, the Europeans exchanges between men. Neither is intrinsically superior to the other, and we always need both at once; if we win on only one level, we necessarily lose on the other. But at the same time I have been led to observe an evolution in the "technology" of symbolism; this evolution can be reduced, for simplicity's sake, to the advent of writing. Now, the presence of writing favors improvisation over ritual, just as it makes for a linear conception of time or, further, the perception of the other. Is there also an evolution from communication with the world to communication between men? More generally, if there is such an evolution, does not the notion of barbarism recover a nonrelative meaning?

The solution of this aporia, as I see it, does not reside in the abandonment of one of the two statements, but rather in the recognition, for each event, of multiple determinations which condemn any attempt to systematize history to failure. This explains why technological progress, as we know only too well today, does not involve a superiority on the level of moral and social values (nor, moreover, an inferiority). Societies that employ writing are more advanced than societies without writing; but we may hesitate to choose between sacrifice societies and massacre societies.

On yet another level, our recent experiences are discouraging: the desire to transcend the individualism of egalitarian societies and to accede to the sociality characteristic of hierarchical societies reappears, along with others, in totalitarian states. These resemble that monstrous child Bernard Shaw foresaw as the result of the union proposed to him by Isadora Duncan: as ugly as he and as stupid as she. These states, certainly modern in that they cannot be identified either with sacrifice societies or with massacre societies, nonetheless unite certain features of both, and deserve the creation of a portmanteau word: they are *massacrifice* societies. As in sacrifice societies, a state religion is professed; as in massacre societies, behavior is based on the Karamazovian principle of "everything is permitted." As in a sacrifice, killing is performed first of all on home ground; as in a massacre, the very existence of such killing is dissimulated and denied. As in a sacrifice, the victims are chosen individually; as in a massacre, they are exterminated without any notion of ritual. The third term exists, but it is worse than the preceding two; what is to be done?

The form of disclosure I have resolved upon for this book, that of the exemplary history, also results from the desire to transcend the limits of systematic writing, yet without "returning" to pure myth. By comparing Columbus and Cortés, Cortés and Montezuma, I have become aware that the forms of communication—production as well as reception—even if they are universal and eternal, are not accessible to the writer's free choice, but are correlated to the ideologies in force and can thereby become their sign. But what is the discourse appropriate to our heterological mentality? In European civilization, *logos* has conquered *mythos;* or rather, instead of polymorphous discourse, two homogeneous genres have prevailed: science and everything related to it derive from systematic discourse, while literature and its avatars practice narrative discourse. But this second terrain is shrinking day by day: even myths are reduced to double-entry ledgers, history itself is replaced by systematic analysis, and novels vie with each other against temporal development and toward spatial form, tending to the ideal of the motionless matrix. I could not separate myself from the vision of the "conquerors" without at the same time renouncing the discursive form they had appropriated as their own. I feel the need (and in this I see nothing individual, it is why I write it) to adhere to that narrative which proposes rather than imposes; to rediscover, within a single text, the complementarity of narrative discourse and systematic discourse; so that my "history" perhaps bears more of a generic resemblance to Herodotus's (all questions of genre and value aside) than to the ideal of many contemporary historians. Certain facts that I report here lead to general assertions; others (or other aspects of the same facts) do not.

Alongside the narratives I submit to analysis there remain others, unsubmissive. And if, at this very moment, I am "drawing the moral" of my history, it is with no thought of yielding up and "fixing" its meaning—a narrative is not reducible to a maxim—but because I find it more honest to formulate some of the impressions it makes upon me, since I too am one of its readers.

Exemplary history has existed in the past, but the term now has a different meaning. Since Cicero, we have repeated the adage *Historia magistra vitae*, which suggests that since man's fate is unchangeable, and that we can base his present conduct on that of the heroes of the past. This conception of history and of fate has perished with the advent of modern individualist ideology, for we now prefer to believe that a man's life belongs to himself and has nothing to do with anyone else's. I do not think that the narrative of the conquest of America is exemplary in the sense that it represents a faithful image of *our* relation to the other: not only is Cortés not like Columbus, but we are no longer like Cortés. If we are ignorant of history, says another adage, we risk repeating it; but it is not because we know history that we know what to do. We are like the conquistadors and we differ from them; their example is instructive but we shall never be sure that by *not* behaving like them we are not in fact on the way to imitating them, as we adapt ourselves to new circumstances. But their history can be exemplary for us because it permits us to reflect upon ourselves, to discover resemblances as well as differences: once again self-knowledge develops through knowledge of the Other.

For Cortés, the conquest of knowledge leads to the conquest of power. I take the conquest of knowledge from his example, even if I do so in order to resist power. There is a certain frivolity in merely condemning the wicked conquistadors and regretting the noble Indians —as if it sufficed to identify evil in order to oppose it. I am not eulogizing the conquistadors by acknowledging their occasional superiority; it is necessary to analyze the weapons of the conquest if we ever want to be able to stop it. For conquests do not belong only to the past.

I do not believe that history obeys a system, nor that its so-called laws permit deducing future or even present forms of society; but rather that to become conscious of the relativity (hence of the arbitrariness) of any feature of our culture is already to shift it a little, and that history (not the science but its object) is nothing other than a series of such imperceptible shifts.

Bibliographic Note

In the list of *References* below will be found the publication data for the works cited in the text, in Spanish, French, and English; here I give some additional bibliographical information. Modern commentators are cited according to a single criterion: their possible influence on my own text. Hence, this notice is no more than a *Tabula gratulatoria.*

DISCOVERY

The texts used in this section are principally those of Columbus, then of his contemporaries and companions (Chanca, Cuneo, Mendez), then the writings of contemporary historians: Peter Martyr, Bernáldez, Ferdinand Columbus, Oviedo, Las Casas. Among the modern biographies, Madariaga's *Christophe Colomb* (Paris: Calmann-Lévy, 1952; Le Livre de Poche, 1968) remains agreeable to read, despite its racism. A very extensive biography has just appeared in French: J. Heers, *Christophe Colomb* (Paris: Hachette, 1981). Olschki's study, "What Columbus Saw on Landing in the West Indies," *Proceedings of the American Philosophical Society* 84 (1941), 633–59, is one of the rare texts to deal closely with the subject discussed here; Olschki's conclusions are at first glance quite different, which is in part explained by the generality of his statement, in part by his Europeocentrist ideology. A. Gerbi in *La Naturaleza de las Indias Nuevas. De Cristobal Colón a Gonzalo Fernández de Oviedo* (Mexico: Fondo de Cultura Economica, 1978; Italian original, 1975).

On the general phenomenon of discovery, I shall indicate three works. That of P. Chaunu (*Conquête at exploitation des nouveaux mondes, xvie siècle*, Paris: Presses Universitaires de France, 1969) contains an enormous bibliography and a great deal of information. J. H. Elliott's little book *The Old World and the New, 1492–1650* (Cambridge: Cambridge University Press, 1970) is suggestive. E. O'Gorman's book *The Invention of America* (Bloomington: Indiana University Press, 1961) is devoted to the evolution of the geographical conceptions linked to the discovery of America.

CONQUEST

There exists an inexhaustible mine of historical and bibliographical information in the four volumes of the *Guide to Ethnohistorical Studies*, published under the direction of H. F. Cline, which constitute volumes 12 to 15 of the *Handbook of the Middle American Indians* (1972-75).

For the knowledge of Aztec society the most valuable sources are (a) the descriptions, compilations, and translations of the Spanish monks (I have used those of Motolinia, Durán, Sahagún, Tovar, de Landa, the *Relación de Michoacán*), to which must be added the description of a layman, A. de Zorita; (b) the writings, in Indian languages or in Spanish, of Indians or of half-castes (thus Tezozomoc, Ixtlilxochitl, J. B. Pomar, the *Chilam Balam*, *Annales des Cakchiquels*, Chimalpahin). References to Sahagún are sometimes to the *Florentine Codex*, which is the illustrated and bilingual version of his book (for all the passages for which we possess the Nahuatl text), sometimes to his *Historia general de las cosas de Nueva España*.

Among the conquistadors, the most important authors are Cortés (reports to Charles V and other documents) and Bernal Díaz *(Historia verdadera de la conquista de la Nueva España)*. I have also used the shorter chronicles of J. Díaz, F. de Aguilar, A. de Tapia, D. Godoy. The first historians—such as Peter Martyr, Gomara, Oviedo, and Las Casas—also furnish unpublished documents.

For the reasons for the Spanish victory, one may consult J. Soustelle, *Recontre de la civilisation hispanique et des civilisations indigènes de l'Amérique* (Paris: no date, roneograph). On the *huehuetlatolli* I have used the study of Thelma D. Sullivan, "The Rhetorical Orations, or *Huehuetlatolli*, Collected by Sahagún," in M. S. Edmondson (ed.), *Sixteenth-Century Mexico, The Work of Sahagún* (Albuquerque: University of New Mexico Press, 1974, pp. 79-109). On the myth of Quetzalcoatl, see the fundamental book by J. Lafaye, *Quetzalcoatl et Guadalupe* (Paris: Gallimard, 1974, of which an English translation exists), as well as the notes by A. Pagden to his remarkable English translation of Cortés's letters. On Aztec thought, I have benefited from the book by M. Leon-Portilla, *Filosofía nahuatl* (Mexico: UNAM, 1959; English translation, *Aztec Thought and Culture: A Study of the Ancient Nahuatl Mind* (Norman: University of Oklahoma Press, 1963). Octavio Paz's books—for example *The Labyrinth of Solitude* (Paris: Gallimard, 1972; English translation, 1961) and *The Other Mexico: Critique of the Pyramid* (Paris: Gallimard, 1972; English translation, 1972)—are a valuable source of reflection for anyone interested in the history of Mexico.

The context that permits me to compare Aztecs and Spaniards owes a great deal to Louis Dumont's works of comparative sociology, notably *Homo hierarchicus* (Paris: Gallimard, 1966; translated into English as *From Mandeville to Marx*); *Homo aequalis* (Paris: Gallimard, 1977); "La Conception moderne de l'individu," *Esprit* (February 1978, pp. 3-39). On the effects of the presence or absence of writing, see J. Goody, *The Domestication of the Savage Mind* (Cambridge University Press, 1977; French translation, *La Raison graphique*, Paris: Minuit, 1978).

The notion of improvisation as a characteristic of Western civilization in the Renaissance comes from an essay by Stephen Greenblatt, "Improvisation and Power," in E. Said (ed.), *Literature and Society* (Baltimore and London: Johns Hopkins University Press, 1980, pp. 57-99); he also cites the story of the Lucayos in Peter Martyr.

On the relation between linear perspective and the great discoveries in the Renaissance, consult among others S. Y. Edgerton, Jr., "The Art of Renaissance Picture Making and the Great Western Age of Discovery," in *Essays Presented to Myron P. Gilmore* (Florence: La Nuova Italia Editrice, 1978, vol. 2, 133–53). For the formal characteristics of representation among the Mexicans, the writings of D. Robertson are authoritative—for instance, "Mexican Indian Art and the Atlantic Filter: Sixteenth to Eighteenth Centuries," in F. Chiapelli (ed.), *First Images of America* (Berkeley, Los Angeles, and London: University of California Press, 1976, vol. 1, 483–94).

LOVE

Many of the sources used in this chapter are the same as for the preceding one. To them must be added Las Casas's other works, the treatises of Sepúlveda and Vitoria, and several documents issued by the civil or religious authorities.

The demographic historians who have transformed our ideas on the Indian population before and after the conquest are often designated as forming the "Berkeley School." See in particular the works of S. Cook and W. W. Borah, *The Indian Population of Central Mexico, 1531–1610* (Berkeley, Los Angeles, and London: University of California Press, 1960); *Essays in Population History: Mexico and the Caribbean* (1971). On the Las Casas–Sepúlveda debate and around it, I have used the works of L. Hanke (notably *Aristotle and the American Indian*, Bloomington: Indiana University Press, 1970; first edition, 1959; and *All Mankind Is One*, Dekalb: Northern Illinois University Press, 1974); S. Zavala (for example, *L'Amérique latine, Philosophie de la conquête*, Paris, The Hague: Mouton, 1977; an English translation exists); M. Bataillon (*Etudes sur Bartolomé de Las Casas*, Paris: Centre de Recherches de l'Institut d'Etudes Hispaniques, 1965); and the collection *Bartolomé de Las Casas in History*, published under the direction of J. Friede and B. Keen (Dekalb: Northern Illinois University Press, 1971).

Much information is to be found concerning the image of the Aztecs in the West in B. Keen, *The Aztec Image in Western Thought* (New Brunswick, N.J.: Rutgers University Press, 1971); and on the general impact of the discovery and conquest of America in F. Chiapelli (ed.), *First Images of America* (Berkeley, Los Angeles, and London: University of California Press, 1976, 2 vols.).

KNOWLEDGE

On Vasco de Quiroga I have consulted S. Zavala, *Recuerdo de Vasco de Quiroga* (Mexico: Porrua, 1965) and F. B. Warren, *Vasco de Quiroga and His Pueblo-Hospitals of Santa Fe* (Washington, D.C.: Academy of American Franciscan History, 1963). On Sahagún, two sources have been particularly useful: the collection published under the direction of M. S. Edmondson, *Sixteenth Century Mexico, The Work of Sahagún* (Albuquerque: University of New Mexico Press, 1974, especially the study by A. Lopez Austin on the questionnaires); and the texts collected in the *Guide to Ethnohistorical Studies* (1973, vol. 13 of the *Handbook* mentioned above). The work of R. Ricard, *La Conquête spirituelle du Mexique* (Paris: Institut d'Ethnologie de Paris, 1933) is still very instructive; that of G. Baudot, *Utopie et histoire au Mexique* (Toulouse: Privat,

1976), contains a great deal of information. I have found suggestive the article by F. Lestringant, "Calvinistes et cannibales," *Bulletin de la Société du protestantisme français,* issues 1 and 2, 1980, pp. 9–26 and 167–92.

EPILOGUE

E. Levinas, the the philosopher of alterity, is the author of *Totalité et infini* (The Hague: M. Nijhoff, 1961). I cite here *L'Humanisme de l'autre homme* (Montpellier: Fata Morgana, 1972). Blanchot speaks of the neutral in *L'Entretien infini* (Paris: Gallimard, 1969), and Barthes in *Roland Barthes* (Paris: Seuil, 1975; English translation, 1977). The reference to Auerbach is to "Philologie und Weltliteratur," collected in *Gesammelte Aufsätze zur romanischen Philologie* (Berne: Franke, 1967); and to E. Said, in his book *Orientalism* (New York: Pantheon, 1978; French translation, Paris: Seuil, 1980). My quotation from Herzen comes from *Sobranie sochinenij,* in 30 vols. (Moscow and Leningrad, 1955, vol. 5, p. 62). L. Dumont evokes several features of modernity in his works cited above and in "La Communauté anthropologique et l'idéologie," in *L'Homme,* 18 (1978), issues 3–4, pp. 83–110. One may gain access to Bakhtine's texts on alterity and exotopy through my book *Mikhaïl Bakhtine et le principe dialogique* (Paris: Seuil, 1981).

On the narrative discourse/systematic discourse opposition, see H. Weinrich, "Structures narratives du mythe," *Poétique* 1 (1970): 25–34; and K. Stierle, "L'Histoire comme exemple, l'exemple comme histoire," *Poétique* 3 (1972): 176–98.

I should also like to thank all those who, by oral or written intervention, have helped me correct earlier versions of this work, and especially Catherine Malamoud, Fedora Cohan, Esther Pasztory, Diana Fane, André Saint-Lu.

References

Acosta, J. de. *Historia natural y moral de las Indias*. Mexico: Fondo de Cultura Economica, 1962. French translation: *Histoire naturelle et morale des Indes Occidentales*. Paris: Payot, 1979. English translation: *The Natural and Moral History of the Indies*. 2 vols. London: The Hakluyt Society, 1880.

Aguilar, F. de. *Relación breve de la conquista de la Nueva España*. Mexico: Porrua, 1954. English translation: P. de Fuentes, *The Conquistadors*. New York: Orion, 1963.

Annales des Cakchiquels. Spanish translation: *Anales de los Cakchiqueles (Memorial de Solola), Titolo de los señores de Totonicapán*. Mexico: Fondo de Cultura Economica, 1950. English translation: *The Annals of the Cakchiquels, Title of the Lords of Totonicapán*. Norman: University of Oklahoma Press, 1953.

Bernáldez, A. *Historia de los reyes católicos don Fernando y doña Isabel*. Grenada, 1856. English translation: *Select Documents Illustrating the Four Voyages of Columbus*. London: The Hakluyt Society, 1930 (bilingual edition), vol. 1.

Bienvenida, L. de. "Carta a Don Felipe," 10.2. 1548, in *Cartas de Indias*, vol. 1. Madrid: Biblioteca de Autores Españoles, vol. 264, 1974, pp. 70–82. French translation: H. Ternaux-Compans, *Recueil de pièces relatives à la conquête du Mexique*. Paris, 1838.

Bologna, F. de. "Lettre à Clement de Monelia." French translation: H. Ternaux-Compans, *Recueil de pièces relatives à la conquête du Mexique*. Paris, 1838.

Bruno, G. "De l'infinito universo e mondi" in *Opere italiane*, vol. 1. Bari, 1907. English translation: "On the Infinite Universe and Worlds," in D. W. Singer, *Giordano Bruno, His Life and Thought*. New York: Schuman, 1950, pp. 225–378.

Cabeza de Vaca, A. N. *Naufragios y comemtarios*. Madrid: Taurus, 1969. French translation: *Naufrages et commentaires*. Paris: Fayard, 1980. English translation: *Adventures in the Unknown Interior of America*. New York: Collier Books, 1961.

"Carta . . . a Mr. de Xevres," 4.6.1516, *Colección de documentos inéditos . . . America*, vol. 7. Madrid, 1867, pp. 397–430. French translation: *Las Casas et la défense des Indiens*. Paris: Julliard, 1971, pp. 61–3 (extracts).

Charles V, "Cedula," 1530, in Diego de Encinas. *Cedulario indiano* (1596), 4 vols.

Madrid: Cultura Hispanica, 1945–46. French translation: S. Zavala. *L'Amérique latine, philosophie de la conquête.* Paris, The Hague: Mouton, 1977.

Chauveton, U. "Aux lecteurs chrestiens." In J. Benzoni, *Histoire nouvelle du Nouveau Monde.* Lyon, 1579.

Chilam Balam de Chumayel. Spanish translation: *Libro de los libros de Chilam Balam.* Mexico: Fondo de Cultura Economica, 1948. French translation: *Les prophéties de Chilam Balam.* Paris: Gallimard, 1976 (poetic version). English translation: *The Book of Chilam Balam of Chumayel.* Norman: University of Oklahoma Press, 1967.

Chimalpahin, F. S. A. M. French translation: *Sixième et septième relations.* Paris, 1889 (bilingual edition).

Colección de cantares mexicanos. Mexico, 1904.

Colón, C. *Raccolta colombiana,* I, vol. 1 and 2, Rome, 1892–94. French translation: *Oeuvres.* Paris: Gallimard, 1961; *La Découverte de l'Amérique.* Paris: Maspero, 1979. English translation: *Journals and Other Documents.* New York: Heritage Press, 1963; *Select Documents Illustrating the Four Voyages of Columbus,* 2 vols. London: The Hakluyt Society, 1930; 1933 (bilingual edition).

Colón, F. *Historie.* Spanish translation: *Vida de Almirante don Cristobal Colón.* Mexico: Fondo de Cultura Economica, 1947. English translation: *The Life of the Admiral Christopher Columbus.* New Brunswick, N.J.: Rutgers University Press, 1959. French translation: *Histoire de la Vie et des Découvertes de Christophe Colomb.* Paris, 1879.

Cortés, H. *Cartas y documentos.* Mexico: Porrua, 1963. English translation: *Letters from Mexico.* New York: Grossman, 1971. French translation: *Lettres à Charles Quint.* Paris, 1896.

Cuneo, M. de. "Lettre à Annari," 28.10.1495. *Raccolta columbiana,* III, vol. 2, pp. 95–107. English translation: C. Columbus. *Journals . . . ,* pp. 209–28.

Dialogues. English translation: "The Aztec-Spanish Dialogues of 1524," *Alcheringa,* 4 (1980), 2, pp. 52–193 (bilingual edition).

Díaz del Castillo, B. *Historia verdadera de la conquista de la Nueva España,* 2 vols. Mexico: Porrua, 1955. French translation: *Histoire véridique de la conquête de la Nouvelle Espagne.* Paris, 1877. English translation: *The True History of the Conquest of New Spain,* 5 vols. London: The Hakluyt Society, 1908–16.

Díaz, J. "Itinerario . . ." In J. García Icazbalceta, *Colección de documentos para la historia de Mexico,* vol. 1. Mexico, 1858, pp. 281–308 (with the Italian "original"). French translation: H. Ternaux-Compans, *Recueil de pièces relatives à la conquête du Mexique.* Paris, 1838. English translation: P. de Fuentes, *The Conquistadors.* New York: Orion, 1963.

Durán, D. *Historia de las Indias de Nueva España e Islas de la Tierra Firme,* 2 vols. Mexico: Porrua, 1967. English translation: *Book of the Gods and Rites and the Ancient Calendar.* Norman: University of Oklahoma Press, 1971 (1st and 2nd parts); *The Aztecs, The History of the Indies of New Spain.* New York: Orion, 1964 (3rd part abridged).

Ferdinand, Isabela, "Carta . . . a D. C. Colón." In M. Fernández de Navarrete, *Colección de los viajes y descumbrimientos,* vol. 2. Madrid, 1825, pp. 21–22.

Florentine Codex, 12 vols. Santa Fe, New Mexico: Monographs of the School of

American Research, 1950–69. (Bilingual edition. Apart from the text of Sahagún, there exists no complete Spanish translation.)

Godoy, Diego. "Relación a H. Cortés." In *Historiadores primitivos de Indias*, vol. 1. Madrid: Biblioteca de Autores Españoles, vol. 22, 1877, pp. 465–70. French translation: H. Ternaux-Compans. *Recueil de pièces relatives à la conquête du Mexique.* Paris, 1838.

Gomara, F. Lopez de. *Historia de la conquista de Mexico.* Mexico: P. Robredo, 1943. French translation: *Histoire générale des Indes occidentales . . .* Paris, 1584. English translation: *Cortés: The Life of the Conqueror By His Secretary.* Berkeley, Los Angeles, and London: University of California Press, 1964.

Ixlilxochitl, F. de Alva. "Relación de la venida de los Españoles." In B. de Sahagún, *Historia general de las cosas de Nueva España.* Mexico: Porrua, 1956. French translation: *Cruautés horribles des conquérants du Mexique.* Paris, 1838 (repr. Paris: Anthropos, 1967).

Ferrer, M. Jaume. "Carta a Colón." 5.8.1495, in M. Fernández de Navarrette, *Colección de los viajes y descumbrimientos*, vol. 2. Madrid, 1825, pp. 103–5.

Landa, D. de. *Relación de las cosas de Yucatán.* Mexico: Porrua, 1959. French translation: *Relation des choses de Yucatan*, 2 vols. Paris: Editions Genet, 1928–29 (incomplete bilingual edition). English translation: *The Maya, Account of the Affairs of Yucatan.* Chicago: J. Philip O'Hara, 1975.

Las Casas, B. de. *Apologética Historia Summaria*, 2 vols. Mexico: UNAM, 1967.

Las Casas, B. de. *Apologia.* Spanish translation: *Apologia . . .* Madrid: Nacional, 1975. English translation: *In Defense of the Indians.* Dekalb: Northern Illinois University Press, 1974.

Las Casas, B. de. *Historia de las Indias*, 3 vols. Mexico: Fondo de Cultura Economica, 1951. English translation: *History of the Indies.* New York: Harper & Row, 1971 (extracts).

Las Casas, B. de, all other writings. *Opusculos, cartas y memoriales.* Madrid: Biblioteca de Autores Españoles, vol. 110, 1958. English translation: *A Selection of His Writings.* New York: Knopf, 1971 (extracts); *The Devastation of the Indies.* New York: Seabury Press, 1974. French translation: *Oeuvres.* Paris, 1822 (extracts); M. Mahn-Lot, *Bernard de Las Casas, L'Evangile et la force.* Paris: Edition du Cerf, 1964 (extracts); *Las Casas et la défense des Indiens.* Paris: Julliard, 1971 (extracts).

Lopez, G. "Carta al Emperador" in J. García Icazbalceta, *Colección de documentos para la historia de Mexico*, vol. 2. Mexico, 1866, pp. 141–54.

Machiavelli. English translation: *The Prince* and *The Discourses.* New York: Modern Library, 1940. French translation: *Oeuvres complètes.* Paris: Gallimard, 1952.

Martyr Anghiera, P. *De Orbe Novo.* English translation: *De Orbe Novo.* 2 vols. New York: Putnam's, 1912. Spanish translation: *Decades del Nuevo Mundo.* Buenos Aires: Bajel, 1944. French translation: *De orbe novo, Les huit décades.* Paris, 1907.

Mendieta, G. de. *Historia eclesiástica indiana.* Mexico: Porrua, 1971.

Motolinia, T. *Historia de los Indios de la Nueva España.* Mexico: Porrua, 1969. English translation: *History of the Indians of New Spain.* Westport, Conn.: Greenwood Press, 1973.

Motolinia, T., and D. Olarte. "Carta de Cholula." 27.8.1554, in *Documentos inéditos del siglo XVI para la historia de Mexico*. Mexico, 1914, pp. 228–32. French translation: H. Ternaux-Compans. *Recueil de pièces relatives à la conquête du Mexique*. Paris, 1838.

Nebrija, A. de. *Gramática de la lengua castellana*. Oxford, 1926.

"Ordenanzas de Su Magestad . . ." In *Colección de documentos inéditos . . . America*, vol. 16. Madrid, 1871, pp. 142–87. French translation: *Las Casas et la défense des Indiens*. Paris: Julliard, 1971, pp. 265–67 (extracts). English translation: L. Hanke. *History of Latin American Civilization, Sources and Interpretations*, vol. 1. Boston: Little, Brown, 1967, pp. 149–52 (extracts).

Oviedo y Valdes, G. Fernández de. *Historia general y natural de las Indias, islas y Tierra firme del Mar Oceano*, 5 vols. Madrid: Biblioteca de Autores Españoles, vols. 117–21, 1959. English translation: *Natural History of the West Indies*. Chapel Hill, N.C.: University of North Carolina Press, 1959 (extracts).

Palacios Rubios, J. L. "Requerimiento," *De las islas del mar oceano*. Mexico, 1954. English translation: L. Hanke, *History of Latin American Civilization, Sources and Interpretations*, vol. 1. Boston: Little, Brown, 1967. French translation: S. Zavala, *L'Amérique latine, Philosophie de la conquête*. Paris, The Hague: Mouton, 1977.

Paul III, "Sublimus Deus." English translation: F. MacNutt, *Bartholemew de Las Casas*. New York, 1909, pp. 427–31. Spanish translation: *Documentos inéditos del siglo XVI para la historia de Mexico*. Mexico, 1914, pp. 84–86.

Pomar, J. Bautista. *Relación de Texcoco*. Mexico: S. Chavez Hayhoe, 1941.

Quiroga, V. de. *Documentos*. Mexico: Polis, 1939.

Ramírez de Fuenleal, S. "Carta," 3.11.1532 in *Colección de documentos inéditos del Archivo de Indias*, vol. 13. Madrid, 1870, pp. 250–60. French translation: H. Ternaux-Compans. *Second recueil de pièces sur le Mexique*. Paris, 1840.

Relación de las ceremonias y ritos, población y gobierno de los Indios de la provincia de Mechuacan. Madrid: Aguilar, 1956. English translation: *The Chronicles of Michoacán*. Norman: University of Oklahoma Press, 1970.

Sahagún, B. de. *Historia general de las cosas de Nueva España*, 4 vols. Mexico: Porrua, 1956. English translation: *A History of Ancient Mexico*. Nashville, 1932 (incomplete). French translation: *Histoire générale des choses de la Nouvelle Espagne*. Paris, 1888.

Salmeron, Maldonado, Ceynos, V. de Quiroga. "Carta a su Magestad," 14.8.1531. *Colección de documentos inéditos . . . America*, vol. 41. Madrid, 1844, pp. 40–138. French translation: F. Ternaux-Compans, *Second recueil de pièces sur le Mexique*. Paris, 1840.

San Miguel, J. de. "Carta," 20.8.1550, quoted by J. Friede, "Las Casas y el movimiento indigenista en España y America en la primera mitad del siglo XVI," *Revista de Historia de America* 34 (1952): 371.

Sepúlveda, J. Ginés de. *Democrates Alter*. Spanish translation: *Democrates secundo: De las Justas causas de la guerra contra los Indios*. Madrid: Instituto F. de Vitoria, 1951.

Sepúlveda, J. Ginés de. "Del Reino y los Deberes del rey." In *Tratados politicos*. Madrid: Instituto de Estudios Politicos, 1963.

Sumario del residencia. 2 vols. Mexico, 1852–53.

Tapia, A. de. "Relación sobre la conquista de Mexico." In J. Garcia Icazbalceta, *Colección de documentos para la historia de Mexico,* vol. 2. Mexico, 1866, pp. 554–94. English translation: P. de Fuentes, *The Conquistadors.* New York: Orion, 1963.

Tezozomoc, H. Alvarado. *Crónica Mexicana.* Mexico: Vigil-Leyenda, 1944. French translation: *Histoire du Mexique,* 2 vols. Paris, 1853.

Tovar, J. *Origines et croyances des Indiens du Mexique.* Graz: Academische Druck und Verlagsanstalt, 1972 (bilingual edition; also contains the letter to Acosta). English translation: P. Radin, *The Sources and Authenticity of the History of the Ancient Mexicans.* Berkeley: University of California Publications in American Archeology and Ethnology, vol. 17, 1, 1920, pp. 67–123 (extracts).

Valdivia, P. de. *Cartas . . .* Seville, 1929.

Vitoria, F. de. *De Indis, De Jure Belli.* Spanish translation: *Relecciones sobre los Indios y el derecho de guerra.* Buenos Aires: Espasa-Calpe, 1946. English translation: *De Indis et De Jure Belli relectiones . . .* Washington, D.C.: Carnegie Institute, 1917. French translation: *Leçons sur les Indiens et sur le droit de guerre.* Geneva: Droz, 1966.

Zorita (or Zurita), A. de. *Breve y sumaria relación de los señores de la Nueva España.* Mexico: UNAM, 1942. English translation: *Life and Labor in Ancient Mexico: The Brief and Summary Relations of the Lords of New Spain.* New Brunswick, N.J.: Rutgers University Press, 1963. French translation: *Rapport sur les différentes classes des chefs de la Nouvelle Espagne.* Paris, 1838.

Zumarraga, J. de. "Carta a Su Magestad." 27.8.1529, in J. Garcia Icazbalceta, *Don Fray Juan de Zumarraga,* vol. 2. Mexico: Porrua, 1947, pp. 169–245. French translation: H. Ternaux-Compans, *Second recueil de pièces sur le Mexique.* Paris, 1840.

Index